What People Are Saying About
Chicken Soup for the Mother's Soul 2 . . .

"Chicken Soup for the Mother's Soul 2 has reminded me that the privilege of being my children's mother is the greatest role I will ever play. And the whispers of love transcribed on their hearts are the most important words I will author."

Lisa Whelchel
actress, Blair on "The Facts of Life"
author, *Creative Correction: Extraordinary Ideas for Everyday Discipline*

"One of the most crucial needs in the career of motherhood is inspiration. This book is a great resource for exactly that!"

Linda Eyre
author, *A Joyful Mother of Children: The Magic & Mayhem of Motherhood*

"This book is an inspirational read for moms trying to juggle their multiple roles. Its heartwarming stories offer a peaceful respite in our busy lives and celebrate the special spirit of motherhood."

Ellen H. Parlapiano and Patricia Cobe
authors, *Mompreneurs®: A Mother's Practical Step-by-Step Guide to Work-at-Home Success*

"What a gift for all mothers! You'll love the stories of mothers' wisdom, miracles, precious moments and the power of a mother's love."

Bobbi McCaughey
mother of the McCaughey septuplets
author, *Seven from Heaven: The Miracle of the McCaughey Septuplets*

"Reading *Chicken Soup for the Mother's Soul 2* reminds us all of the depth and power of the precious bond between mother and child and uplifts the role of motherhood toward the divine."

Jeanette Lisefski
founder, National Association of
At-Home Mothers and *AtHomeMothers.com*

"Every ordinary mom has extraordinary stories to tell. By assembling such stories, *Chicken Soup for the Mother's Soul 2*, like its predecessor, provides an invaluable service—honoring and celebrating motherhood."

Lynda DeWitt
director of content, Mom.com, Inc.

"The love a mother has for her child is unbounded. *Chicken Soup for the Mother's Soul 2* contains precious stories of inspiration and truth that capture the essence of motherhood. Each story touched me deeply, as it reflected these universal laws of unconditional love."

Laura L. Bordow
elementary school director and mother

"*Chicken Soup for the Mother's Soul 2* reminds us that not only are our children gifts from God to love and cherish, but so also are our mothers!"

Peggy Dunn
mayor of Leawood, Kansas

"As a mom, I say 'Thank you!' *Chicken Soup for the Mother's Soul 2* is a reaffirmation that being a mom is the most important and fulfilling job in the world."

Glo Goodwin
radio personality

CHICKEN SOUP
FOR THE
MOTHER'S SOUL 2

More Stories to
Open the Hearts and Rekindle
the Spirits of Mothers

Jack Canfield
Mark Victor Hansen
Marci Shimoff
Carol Kline

Health Communications, Inc.
Deerfield Beach, Florida

www.hci-online.com
www.chickensoup.com

We would like to acknowledge the many publishers and individuals who granted us permission to reprint the cited material. (Note: The stories that were penned anonymously, that are in the public domain, or, that were written by Jack Canfield, Mark Victor Hansen, Marci Shimoff and Carol Kline are not included in this listing.)

The Call at Midnight. Reprinted by permission of Christie Craig. ©1995 Christie Craig.

A Mother's Love. Reprinted by permission of Pat Laye. ©2000 Pat Laye.

The Green Pajamas and *Learning to Listen.* Reprinted by permission of Marion Bond West. ©1977 Marion Bond West.

Growing Up. Reprinted by permission of Lisa Duffy-Korpics. ©2000 Lisa Duffy-Korpics.

(Continued on page 379)

Library of Congress Cataloging-in-Publication Data

Chicken soup for the mother's soul 2 : more stories to open the hearts and rekindle the spirits of mothers / Jack Canfield . . . [et al.].
    p.   cm.
   ISBN 1-55874-891-1—ISBN 1-55874-890-3 (trade paper)
   1. Mothers—Literary collections. 2. Motherhood—Literary collections.
I. Canfield, Jack, 1944-

PN6071.M7 C48 2001
810.8'03520431—dc21

00-053990

Publisher: Health Communications, Inc.
          3201 S.W. 15th Street
          Deerfield Beach, FL 33442-8190

Cover design by Andrea Perrine Brower
Inside book formatting by Dawn Grove

We dedicate this book with love to everyone's mother—
Mother Earth,
And to all mothers, who, with unbounded generosity,
Create, nourish and sustain life
And fill our world with beauty and love.

"Enough with the *Chicken Soup for the Soul.*
How about some pizza for the son?"

Contents

3. ON MOTHERHOOD

4. BECOMING A MOTHER

5. ON ADOPTION

6. MOTHERS AND DAUGHTERS

7. ON WISDOM

8. MIRACLES

9. SPECIAL MOMENTS

10. LETTING GO

11. A GRANDMOTHER'S LOVE

12. THANK YOU, MOM

Acknowledgments

Chicken Soup for the Mother's Soul 2 has been three years in the making and has been a labor of love for all of us. One of the greatest joys in creating this book was working with people who gave this project not just their time and attention, but their hearts and souls as well. We'd like to thank the following people—without their support, this book could not have been created.

Our sincerest thanks to:

Our families, who have been chicken soup for *our* souls!

Inga, Travis, Riley, Christopher, Oran and Kyle for all their love and support.

Patty, Elizabeth and Melanie Hansen, for once again sharing and lovingly supporting us in creating another book.

Carol's husband, Larry, for being the rock of kindness and strength that he is, and to her stepchildren, Lorin and McKenna Kline, for their inspiration, affection and for pitching in to help when things got crazy! And to Carol's family, her mother, Selmajean Schneider, and her late father, Raymond Zurer, and her brothers and sisters, Jim, Diana, Barbara, Wilbur, Burt, Pam and Holly, for their encouragement, common sense and best of all, their love.

Sergio Baroni, for being a steady reflection of love, light and truth, and being a reminder to keep the heart open, humble and full of gratitude.

Marci's always loving and supportive parents, Marcus and Louise Shimoff, and Lynda, Paul, Susan, Aaron, Jared, Tony and Vickie for being the wonderful family that they are.

Jennifer Read Hawthorne, for providing the foundation for this book by coauthoring the first *Chicken Soup for the Mother's Soul.* We deeply appreciate your helpful input, superb editing and generous encouragement on this book.

Sue Penberthy, for being the true mother that she is in taking care of us and this book in so many ways. We thank you for putting your heart into reading and acknowledging thousands of stories and handling all the details.

Suzanne Lawlor, for her steady, devoted care in helping us finish this book and for being the "mother at home" in this process.

Bryan Aubrey and Natalie Cleeson, for being such fine editors. This book benefited tremendously from your marvelous writing and editing talents. We especially appreciate how much fun it is to work with you. You are the best!

Craig Herndon, for once again coming to the computer rescue. Thanks for your precision and your dedication to doing the job right.

Patty Aubery, for being a great role model to us all— you are the glue that holds the *Chicken Soup for the Soul* family together. We truly value and appreciate your special friendship, loving heart and brilliant business sense.

Our publisher, Peter Vegso, who continues to support us and keeps bringing *Chicken Soup for the Soul* to the world.

Heather McNamara and D'ette Corona, for producing our final manuscript with magnificent ease, finesse and care. Thanks for making the final stages of production such a breeze!

Nancy Autio and Leslie Riskin for sending us stories and cartoons along the way, and for diligently overseeing the thankless task of ensuring permissions. We love how you look out for us in so many ways.

Deborah Hatchell, for being the *Chicken Soup* liaison extraordinaire. You have done an amazing job organizing the *Chicken Soup* process and we've found your help invaluable.

Mark and Chrissy Donnelly, our friends and colleagues, for their exceptional marketing skills and for representing *Chicken Soup* in such great style.

Veronica Romero, Teresa Esparza, Robin Yerian, Cindy Holland, Vince Wong, Sarah White, Lisa Williams, Michelle Adams, DeeDee Romanello, Trudy Marschall, Tracy Smith, Shanna Vieyra, Joy Pieterse, Kristi Knoppe, and David Coleman, who support Jack's and Mark's businesses with skill and love.

Maria Nickless, for her marketing and public relations support and expertise and her boundless enthusiasm.

Patty Hansen, for her thorough and competent handling of the legal and licensing aspects of the *Chicken Soup for the Soul* books. Thanks for doing one of the most challenging jobs of all!

Laurie Hartman, for being a good guardian of the *Chicken Soup* brand.

Christine Belleris, Lisa Drucker and Susan Tobias, our editors at Health Communications, Inc., and especially Allison Janse, our managing editor, for their devotion to excellence. We love how easy and joyful it is to work with you.

Tom Sand, Terry Burke, Irena Xanthos, Jane Barone, Lori Golden, Kelly Johnson Maragni, Karen Bailiff Ornstein, Randee Feldman, Patricia McConnell, Kim Weiss, Maria Dinoia, Kimberley Denney, Claude Choquette, and Terry Peluso, the marketing, sales, administration and PR departments at Health Communications, Inc., for doing a wonderful job supporting our books.

Thanks to the art department at Health Communications, for their talent, creativity and unrelenting patience in producing book covers and inside designs that capture the essence of *Chicken Soup:* Larissa Hise Henoch, Lawna Patterson Oldfield, Andrea Perrine Brower, Lisa Camp, Anthony Clausi and Dawn Grove.

George and Felicity Foster, for helping with the book cover design. Working with you is a delight.

Fairfield Printing, for coming through once again, when we needed something done "yesterday."

Lynda DeWitt, at Mom.com, Inc., for helping us run our story contest on Mom.com's wonderful Web site.

Sid Slagter, for his invaluable computer advice, for his good cheer and for always having a scanner at the ready. Thank you for everything.

Elinor Hall, our "second opinion" reader, for her loving feedback and her marvelous sense of what makes good *Chicken Soup*. We love you.

We deeply appreciate all the *Chicken Soup for the Soul* coauthors, who make it a joy to be part of this Chicken Soup family: Raymond Aaron, Patty and Jeff Aubery, Nancy Mitchell Autio, Marty Becker, Cynthia Brian, Cindy Buck, Ron Camacho, Barbara Russell Chesser, Dan Clark, Tim Clauss, Barbara De Angelis, Mark and Chrissy Donnelly, Irene Dunlap, Bud Gardner, Patty Hansen, Jennifer Read Hawthorne, Kimberly Kirberger, Tom Lagana, Hanoch and Meladee McCarty, Heather McNamara, Paul J. Meyer, Marion Owen, Maida Rogerson, Martin Rutte, Amy Seeger, Barry Spilchuk, Pat Stone, Carol Sturgulewski, Jim Tunney and Diana von Welanetz Wentworth.

The following people who completed the monumental task of reading the preliminary manuscript of this book.

They helped us make the final selections and made invaluable comments on how to improve the book: Bryan Aubrey, Linda Beckwith, Christine Belleris, Cindy Buck, D'ette Corona, Randee Feldman, Elinor Hall, Ceil Halpern, Amy Hawthorne, Jennifer Read Hawthorne, Deborah Hatchell, Betsy Hinchman, Becky Huggins, Carol Jackson, Allison Janse, Rita Kline, Cindy Knowlton, Suzanne Lawlor, Jeanette Lisefski, Barb McLaughlin, Heather McNamara, Linda Mitchell, Holly Moore, Sue Penberthy, Staci Richmond, Carol Richter, Heather Sanders, Selmajean Schneider, Maria Sears, Marc and Louise Shimoff, Elizabeth Songster, May Story, Carolyn Strickland and Lynda Valles. Your feedback was priceless.

We also wish to acknowledge the hundreds of people who sent us stories, poems and quotes for possible inclusion in *Chicken Soup for the Mother's Soul 2*. While we were not able to use everything you sent in, we were deeply touched by your heartfelt intention to share yourselves and your stories with us and with our readers. Many of these may be used in future volumes of *Chicken Soup for the Soul*. Thank you!

Because of the size of this project, we may have left out the names of some people who helped us along the way. If so, we are sorry—please know that we really do appreciate all of you very deeply.

We are truly grateful for the many hands and hearts that have made this book possible. We love you all!

Introduction

A mother is not to be compared with any other person—she is incomparable.

African Proverb

There is no one like a mother. Our mothers give us life, love us, take care of us and want the best for us, no matter how old we are. They never stop being our mothers. There is no way to adequately describe the gift they have given us.

And no other experience in the world compares to *being* a mother. Being pregnant, going through labor and childbirth, and for both adoptive and biological mothers, seeing your baby's face for the very first time—these powerful occurrences are just the start of the uniquely compelling role in life we call motherhood.

It is because mothers have such a special place in our hearts that the first *Chicken Soup for the Mother's Soul* was created. This book, *Chicken Soup for the Mother's Soul 2,* was put together to answer the overwhelming demand of readers around the world who loved our first *Chicken Soup* book for mothers and wanted another helping. The books can be enjoyed in any order—you don't have to read the first book first. But, according to our readers, once you read one, you'll be hungry for more.

Whether you are a mother or treasure your relationship with your mother, the stories in this book will delight, inspire, move and touch you. For sons and daughters, these stories showcase the many ways mothers enrich our lives. For mothers, these true-life tales celebrate and acknowledge the multifaceted and demanding nature of your role.

Who else must juggle all the jobs necessary to raise a family in this day and age? At any given time, a mother may be called upon to be a breadwinner, food-provider, chauffeur, dishwasher, maid, social secretary, nurse, cheerleader, disciplinarian, personal shopper, confidante and so on. Sometimes a mother must perform all these jobs at once! It's clear that mothers are the original multitaskers.

These different aspects of a mother's life are described in the various chapters of *Chicken Soup for the Mother's Soul 2* The first chapter contains stories about that most fundamental ingredient of human life—love. These stories highlight the bond of love that connects mothers to their children. We also have included chapters about mothers' courage in the face of challenge, about the wisdom mothers share with their children, about miracles, about those special moments that create our fondest memories and about the amazing process of becoming a mother, either through birth or adoption.

We've added a chapter called "Mothers and Daughters" dedicated to the special relationship mothers and daughters share. Our chapter "On Motherhood" touches on a wide variety of subjects, some humorous, some poignant, all of which will resonate with mothers everywhere.

The chapter "Letting Go" includes stories that deal with

losing a mother or a child. This chapter provides comfort and inspiration to mothers and children coping with these devastating losses.

No book about mothers would be complete without tributes to our moms; so our final chapter, "Thank You, Mom," is a collection of stories that express gratitude for the priceless gifts bestowed by mothers.

This entire book was created as a tribute to mothers of all ages, and to serve as a source of inspiration, a sharing of experiences and a comfort in tough times. In addition, we hope that this book will provide practical wisdom for mothers. Carol's mother, after reading our initial manuscript, wrote Carol the following note: *"There are lots of things in these stories that I wish I had done as a mother. There are still things I can do. One thing I am going to do is tell my children and grandchildren and great-grandchildren how much I love them, and how much they mean to me."* Our sincere desire is that everyone reading this book is moved in a similar way.

The question remains: How can we ever adequately thank our mothers for the gift of life and unconditional love? How can we honor our daughters, wives, friends and other relatives who are mothers for the enormously important job they do? To start, we can remember to express all the love and gratitude we feel for them. In addition, we at *Chicken Soup* offer this "bouquet of stories" to mothers, and their children, everywhere. We hope it will warm your heart, make you laugh and give mothers a renewed sense of purpose and courage to continue what so many feel is life's most rewarding—and challenging— occupation.

Jack Canfield, Mark Victor Hansen,
Marci Shimoff and Carol Kline

Share with Us

We would love to hear your reactions to the stories in this book. Please let us know what your favorite stories were and how they affected you.

Also, please send us stories you would like to see published in future editions of *Chicken Soup for the Mother's Soul*. You can send us stories you have written or ones you have read and liked.

Send your stories to:
Chicken Soup for the Mother's Soul 2
P.O. Box 30880
Santa Barbara, CA 93130
To e-mail or visit our Web site:
www.chickensoup.com

1

ON LOVE

When Mother Teresa received her Nobel Prize, she was asked, "What can we do to promote world peace?" She replied, "Go home and love your family."

Reprinted by permission of Mike Shapiro.

The Call at Midnight

*One of the oldest human needs is having some-
one to wonder where you are when you don't
come home at night.*

Margaret Mead

We all know what's it like to get that phone call in the
middle of the night. This night's call was no different.
Jerking up to the ringing summons, I focused on the red
illuminated numbers of my clock. Midnight. Panicky
thoughts filled my sleep-dazed mind as I grabbed the
receiver.

"Hello?"

My heart pounded, I gripped the phone tighter and
eyed my husband, who was now turning to face my side
of the bed.

"Mama?" I could hardly hear the whisper over the sta-
tic. But my thoughts immediately went to my daughter.
When the desperate sound of a young crying voice
became clearer on the line, I grabbed for my husband and
squeezed his wrist.

"Mama, I know it's late. But don't . . . don't say anything, until I finish. And before you ask, yes, I've been drinking. I nearly ran off the road a few miles back and. . . ."

I drew in a sharp shallow breath, released my husband and pressed my hand against my forehead. Sleep still fogged my mind, and I attempted to fight back the panic. Something wasn't right.

"And I got so scared. All I could think about was how it would hurt you if a policeman came to your door and said I'd been killed. I want . . . to come home. I know running away was wrong. I know you've been worried sick. I should have called you days ago, but I was afraid . . . afraid. . . ."

Sobs of deep-felt emotion flowed from the receiver and poured into my heart. Immediately I pictured my daughter's face in my mind and my fogged senses seemed to clear. "I think—"

"No! Please let me finish! Please!" She pleaded, not so much in anger, but in desperation.

I paused and tried to think what to say. Before I could go on, she continued. "I'm pregnant, Mama. I know I shouldn't be drinking now . . . especially now, but I'm scared, Mama. So scared!"

The voice broke again, and I bit into my lip, feeling my own eyes fill with moisture. I looked at my husband who sat silently mouthing, "Who is it?"

I shook my head and when I didn't answer, he jumped up and left the room, returning seconds later with the portable phone held to his ear.

She must have heard the click in the line because she continued, "Are you still there? Please don't hang up on me! I need you. I feel so alone."

I clutched the phone and stared at my husband, seeking guidance. "I'm here, I wouldn't hang up," I said.

"I should have told you, Mama. I know I should have told you. But when we talk, you just keep telling me what

I should do. You read all those pamphlets on how to talk about sex and all, but all you do is talk. You don't listen to me. You never let me tell you how I feel. It is as if my feelings aren't important. Because you're my mother you think you have all the answers. But sometimes I don't need answers. I just want someone to listen."

I swallowed the lump in my throat and stared at the how-to-talk-to-your-kids pamphlets scattered on my nightstand. "I'm listening," I whispered.

"You know, back there on the road, after I got the car under control, I started thinking about the baby and taking care of it. Then I saw this phone booth, and it was as if I could hear you preaching about how people shouldn't drink and drive. So I called a taxi. I want to come home."

"That's good, Honey," I said, relief filling my chest. My husband came closer, sat down beside me and laced his fingers through mine. I knew from his touch that he thought I was doing and saying the right thing.

"But you know, I think I can drive now."

"No!" I snapped. My muscles stiffened, and I tightened the clasp on my husband's hand. "Please, wait for the taxi. Don't hang up on me until the taxi gets there."

"I just want to come home, Mama."

"I know. But do this for your mama. Wait for the taxi, please."

I listened to the silence in fear. When I didn't hear her answer, I bit into my lip and closed my eyes. Somehow I had to stop her from driving.

"There's the taxi, now."

Only when I heard someone in the background asking about a Yellow Cab did I feel my tension easing.

"I'm coming home, Mama." There was a click, and the phone went silent.

Moving from the bed, tears forming in my eyes, I walked out into the hall and went to stand in my sixteen-year-old daughter's room. The dark silence hung thick. My husband came from behind, wrapped his arms around me and rested his chin on the top of my head.

I wiped the tears from my cheeks. "We have to learn to listen," I said to him.

He pulled me around to face him. "We'll learn. You'll see." Then he took me into his arms, and I buried my head in his shoulder.

I let him hold me for several moments, then I pulled back and stared back at the bed. He studied me for a second, then asked, "Do you think she'll ever know she dialed the wrong number?"

I looked at our sleeping daughter, then back at him. "Maybe it wasn't such a wrong number."

"Mom, Dad, what are you doing?" The muffled young voice came from under the covers.

I walked over to my daughter, who now sat up staring into the darkness. "We're practicing," I answered.

"Practicing what?" she mumbled and laid back on the mattress, her eyes already closed in slumber.

"Listening," I whispered and brushed a hand over her cheek.

Christie Craig

A Mother's Love

I am convinced that the greatest legacy we can leave our children is happy memories.

Og Mandino

When I think of Clara Harden's family, happiness is what comes to mind. The sounds of laughter always greeted my visits.

Their lifestyle was so very different from mine. Clara's mother believed nurturing the mind was more important than trivial chores. Housekeeping wasn't a high priority. With five children ranging in age from Clara, the oldest at twelve, to a two-year-old baby, this lack of order sometimes bothered me but never for long. Their home was always in some state of chaos with at least one person's life in crisis, real or imagined. But I loved being part of this boisterous bunch, with their carefree, upbeat attitude toward life. Clara's mother was never too busy for us. She'd stop ironing to help with a cheerleading project, or switch off the vacuum cleaner and call us all to trek into the woods to gather specimens for a child's science project.

You never knew what you might do when you visited

there. Their lives were filled with fun and love—lots of love.

So the day the Harden children stepped off the school bus with red, swollen eyes, I knew something was desperately wrong. I rushed to Clara, pulled her aside, begging to hear what had happened but not prepared for her answer. The night before, Clara's mother had told them she had a terminal brain tumor, with only months to live. I remember that morning so well. Clara and I went behind the school building where we sobbed, holding each other, not knowing how to stop the unbelievable pain. We stayed there, sharing our grief until the bell rang for first period.

Several days passed before I visited the Harden home again. Dreading the sorrow and gloom, and filled with enormous guilt that my life was the same, I stalled until my mother convinced me that I couldn't neglect my friend and her family in their time of sadness.

So I visited. When I entered the Harden house, to my surprise and delight, I heard lively music and voices raised in animated discussion with lots of giggles and groans. Mrs. Harden sat on the sofa playing a game of Monopoly with her children gathered round. Everybody greeted me with smiles as I struggled to hide my bewilderment. This wasn't what I had expected.

Finally Clara freed herself from the game, and we went off to her room where she explained. Her mother had told them that the greatest gift they could give her would be to carry on as if nothing was amiss. She wanted her last memories to be happy, so they had agreed to try their hardest.

One day Clara's mother invited me for a special occasion. I rushed over to find her wearing a large gold turban. She explained that she'd decided to wear this instead of a wig now that her hair was falling out. She placed beads, glue, colored markers, scissors and cloth on the table, and instructed us to decorate it, while she sat like a regal maharaja. We turned the plain turban into a thing of gaudy beauty, each adding his or her own touch. Even as we squabbled over where the next bauble should be placed, I was conscious of how pale and fragile Mrs. Harden appeared. Afterwards, we had our picture taken with Clara's mother, each pointing proudly to her contribution to the turban. A fun memory to cherish, even though the unspoken fear of her leaving us wasn't far beneath the surface.

Finally the sad day arrived when Clara's mother died. In the weeks that followed, the Hardens' sorrow and pain were impossible to describe.

Then one day I arrived at school to see an animated Clara laughing, gesturing excitedly to her classmates. I heard her mother's name mentioned frequently. The old Clara was back. When I reached her side, she explained her happiness. That morning dressing her little sister for school, she'd found a funny note her mother had hidden in the child's socks. It was like having her mother back again.

That afternoon the Harden family tore their house apart hunting messages. Each new message was shared, but some went undetected. At Christmastime, when they retrieved the decorations from the attic, they found a wonderful Christmas message.

In the years that followed, messages continued sporadically. One even arrived on Clara's graduation day and another on her wedding day. Her mother had entrusted the letters to friends who delivered them on each special day. Even the day Clara's first child was born, a card and poignant message arrived. Each child received these short funny notes, or letters filled with love until the last reached adulthood.

Mr. Harden remarried, and on his wedding day a friend

presented him with a letter from his wife to be read to his children, in which she wished him happiness and instructed her children to envelop their new stepmother in love, because she had great faith that their father would never choose a woman who wouldn't be kind and loving to her precious children.

I've often thought of the pain Clara's mother must have experienced as she wrote these letters to her children. I also imagined the mischievous joy she felt when she hid these little notes. But through it all I've marveled at the wonderful memories she left those children, despite the pain she quietly suffered and the anguish she must have felt leaving her adored family. Those unselfish acts exemplify the greatest mother's love I've ever known.

Pat Laye

The Green Pajamas

I often watched from inside the house as my mother lugged a bucket of coal up the back steps. There were seventeen steps, and she usually brought up three loads of coal. She'd smile at me when she passed the window. Many times I'd shout through the glass, "Let me help!"

Her answer remained the same. "No. You stay inside where it's warm, Mannie. This only takes a minute. Besides, there's only one bucket." I must have been about nine years old.

You shouldn't have to do this, Mama. You've already worked all day in an office. I know you are tired.

Sometimes I wouldn't watch out the window. I'd busy myself in some other part of the house until I knew the coal for the next day had been brought up. Often I'd think about my friends who had fathers who could bring coal in. My own father had died before I was two.

Yet, even though my mother had to go to work each day and I missed not having a father, our life together in our small house included a lot of happiness.

As I grew older, I'd bring up the coal some days before my mother got home from work. It was terribly heavy, and I could never seem to get an adequate supply. I longed to find some way to make things better for her.

Unexpectedly, when I was about thirteen, I got a temporary job wrapping Christmas gifts at a local department store on the weekends. Although I was young and inexperienced, I worked quickly and earned twenty-three cents an hour. I was to get paid just before Christmas.

I wanted to get my mother something special that year—something to make life easier for her. After work one evening, I went window-shopping. I saw what my mother must have. A dark-haired mannequin modeled it. She had a radiant smile, and there were no tired lines on her face. She appeared pampered and relaxed in the moss-green satin lounging pajamas and short matching robe. She was about the size of my mother, I thought. I strained to see the price tag, turning my head almost upside down.

Twenty-five dollars and ninety-five cents. It was a fortune in 1950!

I had no idea if I would earn that much money. And even if I did, someone else might buy the beautiful set before I did. "Dear God," I prayed, looking intently at the pajamas, "hold them for me. Don't let anyone buy them, and let me make $25.95 at least."

Many evenings after work I stood in front of the shop window looking at the pajamas, smiling with deep satisfaction, relieved that they were still there.

Two nights before Christmas, I got paid. I poured the money out of my pay envelope and counted it. *Twenty-seven dollars and thirteen cents!* I had more than enough. I ran to the store with the money in my pocket. I entered out of breath and said to the saleslady, "I want to buy the beautiful pajamas set in the window. It's $25.95."

The saleswoman knew my mother and me. She smiled warmly, but suggested, "Marion, don't you think your mother would rather have something more . . . practical?"

I shook my head. I didn't even understand her subtle and kindly meant suggestion. Nothing on earth could have changed my mind. Those pajamas were for my mother. God had kept everyone from buying them, and I had the money to pay for them. I watched almost breathlessly as the woman took the pajamas and robe out of the window. While she got a box, I reached out and touched the soft satin. It was an exquisite moment. She wrapped the gift in soft tissue paper first, then in Christmas paper.

Finally, with the large package under my arm, I headed home. I put my mother's gift under the tree wondering how I'd wait until Christmas morning.

When it dawned, I couldn't open any of my gifts until my mother opened hers. I watched with a pounding heart.

She pulled back the tissue paper and her mouth formed a silent "O." She touched the pajamas with one finger—then held up the robe. She looked at me and said, "Oh, Mannie! It's the most beautiful thing I've ever seen. I don't know how you managed it, but I love it!"

I smiled and said, "Put it on, Mama."

She did and cooked breakfast in the outfit. All morning and afternoon she told me how much she loved the gift. I knew she would. She showed it to everyone who came by.

Through the years, even after they'd fallen apart, my mother would still tell people about those pajamas.

I reasoned that somehow my gift had made up for her having to bring in coal, build fires and walk to work. Each evening my mother would put on her satin pajamas and we'd sit by the fire listening to the radio, reading or talking.

As a child, I never realized that I should have gotten her a sweater or boots. No one could have talked me into it, for the green satin pajamas seemed to transport us into another world, just as I knew they would.

Many years later, after I had children of my own, my

mother was visiting with us one Christmas. Despite the joy of the season, I was a bit weary. It seemed like I'd been tired for months—maybe years. I'd finally come to realize that motherhood is a full-time, often mundane job, *every day*. The demands of raising a family had begun to show on my face and in my attitude.

The children squealed and tore into their presents. We were knee-deep in paper, which, I thought with irritation, I'd later have to clean up. Just then my mother handed me a present. "Merry Christmas, Mannie," she said softly.

She hadn't opened her gifts. She watched me as I carefully opened the large golden package. I folded back pink tissue paper and caught my breath. Slowly I lifted out the most beautiful, elegant pink-and-gold silk lounging robe I'd ever seen. I ran my hand over the gold-embossed design. "Ohhh," was all I could manage for a few moments. Then I said, "I can't believe it's for me. It's not something a mother would wear." I looked down at my worn flannel robe through a blur of tears.

"Put it on," my mother urged.

As I threw off the old robe, it seemed that I shed discouragement and weariness, too. I stood up wrapped in the lovely silk robe, knowing fully how Cinderella must have felt.

"Hey," one of the children said, "look at Mama. She's pretty." Everyone looked at me. My husband smiled.

Standing there that Christmas morning in the elegant robe, I suddenly remembered back through the years and recalled those green satin pajamas. I looked at my mother. I believe she remembered them, too. She must have, to have known how desperately I needed that robe. There was no need to say anything. We both understood the gifts too well.

Marion Bond West

Growing Up

Children are the anchors that hold a mother to life.

Sophocles

My mother had been reading me the story of *The Borrowers*, tiny visitors who hid in the nooks and crannies of a house. Captivated, I had set up a tiny dining room under a bookcase with dollhouse furniture. For weeks, I'd left out crumbs and a little bowl of water—the cap of the ketchup bottle—before I went to bed. Each morning before school, I would check to see if the Borrowers had returned. The water and crumbs would be gone. Sometimes there would even be a minuscule thank-you note left for me.

At nine, I should probably have been too old to really believe in the Borrowers. And though I suspected that my tiny visitors might be my mother's doing, I still held on to my belief that they just might be real. Then one day I came home from school, and my mother was gone. So were the Borrowers.

"Mommy is very sick," my father said to me, his usually

bright blue eyes looking tired and sad. "She's going to be in the hospital for a while until she gets better. Her kidneys aren't working right, and the doctors are going to make her better, but it's going to be a few weeks until you can see her because the doctors need that time to fix everything, okay?"

At first it seemed almost like a holiday. Everyone was especially nice to me; my father made my favorite meals or we would go out to dinner. He would bring home letters from my mother, "Make sure you ask Daddy to help you brush your hair; once the knots start, they are so hard to brush out." My hair, fine and wavy, was prone to tangles.

"Why can't I go and see Mommy?" I would ask him.

But his answer was always the same, "Not yet. She's too weak right now . . . but soon."

It was difficult to imagine my mother weak. We went swimming together every day in the summer, walking the five or so miles to the community pool and back again. Sometimes we chased each other around the house playing tag until the downstairs neighbors became so aggravated they would bang on the ceiling for us to stop. Then we'd collapse on the floor from laughing so hard, each of us trying in vain to be quiet.

And no matter how busy she was, she always had enough time to sit on the floor and play dolls with me. In her games, my dolls were never just going to parties, they were architects or doctors, or even running for Congress! I was probably the only nine-year-old whose mother introduced her to *Jane Eyre* and *Gone with the Wind.* I would read a bit of the book each day, and we would sit and discuss it over tea and cookies.

"The women in these books are strong, Lisa. They go through very difficult situations and learn that they can take care of themselves," my mother would tell me. She admired the strength in Jane and Scarlett, and she wanted me to value it as well.

But then things had begun to change. More often I would get up in the morning to fix my own breakfast, or come home from school to find a neighbor waiting to bring me to her home after school. Sometimes my parents would be in their bedroom talking with the door closed. The day the Borrowers stopped coming, I knew something was really wrong.

With my mother gone, I noticed that my father rarely went into my parents' bedroom anymore. I'd sometimes get up in the middle of night and find him lying asleep on the couch in the flickering light of the television, still in his work clothes. Pulling the blanket up over him and turning off the TV, I was a girl who was growing up. A girl who no longer believed in the Borrowers.

"Daddy?" I asked my father one day, "Is Mommy going to die?" He looked at me for what seemed forever, then grabbed my arms and pulled me to him. "Maybe," he said and then lowered his head and began to weep. I wrapped my arms around his neck and held him close. We sat there and cried, for the first time, together.

Then he told me that my mother had been diagnosed with end-stage renal failure, which meant that her kidneys had failed and that unless she had a kidney transplant, she would probably die. In the early 1970s, dialysis as a treatment for renal failure was in its early stages. My mother was at the County Medical Center where they had access to new medical technology. It had been touch-and-go for several weeks, and at times it appeared as though they might have waited too long to be able to help my mother. I told my father I wanted to see her.

At the hospital, my father shouted at the nurse at the desk in the intensive care unit, "I don't care if it's not allowed."

"It will be too disturbing for the child," the nurse said to my dad in a low voice, motioning for him to lower his voice as well.

My father walked over to me where I was sitting on a bench against the wall. "Listen, Honey, I'm going to go and talk to the chief of staff about you seeing your mommy. Sit here and draw me a picture, and I'll be back in a few minutes, okay?" I nodded my head and watched him walk off down the hall with the nurse.

The large double doors had the words "Only Medical Staff Allowed" written on them in large bold letters. A sign in front of the bench said "Children under fifteen not admitted." The sounds coming from behind the double doors frightened me and the thought that my mother was in there frightened me even more.

But as I sat there, my fear dissolved and I became angrier and angrier. *Who were these strangers to keep me away from my mother? Scarlett O'Hara wouldn't have sat by and let people tell her what she could and couldn't do.* My mother was behind that door, and I was going to go in and find her.

Putting both hands on one side of the ICU door, I pushed as hard as I could. Inside, bright fluorescent lights illuminated the room, people in white scurried around and loud beeping filled the air. Without knowing how I knew, I turned to my right and started to walk toward a bed where most of the activity was being focused. No one seemed to notice me.

The woman on the bed seemed very small and was surrounded by tubes and machines with blinking lights. She looked like my mother, except paler and smaller than I remembered. Her eyes were closed and her long dark hair was spread out on her pillow.

"She's not responding!" a white-coated man shouted.

"Her pressure is too low," a nurse shouted back to the man in the white coat.

"Mommy," I said quietly, then again louder. *"Mommy?"*

People started running over to me. "Get her out of here!" bellowed the man in the white coat.

"Wait!" shouted the nurse and motioned for me to come over. As I walked over to my mother, everyone stepped back except for the man in the white coat who tried to grab my shoulder. The nurse standing by the bed put her hand up to stop him.

"Look," she said, glancing down at my mother.

My mother had opened her eyes. "Lisa?" She turned her head to look at me and smiled. The frenetic beeping seemed to slow down.

"Mommy, it's me." I stood next to the bed, wanting to crawl in beside her despite the machines and tubes all around her.

"Come here." She raised her arms, and I let her wrap her arms around me. "Don't be scared by all of this. These machines are going to make me better. We'll have one in our house, and I'll be able to come home to stay." Frowning ever so slightly, she added, "Has anyone been helping you brush your hair?" Laughter from behind me reminded me that we weren't alone. Doctors and nurses were standing around watching us, many with tears in their eyes.

They knew, though I didn't, that only moments ago my mother had actually died. Later she told me that she remembered seeing a young woman lying on a hospital bed connected to tubes and machines. She felt very sorry for the woman until she realized that she was looking at herself and, for the first time in months, she felt no pain or discomfort. In what seemed like a movie, she remembered seeing people rush over to her to try and resuscitate her.

"I felt such peace, such happiness. I didn't want to be

that woman on the bed anymore until I heard a girl's voice that said 'Mommy?'"

When she realized that the voice was mine, she knew that she had to come back. I'm sure that if I hadn't violated hospital policy and been there to call her back, things would have turned out very differently.

Soon after, my mother came home, along with a dialysis machine that became a permanent part of our family. And although the Borrowers never returned, I didn't need them anymore. I was a girl who could brush the tangles out of her own hair. I could fix a meal or two without any help. I was a girl who still had her mother. And that was the most important part.

Lisa Duffy-Korpics

To Have and to Hold

In the summer of 1959, I flew from Washington, D.C., to Los Angeles accompanied by my father. Nineteen years old, pregnant and frightened, I was flying to this distant city to live with total strangers, so that my unborn child could be born far away from prying eyes and gossiping mouths and then be put up for private adoption.

On September 3, I gave birth to a little boy and though I saw him once, lying in the nursery, I was not allowed to hold him. The doctor and nurses felt it would be too painful for me, and I suppose they were right. Shortly after the birth, I flew back to Washington, signed the adoption papers and, as my doctor had suggested, continued on with my life.

Although the pain of the parting diminished with time, I never forgot for a moment that I had a son. Every September third for the next thirty-three years I silently mourned, grieving for the child I had given away. Mother's Day was always the worst. It seemed that every woman I knew was a mom. *I'm a mother, too,* I wanted to say but couldn't.

And so the years passed and turned into decades, and

the memory of my only child lingered just beneath my conscious mind, ready to explode at a moment's notice.

Then on March 26, 1993, I received this message on my answering machine: "Elizabeth," a woman's voice said, "I have some news which I hope will be of interest to you and bring you great joy and happiness."

Her voice broke, and it was quite evident she was crying. "If you are the same Elizabeth Thring who did me a favor thirty-three years ago, please call me in Newport Beach, California. I would very much like to have a chat with you."

I called back immediately and was connected to an answering machine. Three days later, when I finally got through, the woman said her name was Susie. She thanked me profusely for calling and asked if I knew who she was.

"I believe so," I replied, "but I'm not 100 percent sure."

"Oh, Elizabeth," she said, "I adopted your beautiful baby boy thirty-three years ago, and I am just calling to tell you what a wonderful son you have. Bill is married to a terrific girl, and you have two absolutely beautiful little granddaughters."

I couldn't believe what I was hearing. I had fantasized about this very moment in some form or another for years, and now it was a reality. I told her that I couldn't think of another woman I knew with such generosity of spirit. Susie said that one day while watching her two little granddaughters playing, she thought to herself, "What woman wouldn't want to know about such beautiful children?" and so she began to search for me.

She told me that although Bill knew generally that she was looking for me, he had no knowledge of this most recent attempt to locate me, since there was always the possibility that I might not want to see him.

Soon after, I sent Bill a letter. In it I wrote: *Oh, what*

joy—what pure, absolute, sheer joy, to discover after all these years that you are here, on the same earth, under the same blue heaven and stars and moon at night as I—and that you, my darling boy, want to know me as much as I yearn to know, hold and love you. Billy, it is important for me that you know I never, ever forgot you or ceased loving you. I thank you from the bottom of my heart for wanting to know me and not giving up on me. Your loving mother, Elizabeth.

In the middle of April I flew to Los Angeles. On the way, I wrote thirty-three birthday cards to my son with a short description of what I had done for each year of his life. *Bill needs,* I thought, *to learn about me, too.*

DeAnn, Bill's wife, videotaped me coming down the ramp at the airport. With her were my granddaughters, and standing just behind her was a very tall, blond, impeccably dressed man.

When he saw me, Bill stepped from behind his wife and walked toward me with arms open wide. Into this circle of love I stepped, feeling just like every other mother in the world holding her baby for the first time.

Elizabeth Thring

Christmas Joy

We are here to help one another along life's journey.

William Bennett

In one terrible September, both my mother and sister were killed in a tragic car accident. That December, I couldn't imagine celebrating Christmas.

Christmas? *How would I ever crawl through this holiday?* Joy to the world? *How could I rejoice and be merry when my heart was splintered apart?* I, who had always gloried in the joys and wonders of Christmas, wanted to wipe the day off the calendar. But having two small daughters, I numbly moved through all the usual preparations.

As the days moved closer to Christmas, my sorrow deepened and I found myself immersed in the quicksand of self-pity. Wasn't it enough that I had a helpless and handicapped child, and hardly any financial resources? Add the crushing blow of both my mother and sister being killed, and it was more heartache than I could carry.

On the twenty-third of December, I was so deep into the pit of tears, I could hardly function. That evening, my heart aching, I despondently started out for a walk. The magic of Christmas was everywhere: fresh snow, star-sprinkled skies, lighted trees in the windows, wreaths on the doors and candles shining.

As I dragged along, I imagined that everyone was happy except for me. Passing the house of a neighbor, it began to seep into my memory that her husband had died, and this would be her first Christmas alone. I looked at the next house: They were having horrendous problems with their teenager. In the next home, behind those lighted windows, were sorrowing parents, for they had lost a child in the spring.

Silently I walked through our little town, and as I passed each home, for the first time in months, I began to remember other people's suffering instead of my own, and to realize I was not the only person life had punched in the solar plexus. There was hardly a household that didn't have sorrow or tragedy. Did not everyone bear their own burdens and cry their own tears?

Back home, standing at the window, I glanced down the hill at the house on the corner. Within those walls lived a mother, her four children and their grandmother. There were no twinkling lights or wrapped packages under that roof. Everyone in town was aware of their plight and struggles, and although my financial resources might be slim, theirs were downright precarious. What type of Christmas would they be having? Would the little girl, who was my youngest daughter's age, receive a doll or any toy? What would they have for Christmas dinner?

Empathy began to awaken me and nudge the edges of my grief. It dawned on me that I had found the key to unlock myself from misery, for there—right under my nose—was someone worse off than myself. If I could gather my strength and forget about me, I could make a difference in a family's Christmas.

December twenty-fourth was a flurry of activity. I called people and they called others, resulting in a steady stream of cheerful givers crossing my threshold. By afternoon, an amazing assortment of toys, clothing and food was piled high on my dining room table.

Heather, my five-year-old daughter, helped me, while Audrey, my handicapped daughter, looked on. Together we wrapped packages, fixed a box with the makings of a complete dinner and shared the excitement.

Night came, and we were at last finished. Leaving Audrey with her father, Heather and I loaded the over-flowing boxes in the car and coasted down the hill. It was exhilarating to creep from car to porch, sliding the boxes across the wooden boards, all the while tiptoeing and whispering "Sh-h-h-h." When everything was deposited, we knocked on the door and ran like rabbits. We tumbled into the ditch and peered out from behind a bush.

The porch light blazed on. The little girl who was Heather's age opened the door, stood in the glow of light looking at boxes with wrapped gifts spilling out and began jumping up and down, shouting, "Christmas has come! Christmas has come!"

The family crowded onto the little porch, laughing and shouting, the children taking out packages and calling out the names on the tags, the light from within and without shining over them. Then, with merriment, they took everything inside, closed the door, flicked off the porch light and everything was silent.

There in the darkness and stillness of the night, peace poured into my soul, wrapping its sweet warmth around my heart. The warmth didn't extinguish sorrow . . . but made it bearable. It didn't wipe out memories . . . but soft-ened them, so I could once more welcome happiness.

Heather and I scrambled up from the ditch, and I hugged my daughter close while we softly laughed. I had found the secret: In reaching out to others, we heal ourselves; in giving happiness, we receive our peace; and in rising above our sorrows, we find our joy. My soul was filled, for there on that lovely winter's eve, Christmas came into my heart!

Phyllis Volkens

"Because your mother is cold, that's why."

The Sweater

It was too late when I realized I'd made a mistake. I'd been so blinded by my own grief at the rapid decline and death of my father that I hadn't thought through how his death would affect my daughter.

For months, Dad had been complaining of pain in his shoulder, "a pinched nerve"—or so we thought. When he fell ill on vacation and was diagnosed with progressive, primary prostate cancer, we were all shocked.

My dad was one of those special people who was born with a twinkle in his eye. I've never met anyone who didn't think the world of him. Little children, especially, were drawn to him like candy. He would clasp his hands together and grin with such joy that kids would come running. During a visit with my sister in Ireland, he taught the village children how to play American football. The Irish children would often come by in the evenings to ask, "Can Grandpa come out and play?"

So it was no surprise that he was especially close to my five-year-old daughter, Jodi, the last of his grandchildren to reside near him in the United States. They would giggle and laugh together for hours, making up stories and feeding pretend animals in the backyard.

By the time they found Dad's cancer, it had spread to his bones and things went quickly. When we went to visit him, Jodi sat quietly next to the bed, pretending to read from a book to him—there were no more boisterous games. I had explained to her that Grandpa was very sick and that he couldn't play like he used to, but it was hard for her five-year-old mind to comprehend.

Toward the end, I didn't take Jodi along, because I didn't want her to be frightened by Dad's gaunt frame and the look of pain and suffering on the face of the vital man we all adored.

After he died, I didn't know if Jodi understood the finality of death, or if she just thought that Grandpa was out of town, "on vacation." But as the weeks went by, she became very quiet and withdrawn, crying frequently at things I thought odd.

One evening, I sat with her on my lap and gently stroked her hair.

"You seem very sad, Pumpkin," I said. "Can you tell me what's wrong?"

She was silent for a few moments and then broke into sobs.

"I didn't get to say good-bye to Grandpa," she said.

That's when I realized that in my well-meaning way, I'd made a mistake.

Through a haze of mutual tears, we sat and rocked, and talked about Grandpa and all the wonderful times we'd had with him.

"Would you like to say good-bye to Grandpa now?" I asked.

She looked at me as if I were a little strange.

"Close your eyes. Now picture Grandpa's face right in front of you. When he smiles, you can talk to him."

Suddenly she got a huge grin on her face. "He's smiling so big at me!"

"Then tell him whatever you want to tell him."

"Grandpa," she said, "I love you and I miss you so much. I want to say good-bye for now. Good-bye, Grandpa."

Then I remembered the gifts I'd taken for myself when my mother packed my father's clothes away. I had asked her for a couple of his old cozy sweaters that he loved to hang around in on the weekends. I went and got the two blue sweaters and offered one to Jodi.

"These are special sweaters of Grandpa's. If we are sad or missing him, we can put them on and feel as though he is hugging us."

We both wept again as we each pulled one over our heads. Then I held her as she gently drifted off to sleep. For the first time in weeks, she seemed at peace, a slight smile on her face.

Both sweaters were well used over the years. Frequently if Jodi was having a hard time, she retreated to her room. When I checked on her later, usually I'd find her stretched out on her bed with Grandpa's old blue sweater wrapped around her—sleeping peacefully with just the slightest hint of a smile on her face.

Jodi is eighteen now and still loves to wear Grandpa's sweater. Somehow, it always fits perfectly. You see, it's the size of a hug.

Pamela Albee

"Happy Mother's Day!"

Mother's Day Flowers

When my husband calmly announced that, after eleven years of marriage, he had filed for a divorce and was moving out, my first thought was for my children. My son was just five, and my daughter, four. Could I hold us together and give them a sense of "family"? Could I, as a single parent, maintain our home and teach them the ethics and values I knew they would need in life? All I knew was that I had to try.

So every Sunday, we attended church. During the week, I made time to review their homework with them, and we often discussed why it was important to do the right things. This took time and energy when I had little to spare, and worse, it was hard to tell if I was really reaching them.

One Mother's Day, two years after the divorce, as we walked into church, I noticed carts of beautiful flowers in little pots on either side of the altar. During the service, the pastor told us that he thought motherhood was one of the toughest jobs in life, and deserved recognition and reward. He then asked every child to come forward to pick out a beautiful flower and present it to their mother as a symbol of how much they were loved and appreciated.

My son and daughter, hand in hand, went up the aisle

with the other children. Together they considered which plant to bring back to me. We had certainly survived some hard times, and this little bit of appreciation was just what I needed. I looked at the beautiful begonias, the golden marigolds and purple pansies, and started planning where I could plant whichever one they chose for me, for surely they would bring me a beautiful bloom to show their love.

My children took their assignment seriously, and looked over every pot on all the carts. Long after the other children had returned to their seats, and presented the other mothers with a beautiful potted flower, my two were still making their selection. Finally, with a joyful exclamation, they made their selection from the back of one of the carts. With exuberant smiles lighting their faces, they proudly proceeded down the aisle to where I was seated and presented me with the plant they had chosen as their Mother's Day gift of appreciation.

I stared in amazement at the broken, bedraggled, sickly looking stick being held out to me by my son. Mortified, I accepted the pot from him. They had obviously chosen the smallest, sickest plant—it didn't even have a bloom on it. Looking down at their smiling faces, I saw their pride in this choice, and knowing how long it took them to choose this particular plant, I smiled and accepted their gift.

But then I had to ask—out of all those beautiful flowers—*what* had made them pick this particular plant to give to me?

With great pride, my son said, "This one looked like it needed you, Mom."

As tears flowed down my face, I hugged both children close. They had just given me the greatest Mother's Day gift I could ever have imagined. My hard work and sacrifices had not been in vain—they would grow up just fine.

Patricia A. Rinaldi

The Neighbor Lady

When I was in grade school, I used to have a dream that Mrs. Paxton's house next door had fallen down the hill with Mrs. Paxton in it. If that imagined event had actually come to pass, I was sure my life would get much better.

We lived then in a suburb of Pittsburgh—a family neighborhood with lots of kids. It was ideal: big yards, lots of little wooded lots, safe streets, hills for sledding and a few dangerous places to explore. Everything a boy could want. Except for Mrs. Paxton, our neighbor lady.

She was a small, thin woman, who wore spectacles on a black cord around her neck. She had a receding hairline and a ring of gray curls high on her forehead that looked, from a distance, a little like a halo. She never had kids of her own, which seemed to us a lucky break because Mrs. Paxton was any kid's worst enemy: a nosy woman who not only watched us more closely than our own mothers, but reported what she saw.

From her upstairs bedroom window Mrs. Paxton had a view of our backyard, our hillside and the street below. So she could see almost everything we did. Sometimes when we got into fights, she would tap on the glass with a pencil; you would be surprised how far that sound carries. Other times, if we were into something dangerous like hopping curbs on our bikes, she would tell my parents and I would get a lecture . . . at least a lecture.

Our only respite from Mrs. Paxton's constant intrusion on our privacy was on Thursday afternoons in the summer. Then three cars would pull into her driveway, and music teachers from my school would file into her house.

That got my attention because I thought teachers made themselves cocoons or something and just hibernated in the summer. But there they were carrying instrument cases, and after a while we would hear the sounds of a string quartet coming though the open windows.

Mrs. Paxton herself played the viola, and I often listened more attentively when her instrument had the melody. I'd begun piano lessons a few years earlier and had gotten good enough to know how to really listen to music. Still, there was something about the sound the string quartet made, sounds that got to me in a way the piano couldn't.

When Mrs. Paxton played, she made a warm, sweet sound like a song—sweet and mellow as summer.

Quartet-day was good news because it meant that Mrs. Paxton was not at her upstairs window, and we could do the things we did not want our parents to hear about. So my friends and I would head down the hill to the drainage ditch. My own mother said it was "a filthy sewer," but really neat salamanders lived there, so I liked it a lot. Sometimes we would crawl into the forbidden burned-out house—still standing because of some legal tangle. We would peel back water-stained wallpaper looking for hidden messages or sift through ashes, looking for coins.

If we did any of these things unaccompanied by the sounds of string quartets from Mrs. Paxton's house, our parents would know about it immediately. Mrs. Paxton knew everything about our neighborhood and told everything she knew to some grown-up or other. I couldn't imagine why she was like that. Was it because she never had kids of her own that she didn't like us?

By the end of summer, I entered the eighth grade, and signed up for the school orchestra. I got up the nerve and went to see the orchestra director about the possibility of learning on one of the school instruments. But Miss Wagner told me all of the stringed instruments had already been signed out. She said she'd love it if I could help out in the percussion section, though.

That was a long way from what I had in mind, so I moped around the house for a few days. My parents could not afford to buy me an instrument, and I did not want to beg for it.

Though I spent more time than usual running with my friends, I could not get the idea of making music out of my head.

Then one day I came in from riding bikes with my friends to find Mrs. Paxton sitting in our very own living room talking with my mother. I tried to step slowly backwards out the front door, but my mother had already seen me and told me to come in. Mrs. Paxton had something she wanted to say to me.

I felt my body get sort of heavy, and I shuffled into the room. I sat down on a straight-backed chair across the room from Mrs. Paxton. She patted the seat next to her on the couch and told me to come sit beside her. I would rather have been told I had to play with my sister's friends. I delayed moving, and my mother shot me one of her looks—the kind that get you out of your seat in a hurry.

I considered sitting at the far end of the couch, but I knew my mother would consider that noncompliance. So I sat cautiously down next to Mrs. Paxton. To my surprise, Mrs. Paxton smelled like lilacs. She immediately began to quiz me about music, of all things. She wanted to know what I liked and if I really wanted to play a stringed instrument—somehow she even knew that.

I looked at my mother to see if she had blabbed it, but she shook her head telling me she had not. I did not know what to tell Mrs. Paxton about why I wanted to play in the orchestra so badly. I had become obsessed with making a kind of music that was like singing.

But that's just not the kind of thing you say, not even to your own mother. Still, something inside told me to just say it anyway and let everyone laugh if they wanted to.

I said, "I want to play something with strings because you can make them sing the way a voice does."

Mrs. Paxton's eyes widened. She looked at me very curiously as though I had somehow said the magic words. Then she lifted a long black box from the floor and placed it between us on the couch. She opened it, turned back the green velvet cover, took out her viola and held it in her lap. Sort of like the way my mother held babies.

It was the instrument of my dreams. The honey-colored viola glowed and shone. She stroked it gently with her hand and then handed it to me. "I want you to have this. It is a loan until you have your own someday."

I didn't know what to do. I stared at her and then the viola. I couldn't move. She took my hand in hers, which was strangely soft and warm, and put my fingers around the neck of the instrument. I looked at her. She smiled. I looked at my mother. She smiled. I started to shake a little and was really afraid I might cry or do something else disgraceful. But somehow I kept hold of my self-respect.

She did not stay long after that. I wanted to say something really nice to her, but I was so used to hating her I couldn't think of anything at all to say except, "Thank you very much." It seemed lame somehow, considering what the instrument meant to both of us.

Later, I accused my mother of telling Mrs. Paxton about

my wanting an instrument. But she swore she hadn't done anything of the kind. "Mrs. Paxton just knows things," she said.

"But why would she do this?" I asked, still amazed by my good luck.

"Well, she never had children of her own. I think she just loves you." I looked at my mother as though she had lost her last marble. "When you're older . . ." I was out of the room before she finished that dumb line I knew by heart.

Over the years I often thought about Mrs. Paxton and the mystery of why she gave me the thing she loved most in the world. I eventually got good enough to play in a string quartet of my own, to tour Russia, to play in an orchestra in Carnegie Hall, to become principal violist of the Florida Philharmonic.

And after all this time, I see that Mrs. Paxton knew more about me than I ever imagined, knew me almost as well as my own mother.

I think she watched out for me and cared about me just as she might have done for a son of her own. And I think that if she had been able to have children they would have been very lucky. She would not only have watched over them, but she would have opened doors they never knew existed, opened doors to joy and happiness and the immeasurable pleasure of finding the thing you loved to do most in the world—just as she had done for me.

So now as I get ready to begin Fort Lauderdale's Beethoven at the Beach concert, I put on the festival T-shirt that the orchestra wears for these performances. And I hope that my playing will have a sound like singing, a sound I heard long ago coming from Mrs. Paxton's open windows on a summer afternoon.

Michael McClelland

A Time for Memories

Loving a child is circular business. . . . The more you give, the more you get, the more you get, the more you want to give.

Penelope Leach

One balmy summer afternoon, I sat on an old blanket under a pine tree chatting with my mother. For years, we had been coming to this park for family picnics and gatherings, and my mother and I often sat in this same spot.

In recent years, we usually just talked about life, but sometimes we recalled events from my childhood. Like the time I was thirteen and had my first date, when Mother brought me to this spot under the tree and told me about the facts of life. Or the time a few years later, when my hair turned out pink for my senior prom and she'd held me while I cried. But the most special event that occurred next to this tree was when I told Mother I was getting married. Tears filled her eyes and this time I held *her* while she cried. She told me she was sad to lose her little girl but happy to see that I had turned into a beautiful young woman.

Over the years, we'd watched the pine trees in this park grow tall and straight until their needles seemed to touch the clouds. Each year of their growth seemed to match our increasingly close relationship and the deepening love we had for each other.

On this particular sunny afternoon, Mother and I sat quietly breathing in the scent of freshly mown grass. She was unusually solemn and took me by surprise when she asked me, "Who will you bring here after I'm gone?"

I gave her one of my arched-eyebrow inquiries, then smiled. After a few moments, when she didn't return my smile, I began to wonder what made her ask such a disturbing question. Mother picked up a blade of grass and began to shred it with her fingernail. I'd become well acquainted with my mother's habits, and this particular one indicated she had something serious on her mind.

For several minutes, we sat in silence gathering our thoughts. A couple of bluejays squawked nearby and an airplane flew overhead, but they didn't ease the awkward moment between us. Finally, I reached over and took my mother's hand in mine. "There's nothing you can't tell me, Mother," I said. "We will handle this together, like we always have."

She looked into my face, and her eyes filled with tears that spilt down her cheeks—cheeks that were alarmingly pale. Even before she said it, I knew what was coming. Mother was dying.

I held her tightly while she told me that her heart condition was worsening and couldn't be repaired. I think I had known for quite a while but had not been willing to admit it to myself. She'd had several heart attacks and, a few years ago, even open-heart surgery. What I didn't know, and what she had kept from me, was that her condition wasn't improving. We talked about her options, which were few; we cried, held each other and wished for more time together.

That was many years ago now. Mother died soon after that day, before my sons had a chance to know her. I still come to the park, but now I bring my boys. I still sit under that same sturdy pine tree on an old blanket and talk to my sons of family picnics, gatherings and the grand-mother they never knew. Just as my mother did with me, I tell my children about their youthful antics and praise them for their accomplishments as young adults. We come to this special place to create our own memories—memo-ries that I know would make my mother smile with pride.

Not long ago my oldest son wanted to come to the park and talk, so we came and sat under our tree. He hemmed and hawed for a few minutes, then he finally told me he was getting married. I cried tears of joy as my son hugged me—his hug a rare and special treat. I told him how proud I was of the man he had become.

As I sat there that cool April afternoon soaking up the sun and the smell of freshly mown grass, I felt I had come full circle under this giant pine tree. Holding my son in my arms, I was happy for him, just the way I knew my mother had been happy for me all those years ago when I told her I was getting married.

Looking over my son's shoulder, I saw that several young pine saplings had been planted recently. *As these trees grow straight and tall,* I thought, *will the lives of my family continue to grow with them?* I wanted to share this spot with my grandchildren, too.

The branches above were swaying in the breeze and in them I heard a whispering voice: Who will you bring here when I'm gone? It was my mother's voice, and I tightened my arms around my son.

Sharon Wright

2

ON COURAGE

There are some things you learn best in calm, and some in storm.

Willa Cather

Mother of Three Thousand Sons

Who gives to me teaches me to give.

Ancient Proverb

Thirty years ago, when I was a journalist in Philadelphia, I founded a small magazine called *Umoja* (Swahili for unity), which dealt with the issues confronting African-Americans.

Because of the many letters the magazine received about the gang problem in our city, I asked my husband, Dave, to do some research. He began walking the streets, asking questions, talking to people and observing the problem firsthand.

My interest in the subject was purely professional— until the day Dave returned from a fact-finding mission and reported that our second son, Robin, was a member of a gang. Even worse, Robin was the gang's favorite, called the "heart of the corner." The heart is the favorite target if gang wars occur. I was shocked and frightened. How could this be happening in *my* home, in *my* family? But it was true. My son was a walking bull's-eye.

We had six sons, ranging in age from eleven to eighteen. I looked carefully at sixteen-year-old Robin that evening when he came home. I hadn't noticed it before, but Robin *was* different. He wore his clothing differently, and his manner was tougher. I confronted him, and he didn't lie. Yes, he was a gang member—and nothing I said or did was going to change that.

It was as if the bottom dropped out of my world. I stopped eating; I couldn't sleep. In an effort to save my son, I talked to social service agencies and the police, but no one seemed to have an answer. No one seemed able to do anything.

But everyone agreed that the breakdown of the family was the main source of the gang problem. I thought our family was strong, but for Robin, obviously something was missing.

Then an idea came to me. If family was the problem, could family also be the solution? Why not invite Robin's gang to live in our home? We could show them how real families work.

"Are you out of your mind?" Dave said when I told him my idea.

But I was on fire with my idea and wouldn't give up. Eventually he agreed to give it a try. Our other sons were more or less open—they knew Robin's life was on the line. Robin was thrilled with the idea—his boys *and* his family all under one roof.

Robin's gang leader, in serious trouble on the street, needed a place to hide out. He jumped at the chance to live with us, and the rest of the gang followed his lead. I called every parent I could reach to inform them of our plan, and they all agreed to let their sons come to us.

Our house was a small one, hardly large enough for our original family. When fifteen more boys moved in, it felt as crowded as a sardine can. But we made it work. All the boys slept in sleeping bags on the living room floor, and at mealtime the sleeping bags were rolled and stowed and folding tables and chairs were set up.

The first few weeks were difficult. Many times I wondered if Dave had been right about me being out of my mind. The boys chafed at doing chores, wouldn't participate in our family meetings and didn't want to get the part-time jobs I insisted on. But I was determined. I looked at the situation as if it were a puzzle and knew we'd have to find the right pieces if we were going to save the lives of these kids.

Finally we asked the boys to devise rules we could all live by. We were a little nervous about this because if we didn't like their rules, it would be difficult to enforce our own. But I breathed a sigh of relief when they read out their four rules: 1) No fighting in the house, 2) No drugs or drinking, 3) No girls in their rooms, and 4) No gang warring.

Maybe, just maybe, this will work, I thought. We found that since the boys had made up the rules, they were very good about keeping them.

The biggest and most pressing challenge was getting enough food. Our small savings were soon exhausted, but I had the idea to sell back issues of the magazine, *Umoja,* that were stored in our basement. The boys took stacks and peddled them all over Philadelphia, bringing home money to buy food.

We also approached a local church and told them we needed food. They were very supportive and sent notices to affluent parishes asking for food donations. The response was overwhelming. Soon we were inundated. Trucks loaded with food began coming down our block, headed for "The House of Umoja."

Now we had more food than we could use. We decided to give some away to people in the area who could use it.

The boys were excited about distributing food. For most of them, it was the first time they had ever found themselves in the position of benefactors—giving something to help others.

After that, things began to fall into place. The boys got jobs and began contributing money to cover our household expenses. This new "gang" organized yard sales, sold candy door-to-door, and escorted elderly people to the bank.

We faced our largest hurdle the day George, one of the old gang's bitterest rivals, showed up asking to join our family. He realized he needed to take this drastic step, or he would end up in jail or dead. The boys were silent, wrestling with their hatred for their former enemy. But something new had entered their hearts—commitment to family, compassion, kindness—squeezing out their old "turf mentality." The tension broke as the boys accepted George into our new family.

As the weeks went by, I found myself falling in love with the boys; they became like my own children. Some of them even started calling me Mom. When the gang had first arrived, they'd all had street names like Killer, Snake Eyes, Bird, Crow and Peewee. I began to give them African names with special meanings. These were names that acknowledged their bravery or discipline or strength. Although it was never stated, the boys knew they had to earn those names.

Stories about our family spread all over the city. More and more boys came wanting to live with us. Finally, the state of Pennsylvania offered us a contract to officially care for these boys under the banner of foster care. We became "House of Umoja–Boystown," and with our new funds, we were able to expand, buying more houses on our street and hiring staff. The flow of boys kept coming . . . and we just kept opening our arms to gather them in.

It wasn't always easy living with these street kids. Most people had given up on them, and for good reason. Everyone else told these boys what to do, but I decided to listen to them instead. I tried always to see them through a mother's eyes, focusing on the good in them. It didn't always work, but enough of the time, it did.

It didn't work with one boy named Spike. From the first moment he arrived he was a troublemaker—picking fights, refusing to work, disrupting meetings. When he left, I shook my head in despair. I had tried so hard to show him what it felt like to be a member of a loving family. I hated to lose any of the boys.

Some years later, a man came bursting into my office with a baby in his arms. It was Spike! "Mom," he said, placing his tiny daughter in my arms, "I want you to give her a name."

I was speechless with surprise, but as I looked at the beautiful child in my arms, her name came to me: "Fatima," I said softly, "it means 'Shining One.'"

Spike took Fatima from me and said, "I want to raise her like you showed me. I want her to be part of our family." Spike had heard me after all.

There have been other boys, too, who have surprised me by the depth of their dedication and commitment to our family. Two years after we started our experiment, we decided to have a gang conference. We asked the kids who lived with us, as well as the young men who had gone on to careers and their own homes, to go back to their old gangs and ask the new leaders to come to the conference to discuss ending gang deaths citywide. When one boy approached his old gang, they beat him up so badly he ended up in the hospital for a few days. But the minute he was released, that boy went straight back and again asked the gang leader if he would come to our house for the conference. Out of respect for his bravery, the gang leader attended.

Those were the first boys. In the thirty years since, over three thousand have followed. They are all my sons. Though some are now middle-aged men, they still come back to the house for advice or just to visit, play basketball and talk to the current group of young men who make up the family at the House of Umoja. They often bring their wives and children to celebrate birthdays and anniversaries.

I began with only the intention to save my son's life, but that simple act of motherly love grew, blossoming into a full-time service that has saved thousands of lives. While no one person can do everything, *anyone* can start something.

Unity, love, family—these are the things that saved my sons and will save many more sons to come. There is no limit to this love. My own name, Falaka, means "new day." Every day for me is another opportunity to be a mother to these boys who, more than anything, simply need love.

Falaka Fattah

Love in the Mail

More people ask the Lord to lighten their burdens
than ask him to strengthen their backs.

Author Unknown

One fall, my eight-year-old son Andy came down with
bronchitis. We went to the pediatrician, who gave us medication and sent us home. But over the next few days,
Andy became worse, not better. At one point, he was having so much trouble breathing that I rushed him to the
emergency room. Suspecting asthma, they X-rayed his
chest.

That's when our lives changed. The nurses ushered
Andy and me into a small room. Out of the bustling
atmosphere of the ER, everything became very quiet. Too
quiet. It seemed to me that the doctors and nurses were all
whispering. A nurse asked me if I wanted to call my husband. I did. He came and the three of us sat together in
front of the doctor, waiting.

Nothing in the English language changes your life like
the six-letter word: cancer. The chest X ray, the doctor
explained, indicated that Andy had lymphoma in his

chest. In fact two-thirds of his chest cavity was filled with the cancer, putting a great deal of stress on his lungs and heart. Suddenly, my perfectly healthy eight-year-old son was anything but perfectly healthy.

Still in shock, we listened numbly as the doctor explained what would happen now. Andy spent the next five days in the hospital, while the doctors ran test after horrible test, trying to determine exactly what was going on and how best to treat him. I stayed with him, doing my best to keep him from dwelling on how uncomfortable he felt. Fortunately, I had help.

During those five days, Andy received eighty-five pieces of mail. From his class, his Boy Scout troop, his friends and family, distant and near—it was a deluge. I was touched and pleased at this wonderful outpouring of support and love for Andy. And I was surprised by the magnitude of his reaction to the letters and cards; he positively reveled in the attention. He read and reread each piece of mail several times or if it was written in script, asked me to read it to him again and again.

When the five days in the hospital were finally over, Andy was released and came home to begin the biggest battle of his life—for his life. But the mail didn't follow. The deluge became a trickle, and those few letters arriving were only ones forwarded on from the hospital. I understood too well what was happening. It wasn't that people had stopped caring, they just didn't know what to write. How can you say "get well" to an eight-year-old who may not live to see his next birthday?

Andy felt so isolated. He was too sick to go to school and couldn't play with any of his friends. Most of his days were taken up with our trips to the hospital for radiation and chemotherapy. The only thing he asked for was the mail. But there was no mail. One day he asked me, "Did everybody stop loving me?"

"Oh, Honey," I said, fighting back tears, "it's not that. It's just that people have things to do. . . . " But I decided then that if I couldn't control the quantity of his life, I could control the quality of his life. This brave boy was not going to fight this fight alone. I decided to ensure there would be mail for Andy by writing to him as his "secret pal."

I had fun with it. I sent funny cards in brightly colored envelopes with jokey return addresses or no return address at all. Sometimes I fashioned gift wrap or the Sunday comics into envelopes and enclosed little toys from inside cereal boxes. I was sure I was undetected; I even felt a little smug, thinking I'd pulled one over on him. Often I'd ask casually, "Oh, is that from your secret pal?" And Andy would answer, "Yeah! I wonder who it is?" I'd turn away quickly to hide my smirk.

Then one day, Andy handed me an envelope marked "To My Secret Pal." He made me promise I would deliver it. "Only your secret pal will see it," I promised solemnly and set it aside.

When he was finally asleep, I took the picture out of the envelope and examined it. It was a typical Andy picture, bright and colorful. What set it apart and caused my heart to skip a beat were the words printed where the artist's signature usually goes. In crayon letters, Andy had written: P.S. Mom, I love you.

He knew! My secret was out. Yet even though we both knew what was going on, we never said anything. It was simply a new twist to our game together.

Our game continued for the next three and a half years. During those roller-coaster years—treatment, remission, relapse, more treatment—the only thing that Andy could count on in his life was the mail. When he'd hear the mailman come up the steps, it was often the only time all day that I'd see Andy smile.

Being Andy's secret pal was a godsend for me. It gave

me a mission, something to do in a situation where there was nothing I could do. I prayed and poured my creative talents into sending Andy letters, cards and packages. It gave Andy a special kind of hope, and it gave both of us a much-needed break from the needles and procedures.

I thought of our game as a little daily R and R, a light moment in a particularly bleak period of our lives. This time was made even bleaker by our desperate lack of money and my inability to drive. Every day during Andy's treatment, Andy and I would wake up before dawn to catch the first of three buses to the hospital where Andy received his radiation treatment. After the radiation, which made Andy feel sick, we had to catch a bus to another hospital for Andy's chemotherapy, which made him feel even sicker. Then another three buses back home. Often, we'd have to get off a bus before it reached our stop because Andy felt too ill and needed fresh air and solid earth beneath his feet. We'd wait in the bitter cold until he felt well enough to board another bus. Oftentimes, the three buses home became six or seven.

Andy was ill in body, but I was sick at heart. I could hardly stand to wake him in the morning to begin this miserable routine once more. One day as we stood at the bus stop, waiting for Andy to feel better so we could board the next bus, a car went racing past us, spraying us both with gray slush from the gutter. I knelt on the sidewalk by Andy, using a tissue from my pocket to wipe the dirty ice from his frozen little face. I was sobbing, "I'm so sorry. I'm so sorry," over and over.

Andy said, a little sharply, "What are *you* sorry for?"

"Oh Andy, I'm sorry for so many things. I'm sorry I don't know how to drive. I'm sorry I don't have cab fare. I'm sorry it's so cold. I'm sorry you feel sick. I pray all the time, but sometimes all I can say to God is, 'Why me?'"

Without hesitating an instant, my eight-year-old looked

at me and said evenly, "And he parts the clouds and looks down at you and he says, 'Why *not* you?'"

Astonished, I gazed at Andy. *He isn't bitter,* I thought. For him, this whole awful mess is just something that happened. If he could do it, I decided, then I could, too. I was going to be as brave as Andy and never waste another minute wondering why.

It wasn't as hard as I thought it would be. I kept myself busy being Andy's secret pal right up until the time he died, but after he was gone, it was harder. The day I had to go through his things was an especially difficult one. As I pulled his clothes out of his closet, I found a shoebox crammed full of letters to Andy. All from his "secret pal." I was on the verge of dissolving into another round of despairing tears when I noticed that he'd stuck an address book inside the box. I opened it. There were about twenty names—I recognized them as the kids Andy had gone to camp with that summer. All of them were kids with cancer. I considered it a charge from Andrew, his legacy. So, in his memory, I decided to write each and every one of the children in the book.

It felt so familiar, writing a goofy newsy letter like the hundreds I had written to Andy. I wrote a few letters every week and signed each one: Your friend, Linda.

I never expected anyone to answer these letters. But before I was halfway through the list, I received a piece of mail addressed to me. Opening it, I read: *Thank you, thank you, thank you for writing to me. I didn't know anyone knew I lived. Jeffrey*

Holding the sheet of paper in my hand, I thought—as I had thought so many times before, as I watched Andy—how lonely it must feel to fight so hard and be so alone. These two sentences summed up the isolation and depression of so many children who battle cancer. With little time to have made their mark on the world, they often feel that no one knows they are alive . . . and no one ever will.

I hadn't meant to continue writing letters on a regular basis, not even as a hobby—I certainly hadn't expected for this simple gesture to change my life forever. I couldn't get past losing my son, couldn't think beyond how I was going to keep getting up in the morning, making toast . . . living. Now I realized I'd better get it together—and get some more stationery.

I began looking for funny cards again, buying the cereal boxes with the toys inside. That Christmas I bought twenty little jigsaw puzzles with pictures I thought Andy's friends would enjoy and sent them. I had very little money, but any small amount I could scrounge up went to buy stamps. I was having so much fun with my letter writing project.

Then I put up a sign-up sheet at the hospital that Andy had gone to, offering to write to any child who wanted mail. The word spread, snowballed, and soon I was writing over three hundred kids on a regular basis. It had become more than a hobby, more than a project—it felt like what I was alive to do.

Eventually, I founded an organization called Love Letters. Today there are over sixty local volunteers who give of their time to brighten the lives of children who are medically fragile, children with catastrophic illnesses like AIDS, muscular dystrophy and cancer; burn victims, accident victims and survivors of abuse.

I always knew there were children like these, but before Andy, they existed in a world that didn't touch mine. Now, through Love Letters, over one thousand of these children a week receive letters, cards and gift packages. We celebrate Christmas twice a year, in December of course, and again in July for all the kids who might not be alive when winter rolls around again.

Keeping Love Letters going is a struggle financially. And it's hard when we lose a child we've come to love. But I know from experience how important this work is. One little boy sent us our own "love letter," and I framed it for our office. He drew a picture of a brightly colored quilt and wrote underneath the picture, "Love Letters like a quilt keep me warm." I love to look at it. It brings me back to the days when I was Andy's secret pal, and love came through the mailbox in colored envelopes with goofy drawings and return addresses that no mailman would ever find. But of course, love needs no return address, for it is always returned to the sender—multiplied.

Linda Bremner

Speaking

I was no different from any other mother.

When my little boy, Skyler, was born, I longed for the day he would talk to me. My husband and I dreamed about the first sweet "Mama" or "Dada." Every cry or coo was a small glimpse into my son's mind.

My baby's noises were even more precious to me because Skyler had been born with several health problems. At first, the problems had delayed his development, but once they were safely behind us, I looked forward to my son's first words. They didn't come.

At age three, Skyler was diagnosed autistic, a developmental disability destined to affect his social and emotional well-being his entire life. Skyler couldn't talk—wouldn't talk. I would probably never hear any words from him at all. In a store, I would hear a child calling "Mommy," and I would wonder if that were what my little boy might sound like. I wondered how it would feel to hear my child call out for me.

But I could have learned to live with his silence if it weren't for another hallmark characteristic of autism: Skyler formed no attachments. He didn't want to be held, much preferring to lie in his bed or sit in his car seat. He wouldn't look at me; sometimes, he even looked through me.

Once, when I took him to the doctor, we talked to a specialist who was my size, age and who had the same hair color. When it was time to go, Skyler went to her instead of me—he couldn't tell us apart. When Skyler was three, he spent three days at Camp Courageous for disabled children in Iowa, and when he returned he didn't even recognize me.

This pain was almost unbearable. My own son didn't even know I was his mother.

I hid the pain, and we did the best we could for Skyler. We enrolled him in our local area educational agency preschool, where the teachers and speech pathologist worked hard to help Skyler connect with the world around him. They used pictures and computer voice-machines that spoke for him, and sign language. These devices gave me little glimpses of who Skyler was, even if he didn't understand who I was. "He will talk," the speech pathologist insisted, but inside, I had given up hope.

The one dream I couldn't let go was to have Skyler understand that I was his mom. Even if I never heard him say, "Mom," I wanted to see the recognition in his eyes.

The summer of Skyler's fourth year was when it started. A smoldering ember of understanding in him sparked, and fanned by our efforts, steadily flamed. His first words were hardly recognizable, often out of context, never spontaneous. Then, slowly, he could point to an item and say a word. Then two words together as a request. Then spontaneous words. Each day, he added more and more recognizable words, using them to identify pictures and ask questions. We could see his understanding increase, till his eyes would seek out mine, wanting to comprehend.

"You Mom?" he said one day.

"Yes, Skyler, I'm Mom."

He asked his teachers and caregivers: "You Mom?"

"No, Skyler, not Mom."

"You *my* Mom?" he said back to me.

"Yes, Skyler. I'm *your* Mom."

And finally, a rush of understanding in his eyes: "You my *Mom.*"

"Yes, Skyler, I'm *your Mom.*"

If those had been Skyler's only words ever, they would have been enough for me: My son knew I was his mother.

But Skyler wasn't done.

One evening I leaned against the headboard on Skyler's bed, my arms wrapped around him. He was cozily tucked between my legs, our bodies warm and snug as I read to him from one of his favorite books—a typical affectionate scene between mother and son, but because of Skyler's autism, one that I could never take for granted.

I stopped reading. Skyler had interrupted me, leaning back his head so he could look me in the eye.

"Yes, Skyler?"

And then the voice of an angel, the voice of my son: "I love you, Mom."

Cynthia Laughlin

The Day I Became a Mom

You cannot discover new oceans, unless you have the courage to lose sight of the shore.

Author Unknown

The day I became a mom was not the day my daughter was born, but seven years later. Up until that day, I had been too busy trying to survive my abusive marriage. I had spent all my energy trying to run a "perfect" home that would pass inspection each evening, and I didn't see that my baby girl had become a toddler. I'd tried endlessly to please someone who could never be pleased and suddenly realized that the years had slipped by and could never be recaptured.

Oh, I had done the normal "motherly" things, like making sure my daughter got to ballet and tap and gym lessons. I went to all of her recitals and school concerts, parent-teacher conferences and open houses—alone. I ran interference during my husband's rages when something was spilled at the dinner table, telling her, "It will be okay, Honey. Daddy's not really mad at you." I did all I could to protect her from hearing the awful shouting and accusations after he returned from a night of drinking. Finally I did the best thing I could do for my daughter and myself: I removed us from the home that wasn't really a home at all.

The day I became a mom was the day my daughter and I were sitting in our new home having a calm, quiet dinner just as I had always wanted for her. We were talking about what she had done in school and suddenly her little hand knocked over the full glass of chocolate milk by her plate. As I watched the white tablecloth and freshly painted white wall become dark brown, I looked at her small face. It was filled with fear, knowing what the outcome of the event would have meant only a week before in her father's presence. When I saw that look on her face and looked at the chocolate milk running down the wall, I simply started laughing. I am sure she thought I was crazy, but then she must have realized that I was thinking, "It's a good thing your father isn't here!" She started laughing with me, and we laughed until we cried. They were tears of joy and peace and were the first of many tears that we cried together. That was the day we knew that we were going to be okay.

Whenever either of us spills something, even now, seventeen years later, she says, "Remember the day I spilled the chocolate milk? I knew that day that you had done the right thing for us, and I will never forget it."

That was the day I really became a mom. I discovered that being a mom isn't only going to ballet, and tap and gym recitals, and attending every school concert and open house. It isn't keeping a spotless house and preparing perfect meals. It certainly isn't pretending things are normal when they are not. For me, being a mom started when I could laugh over spilled milk.

Linda Jones

Stolen Christmas

When I was a child, our Christmas Eve rituals never varied. First, we sat down to an all-fish dinner—which I absolutely dreaded—followed by a talent show run by my bossy older cousin. At midnight, we attended Mass and then, in the wee hours of Christmas morning, we opened some of our presents at Grandma's house.

The year I was seven, my mother, three brothers and I made the long drive home from Grandma's house. Finally, Mom eased the car slowly into our driveway. As she got out of the car, she told us later, she had a strange feeling in the pit of her stomach.

Leaving us safely sleeping in the car, my mother entered the house. But as soon as she opened the door, she realized we had been robbed. She immediately took a short inventory of the house, to make sure that the robbers were gone and to see exactly what had been stolen.

As she surveyed our small home she discovered that food from our freezer—mostly chopped meats and frozen vegetables—and her meager life savings, the nickels, dimes and pennies that she saved in a container hidden in her underwear drawer, were missing. It wasn't much, but to a single mother living on a limited income, the loss was devastating.

Then to her horror, she saw that the robbers had also taken our Christmas tree, the presents, even the stockings—leaving only a few name tags and a roll of wrapping paper. While other parents were putting the finishing touches on bicycles and dollhouses, she stood gazing at the spot where the Christmas tree had been, too heartsick to cry. It was two in the morning. How was she going to fix this? But fix it she would. Her children were still going to have a Christmas. She would see to that.

Carrying us in one by one, my mother put us to bed. Then she stayed up for what was left of the night and, using buttons, cloth, ribbon and yarn, made handmade gifts of finger puppets and shoelaces.

As she sat and stitched, she remembered the Christmas tree lot around the corner, certainly abandoned for the season by then. Just before dawn, she slipped out and came back with a small broken tree, the best one she could find.

My brothers and I woke up early that morning excited to see what Santa had brought us for Christmas. Our house was filled with the wonderful smell of blueberry muffins and hot chocolate. We hurried to the living room and stopped in the doorway, confused by the strange magic that had turned our beautiful Christmas spruce, glittering with decorations, into a small, bare, pear-shaped tree leaning against the wall.

When my little brother asked my mother what had happened to our tree and stockings, she hugged him tight and told us that someone really poor had needed them. She told us not to worry because we were very lucky, we had the most important gift of all—God's love and one another.

As she filled our cups with the steaming hot chocolate, we opened our gifts. After breakfast we made Christmas

ornaments out of old egg cartons and cereal boxes. Together we laughed, sang carols and decorated our new
tree.

It is an odd thing: Although I do not remember now
what I got for Christmas when I was five, ten or even thirteen years old, I have never forgotten anything about that
strange and wonderful Christmas the year I was seven.
The year someone stole our Christmas and gave us the
unexpected gift of joyous togetherness and love.

Christina Chanes Nystrom

Music That Might Never Be Heard

I do not love him because he is good.
I love him because he is my child.

Rabindrath Tagore

Spring had slipped quietly into our neighborhood and across the mountains with wildflowers and the scent of fresh earth reminding me of happy yesterdays. It was Mother's Day and we were celebrating with our three grown children and their families, picnicking and playing volleyball in our backyard. We were having a wonderful time, yet I ached for the one lost sheep.

Our youngest son, Brian, was gone. He had changed from a loving, tender, family-oriented person into an irritable stranger before he'd left school and the tennis team, and disappeared into the streets six months ago.

I longed for the days when he would bounce into the house yelling, "Mom, want to go over to the school and watch me practice my serve?" On Sunday afternoons, he would set up "Olympic" hurdles for his nieces and nephews and cheer them on to victory, making sure they all got a ribbon. Sometimes, he made beds for us all on the deck, inspiring summer sleepovers and star-watching.

We missed him.

Though Brian's sensitivity and compassion had endeared him to adults and small children, he didn't make friends of his own age easily and faced relentless torment all through school.

At seventeen, he battled depression. Unable to cope, he ran away and lived on the streets where he was accepted, but after a short time, he returned home with the promise to obey house rules and get his life together. One winter afternoon, his sobs broke through the house. "Mom, come here," he said. "I'm scared. The world is so ugly."

I ran to my six-foot-three son and cradled him in my arms. Sweat mingled with tears on his cheeks. I wiped his forehead. I could smooth his hair but not his pathway. "Brian," I said. "You're going to come through this hard time. The world needs a boy like you. We'll get professional help, and we'll all work together on this."

But within days he had disappeared again.

I knew when Brian was born I would have to give him up someday—but not like this. At three, he had played outside rain or shine, laughed up at the clouds, shoveled sunlight, built roads and tunnels for his trucks. One morning he ran in breathless. "Mom," he shouted, waving his arms, then whispering his secret, "Mom, my heart is so happy it's tickling me."

During his junior high years, he made friends with folks on his paper route. He would come home laden with plants to begin a garden. One widow gave him her whole stamp collection. Another of his customers was running for reelection as state representative. He left a note in her paper. "Mrs. North, I watched the election on TV last night. I'm glad you won." He later served as page at the State Capitol with her recommendation.

A former teacher was on his route, and he helped with

her sick dog. He sat with them many evenings and listened to tales about Chiquita, who could fit into Mrs. Hall's pocket. The day Chiquita died he took lilacs to his grieving friend and left his dinner untouched.

I had rocked him through nightmares and fevers, panned "gold" with him at the river, led him up mountainsides and run with him in 5Ks. I wouldn't give up on him now.

I opened the door to his room, stung by the lingering trace of his familiar aftershave as the silence screamed at me. I smoothed the quilt on his bed and kneeled down, burying my head in the softness, clutching for his presence, praying as mothers all over the world pray when a child is in need.

I grieved for the music in him that might never be heard, remembering his childhood notes—scrawled messages on paper—sailing under the bathroom door when I was bathing, his teenage knock on the wall to say goodnight after all the lights were out.

All those memories helped me through sleepless nights and dark days. After several weeks, Brian called again. "Mom, do you think I could come back? It's awful here. I think I'm going crazy. Can you meet to talk?"

My feet barely touched the ground as I scrambled for my keys and ran to the car, praying all the way. There, in the dark restaurant, sat my son, hollow eyes peering from his haggard face. He looked like an old man, and at the same time, a lost child. As I approached the booth, he brightened briefly. "Hi, Mom. Thanks for coming."

I sat down facing him, and he said, "I'm so confused. My head feels like it will explode."

I put my hand on his arm. "If you can live by the rules, you can come home. You're stepping in the right direction."

He cupped his chin in one hand and looked out the window. "Last week I walked over to the park where I used to play tennis matches. If I hadn't messed up, I could have earned a tennis scholarship to college. I climbed the hill where you always sat to cheer for me. It was lonely and quiet. I sat there in the rain till dark, then walked back to where I'm staying and slept in someone's car."

The pain in my son's eyes tugged at my already weary heart.

He came back home only to disappear within a few days. Again he was lost to us. Worse, we had to live month after month with the terror of not knowing.

Somehow, the time passed. Mother's Day came, my first without him. Bravely I'd picnicked and played, but in the evening, after our children had returned to their own homes, emptiness jabbed at my insides. I had enjoyed spoiling our grandchildren, grateful for our family day, but the house was all too quiet in the soft twilight. When a knock came at the door, I welcomed the distraction.

There stood Brian, his face thin, clothes wrinkled and stale, but his eyes revealing a faint spark behind the pain. "I had to come," he said. "I couldn't let Mother's Day go by without letting you know I'm thinking of you." He straightened his shoulders and smiled, holding out two pink carnations cradled in baby's breath. I read the card: *Mom, I love you, and you're thought of more often than you'll ever know.*

His arms wrapped around me like sunshine breaking through black thunder, his voice barely a whisper, "Mom, I wanted to take my life, be through with the pain, but I could never do that to you." I leaned against his shoulder and buried my face in the sweet, stale sweat of his shirt.

This time, Brian stayed. It was difficult at first, but now ten years later, he is doing well. And each year on Mother's Day, I celebrate my son's final homecoming, and deep inside I relive the wonder of this secret anniversary of my heart.

Doris Hays Northstrom

Jimmy's New Shoes

My son Jimmy has sky-blue eyes, curly hair and a smile that lights up a room. Two days before Jimmy's fifth birthday, my husband (whose nickname is Chooch) and I took Jimmy to buy a new pair of high-top tennis shoes. At the store, after looking up and down the display of shoes, Dad found a pair in the colors of Jimmy's favorite basketball team. Jimmy's eyes widened as he asked, "Let's try these, okay, Mom?"

I found the style in his size, and he sat down on a nearby stool. I had a lump in my throat as I took off his old shoes and then removed the braces he had worn since he was sixteen months old, when the doctors had told us he had cerebral palsy.

Of course, we had bought shoes before, but never shoes like these. Normally we could only pick shoes that would fit over his braces, but Jimmy's therapy had been going so well, his specialist said he could wear a pair of shoes without braces a few days a week.

I bent down, adjusted his socks and slipped the shoes on Jimmy's feet. I laced them up, and the instant I finished tying the second bow, Jimmy slid off the stool and went to the mirror. He stood for a moment gazing at himself, his hands on his hips, like Superman.

Chooch and I were as excited as he was. "Jimmy," I said, "why don't you walk around and see how they feel?"

He took a few steps and turned to see if we were watching.

"Go on, Honey," I told him. "You're doing great."

I was holding Chooch's hand, and we both squeezed tightly as we watched Jimmy walk faster, and then almost run in his new shoes. Jimmy—almost running! My heart was full to bursting.

Still watching my son march around the shoe department with a great big smile on his face, I asked Chooch, "How much are they?"

We both laughed. "Who cares?" he answered. "Jimmy is getting these shoes."

I put the old shoes in the box, and we paid for the new ones.

As we walked to the car, Jimmy thanked us. On the ride home, he sat up front with Dad, clicking his feet and admiring his new shoes the whole way. I sat quietly in the back, thinking of all we had been through, especially Jimmy, to get to this point.

At home, Jimmy hummed happily as we went inside the house. He was eager to call everyone and tell them about his new shoes, but he accepted my suggestion that we call just a few people and then surprise the rest at his birthday party. After our calls, we went through our nightly routine of a warm bath, lotion massage and a few stretches. I put on his night braces and kissed him good night.

"Thank you for my new shoes," he said again. "I love them!" He fell asleep with the shoes right next to him on the bed.

The next morning, as I helped him dress for school, I

gently reminded him that he would still have to wear his braces most days. "The therapist says you can wear your new shoes only a few days a week. Remember?"

"I know, Mom. My braces are cool," he assured me. "I can wear them, too."

As we walked to the front door to catch the bus, Jimmy smiled up at me and said, "I bet Miss Cindy will say, 'Oh my gosh! I can't believe it!'"

When the bus came and the driver, Miss Cindy, opened the door, Jimmy walked up the steps holding on to the rail and paused at the top. "Look!" he said, "look at my new shoes! And no braces!"

"Oh my gosh! I can't believe it!" Miss Cindy said. Jimmy turned to me and grinned. Then he went to his seat and blew me a kiss, giving me the thumbs-up sign, the way he always did.

I walked slowly back to the house, wondering about how his teachers and friends would react. I wished I could be there. I paced a lot during the day and wrote in my journal. I prepared some snacks for his school birthday party the next day. Chooch was decorating the house and yard for Jimmy's big family birthday party the next night. I couldn't wait to see the smiles of Jimmy's grandparents, aunts, uncles and cousins, as they watched him parade around in his new high-tops. It was something we'd all hoped for but had been afraid to believe was possible.

It was a beautiful day, so I went outside to wait for the bus fifteen minutes early. I couldn't wait for Jimmy to come home. I feel this way every day he goes to school, but that day, when the bus turned the corner, I wanted to run down the street to meet it. But I didn't. I stayed put until the bus pulled up. There was my son, that big smile still on his face.

He blew everyone kisses good-bye. We walked across the street, Jimmy telling me all about his day. One of his teachers, Miss Susan, had "screamed when she saw me," he said. "I think she cried a little, too." He stopped. "Mother, this was my happiest day ever."

I couldn't speak and tears welled up in my eyes as I bent down to hug him. He wrapped his arms around my neck and said, "I know. Me, too." We both cried and hugged each other, then laughed.

Holding hands, we walked slowly up our driveway, both of us getting used to Jimmy's new shoes.

Marie A. Kennedy

A Mother's Valor

*Your children learn more of your faith during
the bad times than they do during the good
times.*

Beverly LaHaye

[EDITORS' NOTE: *Chicago police officer James Love grew up in
the roughest neighborhood, the Robert Taylor Homes, one of the
most notorious housing projects in the country. Now, as an under-
cover narcotics officer, Love's survival skills are a valuable asset in
his efforts to help rid the Chicago projects of drugs. For his hero-
ism in the drug war Love has received a Medal of Valor—the highest honor a policeman can receive.*]

I was conducting search warrants in the projects where
a gang called the Gangster Disciples conducted business
when they ordered a contract on my life. I continued
doing searches, even when I got called into the station and
was told that the contract had gone into effect. I knew this
wasn't a joke, but you can't be out there trying to clean up
the streets if you're going to run from people.

One night I was working with two white officers, and

we were going into the projects. They dropped me off at this dead-end area so I could walk though a viaduct into the projects. After they pulled off to get set up, a van pulled up. The cargo doors opened and I was looking at guns. They told me to get in the van, and I did.

One of the things that you learn from the streets is to always keep talking, always have something to say to keep them off balance, to misdirect them, and that's what I did. There were three guys, two teenagers and an older guy; one of them stayed in the back of the van with me the whole time. At one point they made me lie face down in the van.

One of the kids wanted to shoot me right there, but the adult wouldn't let him. They took me to an abandoned garage of some kind, a warehouse, and there was nowhere to run. I kept talking steadily while at the same time silently asking forgiveness for everything that I ever did wrong. I kept telling myself that it was a bluff—that they were just trying to scare me. But then, I don't know why, I couldn't bet on it anymore and just said, "Shoot me if you're going to." And that's when the kid lit me up. I took four bullets: one above the knee, one bullet fractured my right forearm, and I took two in the sternum.

Something said fall down, play dead, and that's what I did. I had a great vest on, but it is not like television where they show someone getting shot and the guy just takes it in the vest. It hurts and knocks the wind out of you.

I must have laid there for a while. I don't remember that. I do remember looking around and seeing garbage every-where and thinking, *if I'm going to die, I'm going to die looking at the stars.* I remember sitting up in the dirt, my bright yellow shirt was red, my blue jeans were soaked with blood. I took my shoelaces out and used my mouth to tie them around my arm and leg to make tourniquets, and I got up and started walking.

I remember trying to stand up against a fence and the next thing I knew, I had slid down into a seated position. Then I was lying on my side and I could see a woman running toward me with a bunch of towels. That woman cradled me, and it felt like my mother was there holding me. I was okay then. And she kept telling me, "You are going to be all right"—all those things your mother said to you when you were a kid. "You're going to be okay," she said. At that moment it didn't matter whether I lived or died, because I wasn't alone.

I could hear the sirens coming. I was so worried about the precinct notifying my mother that I'd been shot. I thought, *That woman's going to come in here hysterical, with rollers in her hair and house slippers. They're going to have to sedate her.*

They had me in intensive care, and she walked in and I looked up, and there was my mom in a two-piece pants suit, makeup, hair done, and this was about four o'clock in the morning. She was dressed to the nines. I was hooked up to all these machines and I just looked at her, and I smiled at her and she smiled back.

"I knew you were going to be okay," she said, "so I figured I might as well dress up for the occasion." Grown men had been sobbing in the trauma unit because I was such a bloody mess. But my mother leaned over my hospital bed and said, "God spared you for a reason." Just hearing her words gave me a new sense of responsibility.

After I recovered, my mother didn't want me to go back to the job, but she understood why I had to do it. I had to prove that the monkey wasn't on my back. So I went back with her blessing.

The police got the two juveniles the same night I got shot. They got the adult a couple of days later, and they were later sentenced to prison.

If it wasn't for my mother, I could have been one of those kids.

My mother grew up in Mississippi working the fields. She had to quit school, because when harvest time came all the kids had to help my grandfather on the farm; so she never made it past the eighth grade. Her way of providing for her children was also through backbreaking labor. During the times when people didn't have floor buffers, you had women on their knees buffing. My mother was one of them.

Education was always the biggest thing that she pushed—schoolwork, schoolwork, schoolwork—because she knew that was the only way we would be able to compete in the world. So that was her driving force, that her kids weren't going to go through what she did. She was never in a position where she could help us with our homework or things like that. If she received a letter or something, she'd say, "I can't find my glasses. Can you read this letter for me?" She didn't want me to know that she really couldn't read the letter.

But no matter what, my mother can find something to be positive about. That's just the way she is. Every time you thought life was over and you couldn't go any further, she has always been there with some encouragement.

Around the time I found out that the contract was out on me, there were a lot of other things going on in my life. My wife and I were splitting up. Even though we were already separated, I asked her to hold off on the divorce because I just couldn't deal with it at the time. The reality about my son had started to set in: I wouldn't be able to see him when I wanted, and he would not always have a father around who was hands-on.

I was so despondent that I called my mother from a pay phone. I called her to say I was sorry that I had failed. I told her that I just wanted to die. My mother said to hold on, your father wants to talk to you. So I talked with my dad, and I didn't know it, but my mother was already on her way. She knew I was near the expressway on Eighty-seventh Street. She drove all around until she found me.

"If you die," she said, "then I'm going to die with you."

With those words all thoughts of ever wanting to leave this earth left me. So now, regardless of how despondent I may get, I know my mother is depending on me the way I depended on her for so long. She's my hero. I can receive all the awards, all the accolades, but none of them mean anything in comparison to her. What I do, I do because she was there for me.

Maybe if the kid who shot me had a mother like mine, he wouldn't be sitting where he is today.

James Love
From the book, Sacred Bond: Black Men and Their Mothers

3

ON
MOTHERHOOD

What feeling is so nice as a child's hand in yours? So small, so soft and warm, like a kitten huddling in the shelter of your clasp.

Marjorie Holmes

THE FAMILY CIRCUS® **By Bil Keane**

"I figured out a system for getting along with my mom.
She tells me what to do and I do it."

When God Created Mothers

When the good Lord was creating mothers, He was into His sixth day of overtime when the angel appeared and said, "You're doing a lot of fiddling around on this one."

And the Lord said, "Have you read the specs on this order?

"She has to be completely washable, but not plastic;

"Have 180 movable parts . . . all replaceable;

"Run on black coffee and leftovers;

"Have a lap that disappears when she stands up;

"A kiss that can cure anything from a broken leg to a disappointed love affair;

"And six pairs of hands."

The angel shook her head slowly and said, "Six pairs of hands? No way."

"It's not the hands that are causing me problems," said the Lord. "It's the three pairs of eyes that mothers have to have."

"That's on the standard model?" asked the angel.

The Lord nodded. "One pair that sees through closed doors when she asks, 'What are you kids doing in there?' when she already knows. Another here in the back of her head that sees what she shouldn't but what she has to know, and of course the ones here in front so that she can look at a child who goofs and say, 'I understand and I love you' without so much as uttering a word."

"Lord," said the angel touching his sleeve gently, "come to bed. Tomorrow—"

"I can't," said the Lord, "I'm so close to creating something so close to myself. Already I have one who heals herself when she is sick . . . can feed a family of six on one pound of hamburger . . . and can get a nine-year-old to stand under a shower."

The angel circled the model of a mother very slowly and sighed. "It's too soft."

"But tough!" said the Lord excitedly. "You cannot imagine what this mother can do or endure."

"Can it think?"

"Not only think, but it can reason and compromise," said the Creator.

Finally, the angel bent over and ran her finger across the cheek. "There's a leak," she pronounced. "I told you that you were trying to put too much into this model."

"It's not a leak," said the Lord. "It's a tear."

"What is it for?"

"It's for joy, sadness, disappointment, pain, loneliness and pride."

"You are a genius," said the angel.

The Lord looked somber. "I didn't put it there."

Erma Bombeck

Having It All

I was in heaven. I anchored both the weekend *Nightly News* out of New York and also *Sunday Today* out of Washington, D.C. I was living across the map in Los Angeles, commuting to the East Coast on the weekends. I loved the pace. I loved being out in the field doing stories, interviewing the likes of Cory Aquino and King Hussein. I loved traveling, and I loved anchoring. I loved the people I worked with, and I loved the challenge of the job and the stature I'd attained.

Finally, I was respected for being Maria Shriver, anchorwoman, and not because I was a "Kennedy kid." This was what I'd worked so hard for all those years.

So when I got pregnant, I fully expected to keep visible on the air in both my anchor positions, because I couldn't imagine otherwise. Oh sure, I might have to slow down the pace a tad, but hadn't I been told I could/should be able to do it all? I expected nothing less from myself.

Reality started to set in the first time I held my daughter. I fell deeply in love with my child and couldn't imagine being separated from her for one second. But even so, I held on to my unrealistic expectations with both fists, spending most of my maternity leave trying to figure out exactly how I was going to manage this child and the travel and the job. I just knew I'd be able to figure it out, but as I looked around me for guidance and paths to follow, I found none. Apart from the impossible-to-get morning news anchor jobs, which required hardly any travel, there were few network news jobs that seemed compatible with raising kids.

And there was another pressure. My husband, Arnold Schwartzenegger, had made it clear he had no desire to live in New York, where the NBC News operation was based. His career was in LA and was much bigger than mine. So here I was with this beautiful baby and the man I loved in California, this job I loved in New York and Washington, and the stories I wanted to pursue were everywhere else.

So I went back to work and pretended nothing had changed, commuting like a maniac. My baby was accumulating frequent-flier miles. But it didn't take me long to realize I was kidding myself. Nothing was working—neither motherhood nor job. Whichever I was doing, I was worried and guilty about the other. Something had to give.

Finally, with a great deal of sadness, I gave up both my East Coast broadcasts, and went home to Los Angeles where I could devote most of my time to my family *and* work part time for NBC. And that's what I do to this day.

Today overall, I spend much more time being a mother than trying to book an interview with the First Lady. The most important time on my clock is 3:30 P.M. when school is out. I try to turn the phones off from four to eight, so I can focus on playing with the kids and monitoring homework.

On the other hand, I did take my daughter to kindergarten one day in my sweats and full TV makeup and hair, and then changed clothes in the back of an NBC car on the way downtown for the O. J. Simpson verdict. So a normal mom I'm not.

To be sure, it's not always easy. I worry when I say no to a story that requires a lot of travel. Will this be the final straw for my bosses? Each time I turn down an assignment because it conflicts with a child's special performance or a soccer game, I hold my breath for their reaction. Will they fire me now? In my desire to be at home and hands-on, I have made some pretty reckless decisions.

Take the time I interviewed President Fidel Castro for a two-hour special on the Cuban Missile Crisis. It was a big deal, and NBC sent a huge team of producers and technicians to shoot it. We waited and waited. No Castro. Waited some more. No Castro. Now we were approaching the weekend. I was starting to sweat, because Monday was my daughter's first day in preschool. Her father was away on location, and I'd promised her nothing would keep me from taking her.

In my mind, our first child's first day at school was as important as any world event. (First-time mother.) But as Friday came down in Havana, we were informed that Castro was sick—"under the weather," they said—and couldn't be interviewed yet. My boss said we'd wait for him.

Then on Saturday, Castro himself called me in for a meeting. I'd interviewed him before, and he wanted to tell me personally that he was still feeling sick and wouldn't be able to do the interview until Monday. My stomach tightened, and I blurted out, "I can't do that! I have to go back home to take my daughter to school!"

There was stone silence in the room. My boss kicked me under the table and asked me to step outside. "Are you nuts?" he asked. Didn't I know how long we had worked to get this interview? Didn't I realize if I left we would probably never get back in? Castro was so mercurial, you had to take him when you could get him. I understood all that, I told my boss, but I can't *not* go home. Looking back, my little girl probably would never have known what day the first day of school really was, but *I* knew.

I went back inside and told Castro it was my first child and I just had to go, but I'd come back right after, if he would please wait. I thought my boss would have a seizure. But without skipping a beat, Castro said, "Take your daughter to school. I'll be ready next Saturday morning." And he walked out.

I flew home, took her to school (she didn't cry, but I did), and returned to Cuba to shoot one of the most fascinating interviews of my career. By the way, the first thing Castro said was, "How was the first day of school?" I dodged a bullet on that one.

Children do change your career. But they also open you up in ways you never imagined. I'd always expected I'd be operating professionally in what is still very much a man's world. But now I'm also a full-fledged member of the sisterhood of mothers—a gift that's enriched my life.

Maria Shriver

Learning to Listen

One year, I went out of town to attend a writer's conference. As I stepped off the jet back home in Atlanta, my family waited for me. After we had embraced, I started telling them about my trip. At least I tried to. Everyone wanted to tell me something—especially eight-year-old Jeremy. He jumped up and down in order to be heard, and his voice carried above the other children's, even above my husband Jerry's.

Everyone needs something from me, I thought. *They don't want to hear about my trip. What is it Jeremy keeps saying?*

"Poster paper, Mama! I have to have poster paper. We're having a contest at school."

I put him off, promising we'd talk about it later. Back at home I readjusted to the telephone, doorbell, sorting laundry, driving carpools, answering questions and wiping up spills. I fought off the creeping knowledge that, no matter how hard I tried, I couldn't keep up with the needs of my family. As I moved about hurriedly, trying to decide what to do next, Jeremy kept reminding me, "I need the poster paper, Mama."

Gradually though, he began to speak more softly,

almost as though he were talking to himself. So I put Jeremy's request at the bottom of my long list of things to do. *Maybe he'll just hush about the poster paper*, I thought hopefully.

My third day home I managed to salvage about fifteen minutes to try to type an article. Sitting at the typewriter, I heard the dryer stop. Another load of clothes should be put in. Two important phone calls needed to be returned. One of my daughters had pleaded with me several times to listen to her recite part of *The Canterbury Tales*. For over an hour one of the cats had meowed right in my face trying to get me to feed her. Someone had spilled orange Kool-Aid on the kitchen floor and smeared it around with a dry towel. It was past time to start supper, and I hadn't even eaten lunch. Nevertheless, I typed joyfully for a few delicious minutes.

A small shadow fell across my paper. I knew who it would be before I looked up. I glanced up anyway. Jeremy stood quietly watching me. *Oh, Lord, please don't let him say it again. I know he needs poster paper. I need to type.* I smiled weakly at Jeremy and kept typing. He watched for a few more minutes, then turned and walked away. I almost didn't hear his comment. "Contest is over tomorrow, anyway."

I wanted to write so much that, with a little effort, I could have tuned out his remark. But I couldn't ignore the silent voice that spoke urgently to my heart. *Get him that paper—now!* I shut off my electric typewriter. "Let's go get the paper, Jeremy." He stopped, turned around and looked at me without even smiling or speaking—almost as though he hadn't heard.

"Come on," I urged, grabbing my purse and the car keys.

He still didn't move. "Do you have something else you have to get, Mama?"

"No, just your poster paper." I headed for the door.

He lagged behind and asked, "You're going to the store just for me?"

I stopped and looked down at him. Really looked at him. Spots of whatever he'd eaten for lunch at school stained his shirt. Untied, flopping shoes and traces of orange Kool-Aid that turned up at the corners of his small, grim mouth gave Jeremy a clownlike appearance.

Suddenly, a look of utter delight shot across his face, erasing the disbelief. I don't think I'll ever forget that moment. He moved with amazing speed and running to the bottom of the stairs he threw his head back and shouted, "Hey, Julie, Jen, Jon, Mama's taking me to the store! Anybody need anything?"

No one answered him, but he didn't seem to notice. He sprinted out to the car still wearing the Christmas morning expression. At the store, instead of running in ahead of me, he grabbed my hand and started rapidly telling me about the poster contest.

"It's about fire prevention. The teacher announced it a long time ago, and when I first told you, you said we'd see later. Then you went out of town. The contest ends tomorrow. I'll have to work hard. What if I win?" He went on with endless enthusiasm as though he'd only asked me one time for the paper.

Jeremy didn't want an apology from me. It would have spoiled the joy. So I just listened. I listened to him as intently as I ever have anyone in my life. After he bought the poster paper, I asked, "Do you need anything else?"

"Do you have enough money?" he whispered.

I smiled at him, suddenly feeling very rich, "Yes, today I just happen to have lots of money. What do you need?"

"Can I have my own glue and some construction paper?"

We got the other items and at the cashier's, Jeremy, who

usually doesn't confide in strangers, said, "I'm making a poster. My Mama brought me to the store to buy the stuff." He tried to sound matter-of-fact, but his face gave him away.

He worked silently and with great determination on the poster all afternoon.

The winner of the contest was announced over the school intercom two days later. *Jeremy won.* His poster was then entered in the county competition. He won that, too. The principal wrote him a letter and enclosed a check for five dollars. Jeremy wrote a story about the contest. He left it lying on his dresser and I read it. One sentence jumped out at me. "And then my Mama stopped typing and listened to me and took just me to the store."

And a few weeks later, a large yellow envelope came in the mail addressed to Jeremy. He tore into it and read aloud slowly and almost in disbelief the Certificate of Award. "This certifies that Jeremy West has the distinction of reaching the state finals in the Georgia Fire Prevention Theme and Poster Contest." It was signed by the comptroller general of Georgia.

Jeremy fell on the floor and did somersaults, laughing aloud. We framed his certificate and often when I see it I remember that almost—almost I'd turned away from his request to get him some poster paper.

Marion Bond West

Tired?

Children are a great comfort in your old age—
and they help you reach it faster too.

Lionel Kauffman

It was the headline, "Learn to Recognize, Fight Fatigue Symptoms" that initially caught my eye. Having not had a full night's sleep since 1990, the text completely drew me in.

"Feeling too exhausted to complete your daily routines? By mid-afternoon, are you ready for a nap?" the article asked. My autobiography had been written without me even knowing! Spellbound, I read on.

"Fatigue can have a variety of lifestyle causes, including lack of sleep," the author declared.

Really. Well, who would have guessed that I was walking around only half-coherent because I don't get enough sleep? *Who penned this stroke of genius?* I wondered. *Albert Einstein?*

Fatigue has a variety of causes, all right—most of which begin at the moment of conception and continue through the childrearing years. Once spawned and in the world, the tiny barnacle we call "child" will not sleep through the night for, in some cases, twenty-one years. (I am told there will very likely be a three- or four-year period when the child will not wake up. Not having a child who has reached that stage, I have yet to see how this is a bad thing.)

Colic, teething and immunizations perpetuate the fatigue problem in parents of those freshest from God. But later, fielding questions like, "Do tornadoes poop?" and hearing at 11:00 P.M., "Oh, Mom, I forgot to tell you I have to dress like Caesar Augustus tomorrow," serve only to further aggravate the condition.

Some of the symptoms of exhaustion are obvious, such as the presence of bags and/or dark circles under the eyes. Most likely, however, the signs of disease will be more subtle. There are a few simple questions you can ask yourself to determine if you, too, are suffering from sleep deprivation:

1. Have you ever given birth? Is the child still at home? Did you ever give birth again? (It is important to note that each subsequent labor and delivery increases one's chance for developing a lack-of-sleep disorder.)
2. Have you ever been asked, "Why do people look down when they pray when God is up there?"
3. Do you ever provide answers to questions that you know, deep down, don't really answer the question? For example: "Because I'm the Mom, that's why," and "Because I said so!"
4. When your child asks you if you have seen his math paper, have you ever, without so much as blinking, looked in the freezer?
5. Look at your feet. Are you wearing two socks of different hue?
6. Do you have spit-up on one or more of your

shoulders when you leave for work in the morning?

7. Do you eat two or more meals per day in a moving vehicle?

8. Have you ever slept in the living room on a towel wearing nothing but your swimsuit simply because you were asked, in January, "Can we go to the beach?"

9. When playing Candy Land, have you ever become volatile when, two spaces before being named Candy Land champion of the world, you draw the swirly mint card?

If you answered "yes" to one or more of the above questions, there is a good chance you are tired.

But what can you do about it? The article offered several brilliant suggestions for combating fatigue. This was my favorite: "Reduce stress in your life where you can." If tubal ligation had been a prerequisite for graduating from high school, this may have been possible. Unfortunately, there is no going back now.

"Keep your bedroom cool, dark and quiet," the article recommended.

"Not possible," I responded under my breath, because no matter how valiant my efforts, by morning, four Lilliputians will find their way through the dark into my bed.

They will illuminate their path with the "Bug's Life" flashlights they ordered off the back of a cereal box. They will pry both my eyes open with their greasy little fingers and ask, "Are you asleep?"

They will then lie down next to me and begin to breathe, all four of them at different intervals. My oldest son will put one hand under his opposite armpit and flap until flatulence has been successfully simulated. The other three will subsequently giggle, chortle and begin to thrash about.

They will laugh so hard they start to cough, and then they will ask me to get them a drink. That done, they will ask me what time it is.

"Time to go back to sleep," I will say.

They will ask me how long it is until morning.

"Not long enough," I will answer, wearily.

My son will burp. The giggling will begin again. Then the coughing. Then the need for a drink. My temper will heat up and, inevitably, the cool, dark, quiet conditions conducive to obtaining a good night's rest will be shattered.

I am not a doctor. I do not hold a Ph.D. in the sleep sciences. But after having four cesarean sections and then feebly attempting to raise the aftermath, I feel qualified to declare that, as long as one is a mother, there is no way to effectively fight fatigue.

What's worse, even after our children have grown, they will continue to make us tired. We can run, but we can't hide. They will find us in our houseboats off the deserted islands we purchase with our 401(k) money. It will not matter that we left no forwarding address. There they will be, and most likely, they will have reproduced. People will be calling us "Nana."

Of some comfort is that most mothers find they are able to—although, sometimes just barely—secure employment, maintain a semiefficient household, meet the basic needs of their children, create a Caesar Augustus costume in twenty-four minutes and still carry on an adult conversation. (Although those conversations tend to be about how their two-year-old son used the potty for the first time.)

Fatigue, as mothers know and accept, is nothing more than the tradeoff for the comfort of squinting in the night to see the soft rise and fall of your son's tiny chest as he lies sleeping in his bassinet; for the pleasure of kissing his jam-smeared face; for being the one he wants when he is sick; for hearing his teacher say, "He's a great kid." Fatigue is the small price we pay for being our child's safe harbor—for his whisper in the dark, "Can I sleep in your bed?"

Staci Ann Richmond

"I see that at the time you got the ticket you had twelve Cub Scouts, a baby, a toddler, and a sick dog in your van. Ordinarily we don't allow insanity pleas in traffic court, Mrs. Edwards, but in this case I'll make an exception!"

My CEO Is a Four-Year-Old

The most intimidating question I was ever asked as a child was, "What do you want to be when you grow up?" Although this was a common and innocent question, it terrified me. I didn't know.

It wasn't until my son, my firstborn, was six months old that I realized that the one thing that had never changed was that I had always wanted to be a mother. From my dreams when I was a young girl, all through my baby-sitting days while I was a teenager, I always knew that I would have a child of my own. And I've had two.

In a moment of inspiration, I wrote the following poem about my most fulfilling full-time job:

> My CEO is a four-year-old,
> the V.P. is just one.
> From what my friends have told me,
> my "fun" has just begun.
>
> When the work force day is ending,
> mine just seems to start
> with dinner, baths and bedtime,
> and lessons from the heart.

I may not fax and copy
or play that "corporate game,"
but my hours are plenty long,
the work tiring just the same.

"Hostile take-overs" in my job,
involve a toy or two,
and most "successful mergers"
are done with Elmer's Glue.

My vacation time is little,
and sick days are no more.
And all important meetings
are on the bedroom floor.

While most can't wait to retire,
I hope my job NEVER ENDS,
Because in those smiling faces,
I've found my two BEST FRIENDS.

I now proudly distribute business cards to anyone who
will accept one. They simply say:

LLOYD & CLAIRE'S MOMMY

Carol A. Frink

Carol A. Frink

"I phoned your reference. She said you always ate your carrots and picked up your toys."

Reprinted by permission of Benita Epstein.

One of the Boys

"Who's better?" I asked my bridegroom of several weeks, "Cassius Clay or Muhammad Ali?"

My new husband looked at me with wide-eyed terror.

"You're kidding, aren't you?"

I shook my head meekly, wondering what was wrong with my question.

"They're the same person," he said, bursting with laughter as he buried his head back in the sports page.

As a young bride, I was simply trying to acclimate myself to my husband's world of sports. My father and two brothers enjoyed sports, but their interest was nothing compared with my bridegroom's obsession. He watched all the games, knew all the statistics, analyzed all the coaches and listened to all the sports talk shows on the radio.

He tried his best to draw me into his sporting world. "Watch this replay!" he would shout from the TV room.

Dropping what I was doing, I'd dash through the house to catch sight of yet another spectacular catch, block, putt, run or leap. Although it was great stuff, the action didn't grab my attention like a good book, a long walk, stars on a clear night or a Monet on a museum wall.

As our marriage moved through the game plan of life, three sons were born to us. Unwittingly, I had chanced upon the perfect team for a pickup game of pitcher, catcher and batter. While my friends with daughters got all dolled up for outings of lunch and shopping, I threw on my jeans for hours of fielding, refereeing and yelling. "Run! You can make it!"

"Aren't you just a little bit disappointed you don't have a girl?" friends often asked.

"Not at all," I answered truthfully.

"Well, there's a special place in heaven for mothers of three boys," they replied, quoting from a popular parenting guide.

So as each young son grew and took his section of the sports page at the breakfast table, I refused to be benched on the sidelines. So what if I didn't have long hair to braid, sweet dresses to iron or ballet shoes to buy? I wasn't going to be left in the dugout. It didn't take long to figure out I could be the ball girl, or I could step up to bat.

In short order, I became one of the boys. I pitched, I putted, I fished. And a whole new world opened up to me. Activities I never would have chosen turned into wondrous adventures.

As pitcher for the neighborhood pickup game, I discovered the joy of a well-hit ball as well as the earthy smell of trampled grass on a hot summer afternoon.

As driver to the putting green, I marveled at the exactness of nailing a four-foot putt as well as the bird song that serenaded us from a nearby oak tree.

As threader of worms, I caught the excitement of a fish tugging on a line as well as the shade-shifting brilliance of a setting sun.

Just about the time I grew accustomed to these activities, the boys moved into their teenage years, and I found myself thrown into a whole new realm of challenges. Because I was often involved in getting the guys where they wanted to go, I decided there was no point in just sitting and waiting for them to finish. Against my better judgment, I joined the action.

I've spent hours on a cold, overcast day climbing up a forty-foot pine tree, swinging from a rope and yelling "Tarzan" before plunging into the cold waters of a north-woods lake. I rode the fastest, steepest roller coasters of a theme park screaming my head off, and attended years of baseball conventions, running with a crush of fans for autographs from players I didn't even know. I found myself at the top of a snow-covered mountain peak as a novice skier on too steep a slope, simply because my sons knew I would like the view.

"Go for it, Mom," they said. "You can do it!"

And I did.

The highlights of my sporting career came, however, when my sons crossed over into my playing field.

I knew I'd scored when my eighteen-year-old returned from the city and described the personal tour of the art museum he gave his friends; when my sixteen-year-old discussed the contrasting novels of a popular author; and when my thirteen-year-old spotted sparkling Orion in the velvet darkness of the sky and announced that it was his favorite constellation.

Not long ago, as we rode home from dropping off my oldest son at college, my younger sons and husband joined in a spirited game of sports trivia.

"Name three pro basketball teams that don't end in 's.'"

"Who holds the record for most home runs by a catcher?"

I listened vaguely as I watched the silver-beamed headlights of farmers' tractors glide down rows of moonlit cornfields. Breathing in the sweet scent of the summer harvest, I noticed a sudden halt in their questioning. I seized the moment.

"Who was better," I asked, "Muhammad Ali or Cassius Clay?"

Stunned silence.

"Muhammad Ali," answered one.

"Cassius Clay?" guessed the other.

Their father burst out laughing. "They're the same person!" he explained.

"Hey, that's a cool trick question, Mom!" said one son.

"Let's try it on Billy and Greg when we get home," said the other.

Twenty-five years later, I had redeemed myself. Just don't ask me the score.

Marnie O. Mamminga

"Helmet, kneepads, elbow pads, goggles. Okay!
Go have fun!"

Confessions of a Stepmother

When I met Larry, my husband-to-be, he came complete with an eighteen-month-old daughter, McKenna, and a four-year-old son, Lorin—on weekends.

The day I met the children, we walked around a pond, Larry holding the diapered McKenna in his arms while Lorin ran around finding frogs to show me. I was stunned. These children were an enormous piece of the man I loved and yet had really nothing to do with me. How did this stepmother thing work?

I quickly fell in love with Lorin's impish grin and McKenna's pudgy baby body, warm against my chest as I held her. I was completely captivated by my new and charming "instant family," but the children's mother, Dia, was a different story. We had a wary relationship, the edge of hostility between us only thinly veiled. I did my best to ignore her and focused instead on the two adorable children she'd borne.

The children and I got along well, though Lorin was somewhat standoffish. Perhaps it was loyalty to his mother, or being a boy, or at four simply wanting more independence. McKenna, being so little, had no such qualms. She loved me and let me know it, unreservedly and with a sweetness and innocence that took my breath away. I couldn't resist her love and when I fell, I fell hard. Almost immediately, we formed our own mutual fan club—two hearts that beat as one.

In fact, it was McKenna who proposed to me first. We sat together in an airport waiting room, on our way to visit Larry's parents. She was almost three, and she sat facing me in my lap, playing with my necklace and every so often looking into my face with worshipful eyes. I smiled at her, feeling the fullness of love for her present in my own heart. Larry sat beside us and Lorin was motoring around the rows of plastic seats, making engine noises with his mouth. To the casual observer, a typical young family. But we weren't a family because Larry hadn't popped the question yet. And although I didn't want to be pushy, we both knew my patience was wearing thin. What, I wondered, was he waiting for?

Then McKenna pulled her pacifier out of her mouth and returning my smile, said brightly, "Will you marry me?" After a moment of shocked silence, we all laughed till our sides hurt. Me with delight, Larry with the release of tension and the children simply because the grown-ups were laughing. Happily, it didn't take Larry long to follow up with his own proposal.

As time went on, I got used to part-time parenting—and having the children's mother as an unavoidable part of my life. I really liked Dia, but our positions seemed to dictate a certain grumpiness with each other that I did my best to squelch. Sometimes I had the guilty wish that the children's mother would simply disappear. A quick and painless illness and on her deathbed, she would make me promise to raise her children for her. Then the children could stay with us—truly be mine—and we could be a "real" family.

Fortunately that never happened. I didn't really want her to die; I just was jealous that she'd had children with *my* husband. All right, so he was her husband at the time—it still rankled.

I watched the children grow, changing from toddlers to schoolkids. And their mother and I continued our civilized and awkward interactions, arranging for the children to come and go and negotiating vacations and holiday schedules.

My friends all told me that Larry should deal with his ex-wife, and for a while we tried that. But as an active and willing caregiver, I was involved with decisions, so Dia and I went back to our previous arrangement. And as the years went by, I noticed that our phone calls changed. I actually enjoyed talking to Dia about the kids. And I think she realized that there were very few people in the world who were as interested in, charmed by or concerned about her children as I was. We began a slow but perceptible metamorphosis that was completed the year Dia sent me a Mother's Day card, thanking me for "co-mothering" her children.

That was the beginning of a new era for Dia and me. And while it hasn't always been perfect, I know now it's been extraordinary. I have a few thank-yous of my own:

Thank you, Dia, for being big enough to share your children with me. If you hadn't, I would never have known what it was like to hold a sleeping infant and feel the complete trust displayed in the limp, silky-skinned limbs gathered carefully in my embrace. I wouldn't have had the opportunity to marvel at the twists and turns a little boy's mind makes as he tries to make sense of a large and complex universe.

I would never have known that children could cry so loudly when their stomachs hurt or that after they threw up, they could smile so radiantly at you, the tears still wet on their cheeks, their pain already forgotten.

I would never have watched a boy struggle to become his own person, or have been so closely involved with the painful and serious process of "growing a teenager." I would never have had the awe-inspiring privilege of watching that squirty twelve-year-old who could drive you wild with his questions turn into a heartbreakingly handsome hunk with the megawatt smile and charming personality. As he gets ready to leave for college, I know he will drive a new generation of women wild—for entirely different reasons.

I wouldn't have felt the thrill of seeing our beautiful daughter on stage, expressing herself with a grace and depth of emotion that seemed too old for someone so young. Or had the distinctly undeserved (and guilty) thrill of vanity and pride when someone who didn't know us commented that McKenna looked like me.

Thank you for making Christmas morning a communal occasion, so the children never had to feel divided on the holiday they held so dear. I looked around one year as we all sat around the tree, while the children delivered the gifts. There we were, you and your husband, Larry and me, the kids . . . and surprisingly, I felt at home.

I understood then that you didn't have to disappear for us to be a real family.

Carol Kline

"Wait, Dear, you don't have to run away; I will."

A Mother's Mid-Summer Prayer

Dear God,

Grant me the strength to last until Back to School Night.

Give me the energy to drive the swim team carpool, take knots out of wet shoelaces with my teeth and untangle the dog from the sprinkler hose.

Grant me the wisdom to remember the name of the red-headed kid from down the street who hasn't left our house since July.

Walk with me through the backyard over piles of wet bathing suits and empty ice cream cups, to rescue my good lipstick from the bottom of the wading pool.

Give me the courage to accept that everything in the refrigerator either has a bite out of it, had a finger stuck in it or is reproducing in the vegetable crisper underneath the expensive cheese.

Guide me down the hallway to the laundry room, where I can experience five minutes of peace and quiet by turning the lights out and climbing on the dryer so the kids can't see my feet underneath the door.

Help me accept that fact that even if I take the kids to the circus, install a pool in the backyard, go on a safari, and carve a redwood tree into a canoe and sail down the Congo, my children will end each day with "I'm bored."

Grant me the serenity to smile when my husband insists on tossing the Hamburger Helper on the gas grill because "everything tastes better barbecued."

In your infinite wisdom, show me how to disconnect the video game console that hasn't been turned off since June 22.

Comfort me when I realize the color of my earth-tone carpet has changed into a mixture of melted blue Popsicle and the remains of somebody's purple slushie.

And if I ask too much, God, just give me the foresight to know that one day—not too many years from now—the barbecue, television and sprinkler hose will be off; the refrigerator, front door and garage will be closed, and I will wonder where my children—and the little redheaded boy with the glasses—went.

Debbie Farmer

Chicken Pox Diary

Day 1: I'm starting a diary about the kids' upcoming experience with chicken pox. It all started this morning when Vicki called to tell me her kids have chicken pox. She knows I am undecided about whether to have my kids inoculated with the new vaccine, and she said if I wanted to just get it over with, we were welcome to come over and get exposed. She said the incubation period was a week or two, and when I looked at the calendar and counted the days, it turns out we'll have chicken pox right in the middle of our school's break.

Since the kids are going to be home anyway, I figured she was right—why not just get it over with? Plus, my husband is already planning to stay home that week to catch up on paperwork, so he'll be available to back me up when needed.

On the way to her house, I explained to the kids that we were having a playdate with sick friends because we want to get their germs. They asked if this meant there'd also been a policy change about chewing bubble gum that's been picked off the sidewalk.

Vicki made sure all the children shared juice cups, and

we talked about how the timing of this was so perfect, it was almost like a miracle. Perhaps I will submit diary for publication in parenting magazine.

Day 2: Went to grocery store to stock up on calamine lotion and oatmeal bath called Aveeno. Told checker plan for having all four children get chicken pox during school break when husband is home to help. She said, "That's good planning."

Day 12: Keeping bottle of calamine in pocket since chicken pox expected to appear any minute.

Day 18: School break is over; daughters back in school. Husband back at work. Son home with chicken pox. New spots keep appearing; older ones shedding off. After dinner, I dashed to store for more calamine. Mentioned to checker that miracle plan is a bucket of hog slop. Then remembered Vicki's wise words: "It's a rite of passage" and vowed to remain positive.

Day 21: Daughter erupting with chicken pox, so she's staying home with brother. Children's only relief from boredom is connecting red dots on body with permanent marker and demanding exotic snacks.

Day 26: Husband left for out-of-town business trip. Son finished with chicken pox, now has flu. Daughter feeling fine but must remain in quarantine several more days. Second daughter also home with stomachache. Am feeling kinship with pioneer women who gave birth in cornfield and shot rattlesnake off porch while husband away on cattle drive.

Day 30: All kids home from school—one with chicken pox, two with flu, one faking to get in on the snacks. Time together at home giving us a chance to get intimate understanding of each person's special idiosyncrasies, such as those observed by nurse on the job at lunatic asylum.

Day 32: Husband called early from nice hotel while waiting for morning room service. Very understanding when I was unable to remember his name. Described to him last night's dream about oatmeal in which pantry doors in kitchen swung open by themselves revealing huge container of Quaker Oats cereal. Portrait of friendly Quaker pictured on cereal box transformed into scary-looking image of Vicki, that contaminator of children.

Day . . . So tired . . . don't know what day it is and don't care anyway. Very concerned about last night's pizza order. Found pimply faced delivery boy's cap in bathtub and suspect he's the strong one I had trouble wrestling into Aveeno bath. Made note to give extra tip with next order.

Janet Konttinen

Somebody Else's Children

I am often told what beautiful children I have. Many people even comment that they look like me. Pamela, my daughter, I am told has my blue eyes; my son James has my red hair. The truth of the matter is Pamela has her father's eyes, and James, well, his hair color was inherited from his mother—his biological mother. James and Pamela are my husband's children, and I am their stepmother.

Shortly after I met my husband, Carl, his children came for a visit. The visit was to last for two weeks, and then the children would return to their mother. When the two weeks came to an end, their mother called to say she had a job working in a resort community. She would be living in a room provided by the hotel where she worked. The children would have to stay with us until the end of the summer.

But by the end of summer the children's mother had joined the military, and again, they could not live with her. The military does not accept single parents who do not have somebody living with them to care for their children.

Although their mother's military career did not last

through basic training, for a variety of reasons, she never returned for them. Carl and I realized the children were going to stay with us, permanently. I can't say I was thrilled by this realization. I had not wanted children of my own, and raising someone else's children did not appeal to me.

The kids weren't crazy about the idea either. Months earlier, when they had first arrived for their visit, I had been quickly made aware of their feelings toward me. "You're not my mommy! I want my mommy!" they had often shouted at me. After a couple of weeks or so of this, I grew to hate the word "mommy." Then, one day everything changed.

James, who was three years old at the time, had been in the middle of one of his "mommy tantrums" when he suddenly stopped screaming and looked up at me. His face was filled with terror and sadness. "I don't have a mommy no more," he calmly told me.

"James, you do have a mommy," I told him. He didn't believe me, looking at me as if I was crazy.

"No, I don't. Her went away." It was hard to defy his three-year-old logic.

"James, your mommy wants to be with you, but she can't right now. She has to work." When the children asked about their mommy, we had decided this was the best way to explain.

"I don't have no mommy." Fat tears began to roll down his cheeks, and I was beginning to panic. This child needed to know he had a mother, and I didn't know how to make him believe me. I knelt down to wipe the tears from his face.

"Are you my mommy?" he asked. At that moment, I wished that kids came with a manual. I needed answers—fast.

"I'm whatever you want me to be," I said and prayed I

was saying the right thing. "No matter what that is. I'll be your friend, and I'll love you." At that moment, I realized that I meant every word I had just said. I *did* love this child.

James seemed to be satisfied with the explanation I had given him and as quickly as his questions began, they ended. James went outside to play, while I was left to figure out what had just happened.

With Pamela, it had been easier, once we'd come to an understanding. One day while watching television, Pamela looked up at the photographs hanging on the wall. She identified each person in the pictures and who they were to her. When she reached the one of her father, she told me "my daddy."

"Yes, that is Daddy," I told her. My response did not seem to satisfy her.

"*My* daddy!" Pamela said again, pointing to herself. I suddenly understood what she was trying to tell me.

"Pamela," I began, "I don't want to take your daddy away. I know you love him, but I love him, too. Maybe if you will let me, we can both love him. Can we share, if I promise never to take your daddy away from you?"

"Okay. We can share." Pamela was smiling at me. "We both love my daddy."

Carl and I married Christmas Day, the children standing next to us while we exchanged vows. They quickly began telling anyone who would listen, "We got married." I suppose "we" did. Then shortly after the wedding, James and I cleared the mommy issue up once and for all.

It was his fourth birthday, and I had taken the children to the grocery store to get a few things for the party. James, excited about his birthday, was talking a mile a minute. Exactly what he was talking about, I doubt I'll ever remember, because James had said one word that had immediately caught my attention, and I didn't hear anything else he had to say. When James realized what he had said he looked up at me. "I called you Mommy," he giggled.

"Yes, I know." I was trying to behave as if nothing out the ordinary had just happened.

"I'm sorry." James twisted his mouth a bit.

"You don't have to be sorry," I explained. "I don't mind if you call me Mommy."

"Are you my mommy, too?" Why couldn't he just once ask an easy question?

"I'm like a mommy, but you have your mother, and she is your *mommy*. As I told you before, I am whatever you want me to be."

"Okay, Mommy," James said, smiling at me. He was telling me what he wanted.

Recently, James came home from school with a drawing he'd done. "Look what I made for you, Mommy. It's our family. This one is you."

As I looked at the paper he handed me, I felt the tears begin to form in my eyes. He had drawn four red stick figures, holding hands and smiling. James was telling me in his own wonderful way that I am not raising someone else's children—I am raising *my* children.

Trudy Bowler

Wasting Water

It was a Friday evening, and I had just settled into bed with a new novel when I heard it: the kitchen faucet had been turned on. Evidently someone in my family was getting a drink of water before bed. Normally, this action would immediately go in one ear and out the other, but tonight was different. Having just spent several weeks educating our two children about conservation, specifically electricity and water, I was overly attuned to every fan blade turning, every drop of water, every flush.

Anyone who has ever paid the household bills will agree that the humid, unrelenting heat of summer can be especially brutal on the pocketbook. Family funds designated for monthly water usage are flushed down the toilet—literally. Electric bills can fry even the most generous of budgets.

So, it was with a large amount of righteous determination that I laid out the rules: Lights and ceiling fans must be turned off when you leave the room. Don't waste the water. Keep the air conditioner on eighty degrees. Turn off the television when you aren't watching. *Such simple ideas!* I thought. *Of course we can do this!*

On this particular Friday night, perched in bed reading, I turned my attention away from the running faucet and was temporarily lost in the pages of my paperback. One chapter later, I came out of fantasyland long enough to hear the distinct sound of the kitchen faucet still cascading at full speed.

It couldn't be! At least five full minutes had elapsed since the faucet was first turned on, and it hadn't stopped flowing yet! I was mortified, angry and desperately wanted to punish whoever was blatantly ignoring Rule #2, "Don't Waste the Water."

I leaped out of bed, ready to blast into the kitchen and reprimand the evil-doer, realizing nearly too late that my scantily clad self would not get the respect I needed for this particular lecture. So I stuck my head around the corner, saw my ten-year-old son, Christopher, and exploded, "What in the world are you doing? That water's been running for over five minutes. Are you trying to put our last penny down the drain?"

I stomped back to bed and pulled up the covers, satisfied that my point had been made, but it wasn't long before I heard another noise coming from the kitchen. It wasn't the water running. The faucet had been turned off immediately after my verbal assault.

No, the sound was much worse. It was the unmistakable echo of a muffled sob.

Quickly slipping on a pair of shorts, I ran out into the kitchen. What I saw sent my heart into that tiny place in your throat where it sticks and threatens to make camp. I couldn't swallow. I could only cry.

There was my son, carefully wiping down the stove top, his silent tears mixing with window cleaner as they dropped softly onto the range. I looked around the kitchen that I had been too tired to clean before bed. It was spotless. Dishes were put away, the countertops sparkled, and my sink was once again white. Even the microwave was fingerprint-free.

Stunned that Christopher would take such an initiative on his own, and thoroughly disgusted with myself I slowly walked up behind my son, and gently encircled him with my arms.

"I'm so sorry, Son. I was wrong. Terribly wrong," I whispered, my hot tears now dropping onto his back.

"It's okay, Mom," he replied faintly. "I understand."

My son's decency and forgiving nature prevailed over my unfortunate behavior.

So who is the adult here? I wondered, as I turned him around to face me.

"Please forgive me," I half-stated, half-asked, mostly begged. "I shouldn't have flown off the handle without checking first. I should have taken the time to see what was happening. I should have trusted you more. I was wrong."

His hug was strong. We held on to each other as he struggled with forgiveness and I suffered with regret and guilt.

"Christopher," I finally said, "you have taught me to take my time and be cautious when accusing anyone of wrongdoing. You've taught me never to assume anything. You've taught me a great deal about your character and about trust."

He was silent, taking in the apology.

"It's awfully hot tonight, isn't it?" I asked, attempting to establish some positive communication. Then, acting on impulse, I blurted out, "Go get your bathing suit on."

Christopher gave me a questioning look but did as I requested, even though the hands on the kitchen clock were approaching midnight. In two minutes we were both outside in the yard with the sprinklers running hard at full tilt. We raced around in circles, laughing, cooling our bodies and acting silly until finally, Christopher asked the inevitable.

"What about the water bill, Mom? It's going to be huge."

"Water, schmater," I replied, letting a shot of spray hit me directly on the rear end. "It's only money, Honey, and you are much more important than any stack of green paper."

The moonlight cast a strange glow upon his face, and I saw what appeared to be a single teardrop falling from one eye. Or maybe it was just the water dripping from his wet head. It really didn't matter because he walked over to me, gave me a high five and whispered, "I love you, Mom."

We romped and played outside that night for nearly an hour. The water ran continuously, but not once did I envision currency being sucked down the drain. And when the bill came later that month, I paid it, with contentment in my soul and joy in my heart, for now I know the simple truth: To err is human, but to be forgiven by your child is truly divine.

Susan H. Hubbs

The Wonders of Tupperware

Many years ago, in the far distant past of 1966, Tupperware parties were all the rage with stay-at-home moms. Practically all of us "kept house" then, and these parties gave us a pleasant and acceptable way to go out for the evening, usually leaving the dads to handle the kids' bath and bed routine.

We loved actually talking with people older than five, although our conversations mostly centered around those very topics we knew best—kids and housekeeping. While learning the proper way to "burp" a container, we also discussed burping babies. Usually, after about three hours of listening to the demonstrator, playing silly games and filling out our order forms, we would all go home thinking of the wonderful new plastic additions to our already bulging kitchen storage cabinets. We might not see each other again for a month or so until someone else decided to host the next "party."

One day, after a Thursday night Tupperware party at the home of my friend Kay who lived two doors down from me, I was in the backyard hanging out wash (something else we used to do in the olden days, but that's another story). Kay yelled over the back fence that she had some pastries left over and maybe we should gather up some neighbors and finish them off with coffee later that afternoon. This was an unusual idea in our neighborhood. None of us had lived there very long, we all had little ones who took up a lot of our time and we just didn't socialize much except for demonstration parties. I told Kay it sounded good to me, so we called everyone who had been there the night before and made plans to meet at my house at 2:00.

Normally, by 2:00 in the afternoon, most of us had the kids in for a nap, but this time we decided to forgo the naps for just this once and let them play while we ate the pastries and talked. It was raining out, so the little ones had to play in the dining room of my tiny house, out of sight but within hearing distance, while we moms sat talking in the living room. Before we knew it, two hours had gone by and everyone hurried off to start dinner before the men got home from work. But something interesting had happened in those two hours, something that we all knew we wanted to continue.

We continued to meet for three more years, every Friday afternoon at 2:00, bringing the kids along to scatter toys and grind pretzels into the dining room rug of whoever was hosting that week. We didn't mind the mess—we were learning that sometimes *all* mothers lose their cool with their kids, sometimes *every* loving husband was an unfeeling oaf. We weren't alone in the world, and we weren't monsters who sometimes lost control in our frustration with trying to be the best wife and mother. Amazingly, we discovered other women were having the same struggles. And quite often, just talking about it with friends who really *knew* allowed us to handle things better the next time we felt like throwing in the towel or strangling somebody.

Week by week, my sanity was saved and my marriage was strengthened because I found a safe place to vent my frustrations and learn new ways of coping. We moms learned from each other while we developed wonderful friendships among ourselves, and our children learned valuable social skills (such as picking up your own pretzel crumbs) from their tag-along playgroup. And all because of a Tupperware party!

That Tupperware—who knew it could preserve so many things?

Carol Bryant

4

BECOMING
A MOTHER

*When a woman puts her finger for the first
time into the tiny hand of her baby and
feels that helpless clutch which tightens her
very heartstrings, she is born again with a
newborn child.*

Kate Douglas Wiggin

"Notice anything different?"

Reprinted by permission of Benita Epstein.

The Face of God

The drama of birth is over. The cord is cut, the first cry heard: A new life begun. . . . The mother—seeing, hearing, perhaps touching her baby—scarcely notices the world around her, let alone how much her body aches. She just participated in a miracle.

Carrol Dunham

In my years, I have seen the vastness of the Grand Canyon, the splendor of the Alps, the purple mountains' majesty of the Smoky Mountains of Tennessee and the seeming endlessness of the Pacific Ocean. Yet, nothing I have seen, or ever expect to see, compares with what I once witnessed in a dark-paneled, antiseptic birthing room. Then and there, the power and love of God enveloped me.

I was on the last night of my clinical rotation as a nursing student on the labor and delivery floor, and I had yet to see a birth. When my children were born, fathers were relegated to the labor waiting room. Now, at 7:00 P.M. on my last student shift, my nursing instructor suggested I

check into labor room four to see if I could watch the birth.
With some trepidation, I knocked on the door, stuck in my
head, and asked the young couple if I could possibly
observe the birth of their baby. They gave me permission.
I thanked them and found myself a spot in the room that
kept me out of the way but still gave me a good view of
the birth. Then I stood with my hands behind my back,
studiously looking around the room at the preparations
being made by the nurses.

The young mother, covered with blue sterile drapes, lay
in the most uncomfortable and exposed position imaginable and was sweating profusely. Every minute or so, she
would grimace, groan and push with all her might. Her
husband stood beside her, coaching her breathing and
lovingly holding her hand. One nurse dabbed her forehead with a cool washcloth, while another encouraged her
to rest when she could. The doctor worked on a low stool
to ease the birth as best he could. I stood apart, proud of
my unemotional, clinical detachment.

The nurse assisting the doctor said, "Here she comes!" I
looked and was amazed at what I saw: the top of a head
covered with black hair began to appear. I instantly lost
the ability to call this wondrous occurrence something as
medical as "crowning." Then the doctor began gently but
firmly to turn the shoulders of the new life and pull.
Transfixed to my spot, I am sure my mouth was agape.
The doctor continued to turn and pull; the mother
pushed; the husband encouraged; and an event that had
taken nine long months of preparation was over in just a
few seconds. At the sight of the infant's beautiful face, I felt
such wonder that I truly believe angels sing at such times.

My professionalism and clinical detachment had
deserted me, replaced with a warmth that surrounded me.
At a loss for words—congratulations seemed such an
empty and trite thing to say to these two blessed people

at that moment—I nonetheless offered my congratulations anyway. After leaving the room, I walked around the corner into a deserted hallway and allowed my tears to flow.

That night some of my fellow students, all of whom were women and many of them mothers, asked me about the birth. Each time, I welled up again with tears and choked out that it was the most beautiful experience I had ever had. They would hug me or pat my shoulder, and with a gleam in their eyes say, "I know." Days passed before I could speak of the birth in any medical light. Even now, as I review that night, I continue to be in awe.

I have seen many sights in my life. Before my life is over, I will see many more. But none can ever compare to the night I saw the love, hope and beauty of God in the face of a newborn child.

Tony Collins

CLOSE TO HOME. ©*John McPherson. Reprinted with permission of Universal Press Syndicate. All rights reserved.*

Next to My Heart

I looked at this tiny, perfect creature and it was as though a light switch had been turned on. A great rush of love, mother love, flooded out of me.

Madeleine L'Engle

The day I had to stop dead in my tracks in the aisle of a busy supermarket was one of the worst in my whole life.

There I was, pregnant as could be—forty pounds over-weight, a whole month past my due date, with wretched "morning sickness" that lasted twenty-four hours every single day. And now I had cramps in both feet so excruciating I couldn't move.

This wasn't the way I had expected motherhood to be. My own mother, who had six children, glowed when she was expecting. And *her* mother, my grandmother, not only joyfully welcomed sixteen little ones into the world—but also ran a busy store the entire time. Looking forward to holding a little one in your arms, they said, and feeling the miracle of life inside you, should make any woman ecstatically happy. And *healthy!*

In all my magazines, the maternity advertisements showed blissful mothers-to-be in adorable outfits, perfect hairdos—even high heels. And that's the way my expectant friends were. An office-mate with the same due date as me worked right up till her baby came. My next-door neighbor had done everything she wanted to for nine full months while looking absolutely gorgeous. Neither had been ill a minute. And both of them now had adorable, healthy babies.

Meanwhile, I was still pregnant, still miserable, and so large I had long since forgotten what either my feet or my legs looked like. There was only one outfit I could even get on—a sort of muumuu tent. I'd had to give up work, give up church ministries, almost give up hope.

Why was God allowing this to happen to me? He knew I loved him, my husband and this unborn child. My friends had started snickering: "You were due *when?*" Even my doctor grumped at me as if it were all my own fault.

And now during one of the hottest Augusts on record, my ankles swelled so badly in our sweltering apartment, I had to keep them in buckets of ice. Going anywhere was torture. But we were out of milk. *Just a quick dash to the store,* I thought—surely I could do that.

So here I was, frozen in my tracks, stopping carts in both directions.

My face beet-red, I stared at the rows of cracker boxes in front of me, pretending not to notice the angry shoppers whose way I was blocking. And then I heard a little girl's voice: "Mommy, why does that lady look so funny?"

I squeezed my eyes shut, trying to stop sudden tears. *Oh, God, please! That's the last straw! Can't anyone say anything nice about me for a change? I'm so tired of being a medical freak. Won't I ever be normal and comfortable and well again? Won't I ever get to hold this baby in my arms?*

Then that mother said something I will never forget:

"Dear," she murmured, "it's because God has given that woman a tiny baby to carry next to her heart."

When I opened my eyes, mother and daughter were gone. Eventually, so were the cramps. But those words have lasted a lifetime.

For, oh, they were so true. And such a blessing to me during those final miserable days before I did hold my beautiful firstborn in my arms. During my next two pregnancies as well. A blessing I remembered as my three children grew up and married. A blessing I have been privileged to share with my own pregnant daughters-in-law and many other young women I have known over the years.

For even after our children are born, we mothers still carry those precious little ones next to our hearts. And we will our whole lives long.

Bonnie Compton Hanson

No Time for the News

Today, I'd like to share with you my thoughts on the presidential campaign. Unfortunately, I don't have any, because my wife and I just had a baby.

The birth went very well from my perspective, which was the perspective of a person keeping an eye on the contractions via a hospital bedside computer monitor. My wife, who was experiencing the contractions in person, found it more challenging, although I know she appreciated my helpful reports:

Me (watching the monitor): Okay, you're having a contraction now.
Michelle: ARRRRRRGGGGHHHHHH
Me: It looks like a big one.
Michelle: AAAAAAAAAARRRRRRGGGGGGGGGGHHH HHHHHHHHHOOOOOOOOOOOOOOOOOOOOOOOO

The contractions went on for what seemed like two years, although it was really only about fourteen months. In theory, the baby was supposed to be headed toward the exit at that point, but this particular baby seemed to like it in there. This baby was still up in the vicinity of Michelle's sinus cavities. So with month fifteen of labor looming, the doctors decided to remove the baby via cesarean section, a medical procedure named for the Roman emperor Julius Section. They put up a curtain, with Michelle's head on one side and the rest of her body on the other. Michelle and I both stayed on the head side, so we saw nothing; the doctors could have been over there grafting on extra legs, or replacing Michelle's spleen with a harmonica, and we would have had no way of knowing. Finally, the doctors shouted "Stand up, Dad!" This was my signal to stand up, look over the screen and pass out.

No, seriously, I managed to remain conscious, because I was dying to know the baby's gender. There's a test they can do to determine the gender ahead of time; I think they insert a tiny photo of Leonardo DiCaprio into the uterus, and if the baby punches it, it's a boy. We had not had this test done. We had, however, heard many strong opinions from total strangers. For some reason, total strangers feel compelled to do two things whenever they see a pregnant woman:

1. Touch her belly, as though her navel were an elevator button; and
2. Look her over, the way state-fair judges examine a cow, then loudly declare the baby's gender.

There was absolutely no doubt in anybody's mind that this baby was a boy. During the pregnancy at least 600 total strangers assured us of this fact. NOBODY thought it was a girl. So you will not be surprised to learn that when the moment came, the doctors reached in and pulled out seven pounds, nine ounces of Sophie Kaufman Barry.

As a trained journalist, I can state with total objectivity that she is the cutest little girl in the history of the world. The doctors took one look at her and immediately decided that they would shut down the hospital birthing unit, because this baby was so perfect that there was clearly no point in making any more.

Okay, they didn't say that, but they agreed, under intensive interrogation from the father, that the baby was pretty darned cute. She is also, of course, very gifted. I know this because the next morning, I carried Sophie over to the hospital-room window, and we looked out, and I told her that this was the world, and she should not get involved with it. I also told her that our policy regarding boys was that she would never be allowed to date or look directly at them. I could tell by her facial expression that she understood me completely. Although it might also have been gas.

So now we're in that mode—you parents know the mode I'm talking about—where you don't sleep much, and you find yourself celebrating a baby poop the way the French celebrated the liberation of Paris, and you walk around the house at 4:30 A.M. with the baby on your shoulder, trying to remember the words to lullabies ("And if that billy goat don't shed, papa's gonna buy you . . . a squirrel named Ed").

My point is that lately I haven't had time to follow the presidential campaign, or to assess the current crop of candidates. I'm sure they're all fine men. But they're not getting near my daughter.

Dave Barry

"They don't come with a snooze button, Steven."

Alliana's Mother

My husband and I were lying in bed when we heard our daughter, Alliana, call out, "Mommy, Mommy!" I bolted upright and held my breath for a second before running in to comfort her. Was she calling out for me or for Lisa? It was the first time Alliana called me Mommy.

One of Martin's selling points when friends set us up on a blind date was that he was a widower with a three-and-a-half-year-old daughter. If the date worked out, the package deal would come with a wonderful husband and the daughter I had always dreamed of. (I'd been married before and had been unable to conceive.)

Martin and I had been dating for about a month when the three of us spent our first day together. At one point, Alliana scrunched her eyes and snarled at me. "Let's play Black Beauty," she said, giggling and climbing on her father. She bucked like a bronco and hit me smack in the face with her legs. "Oh, sorry," she said, referring to the not-unintentional kick and barely suppressing a cackle.

Later that hot August day, we went canoeing down the Delaware River. In the midafternoon, Martin snapped the photo he now carries in his wallet: We're picnicking on a boulder we've dubbed Lunch Rock. Alliana, in her Pocahontas bathing suit, is smiling broadly as she sits in the crook of my arm. I am radiant.

We were married—all three of us—five months later.

People always want to know if it was hard to step in and love someone else's child. Let me tell you what was hard: It was hard to leave my single-girl loft in Manhattan and what I thought of as my cool single-girl life. It was hard to live in Martin and Lisa's house, filled with all of Martin and Lisa's things, until we found a home of our own. And it was hard to get used to being an "instant family."

There was a honeymoon, but no honeymoon period. There was no nine-month gestation during which I picked out baby clothes, decorated a nursery and made the transition with Martin from couplehood to parenthood. One day Martin and I were chasing each other around my loft, giddy with relief that we'd found each other. Virtually the next we were struggling to get a toddler to eat, rather than sculpt, her mashed potatoes and peas.

But was it hard to love Alliana? I'd wanted her for so long that I'm convinced it wouldn't have been hard to love her even if she hadn't had impish half-moon eyes that lit up when she laughed. Even if she hadn't been funny, adaptive and compassionate. Even if she hadn't decided to trust me and jump into this mommy-daughter thing with both feet and her whole heart from the get-go.

Aside from that one kick in the head, Alliana has challenged my right to mommy her only once. The first time I reprimanded Alliana—for not putting away her toys, I think—she struck back instinctively: "You're not my *real* mommy!" she wailed.

"Yes, I am," I calmly explained. "I'm not your first mommy, but I'm a very real mommy. And I'm yours." As I reassured her, she collapsed, crying, into my arms.

Alliana hasn't forgotten her mother. We talk about Lisa,

and there are pictures of her in Alliana's room. I find it impossible to look at those pictures without sadness for all that Lisa lost—and without feeling like an intruder.

It's not as if I pushed Lisa out of the picture and stepped in to take her place. A horrible thing happened: Lisa died suddenly of a heart attack. And, as Martin assures me, "I came looking for you so Alliana and I could put our lives back together."

Alliana *needed* a mommy. Despite close, loving relationships with her grandparents and with a father who nursed her through all-night earaches, read her two stories and played his guitar for her every evening, and all-around idolized her, Alliana longed for a mommy: a live mommy who could go on class trips, kiss her playground bruises, and explain the mysteries of mascara and moisturizer to her. "I didn't think I'd ever have one again," she told me last Mother's Day, showering me with two homemade cards, a marigold she'd planted herself and a hand-painted picture frame.

"I didn't think I'd ever have a daughter," I said as we covered each other with a million kisses.

I tell Martin—when he asks—that I don't mind having missed Alliana's baby years. It is enough to have her now. But I look at her baby pictures with longing. I wasn't there to see her first step, and I can't talk with other moms about what Alliana went through in her teething days. I can only imagine what it must have been like to see her the moment she was born all pink and smooth, with a patch of black hair sticking straight up from her perfectly round head.

Now, however, I know nearly everything there is to know about Alliana. She likes grilled cheese, cheeseburgers, and macaroni and cheese. Will sit for hours making up stories about her Beanie Babies. She has recently given up bright-green glitter nail polish for a more subdued shade of pastel blue.

And if all goes right, I will be around to hear Alliana tell me about her first kiss, to see her accept her college diploma and to stand next to Martin when Alliana gives birth to our first grandchild.

When I think of the future, and of the inevitable time when Alliana's hormones hit and we are catapulted into the terrible teens, I fear that Alliana will lash out at me by going for the jugular: "My *real* mom wouldn't do that!" I hope I'll have the grace and wisdom to know she doesn't mean to hurt me. I hope she will know how much I've always loved her.

When Alliana was four, she and Martin celebrated their first Hanukkah with me. One night, sitting at the table and drawing, with the candles of the menorah glowing, Alliana reached across the table for a crayon. Luckily, I was sitting next to her, and the few strands of her hair that grazed the flames were barely singed as I quickly pressed them between my fingers. But Alliana refers to the event as the Great Hanukkah Fire, and she still talks about how I saved her life.

Somehow, Alliana understands that she saved my life, too. "You were just plain old Lynn living all by yourself," she said one day, out of the blue. "Just waiting for me and Daddy to come along."

And more than she can ever know, Alliana is right.

Lynn Schnurnberger

A Letter to My Baby

Suddenly she was here. And I was no longer pregnant; I was a mother. I never believed in miracles before.

Ellen Greene

I waited, staring blankly around the white sterile examining room. The nurse had said she would be right back with the test results, but the minutes dragged by. I sat with only a single white sheet covering me, waiting for what turn my life might take. The cold, plastic-cushioned table was becoming uncomfortable, but it did not distract me enough to pull my attention elsewhere. All my thoughts centered around one question. *"What if...?"*

What if... I am pregnant? What will I do? How will I support myself and a baby? These thoughts were interrupted by what felt like the fluttering of butterflies inside my stomach as the door swept open. The nurse entered; I searched her face, but it was empty of expression. When she began to speak, her voice was flat, a dreary monotone. Though I did not catch her words, I knew exactly what she was telling me: I was pregnant.

I didn't say anything, but just sat still, gazing dully at her pasty complexion. There were no encouraging words offered, no squeeze of a hand. Water welled up in my eyes, and I no longer saw or heard anything. I wrapped my arms around myself and wept.

Thoughts and tears both came rushing: I couldn't take care of myself very well. I was always worried about money. Now I was supposed to care and nurture a tiny human being? It scared me so much to think I had been stupid enough to get pregnant. The tears came even faster now. I huddled in my new reality. I was going to have a baby.

The months passed, and as my body grew, so did my fears. I felt so utterly ill-equipped for the business of being a mom. Especially a single mom.

During that time, I talked to friends who did their best to encourage me. I spoke to a counselor once a week. I went swimming every Thursday with another pregnant woman I knew. But most often, when I wasn't working, I sat in front of the television, trying not to think about what would happen after the baby was born.

One day, close to my due date, I sat in my usual spot on my futon couch watching soap opera after soap opera, waiting for the arrival of my daughter, Loreena. (I had picked out her name as soon as I found out she was a girl.) Then it was time for my favorite talk show. The show that day was about parenting. One woman read a letter written to her by her daughter before the daughter had passed away. Though the tears streamed down the mother's face as she read, it obviously brought her great joy and comfort to see the loving words her daughter had set down on paper for her mom.

I was immediately inspired to write to my unborn daughter. Suddenly, it was the most important thing in the world to let her know—on paper—that I would always love her and cherish her and that I would do my best to make up for the absence of a father in her life. When Loreena first moved inside of me, I had realized she was "real." But as I watched the TV show, it was the first time that I thought of Loreena as a person, with her own needs and wants, rather than "the baby I would have to care for *somehow.*"

I was excited to write to her. I waddled over to my desk and got out my stationery. I sat to write, pen poised above the paper. I closed my eyes for a moment, connecting to Loreena, wondering how to say what was in my heart. Opening my eyes, I began to write.

Dear Loreena,   *4-8-99*

Here we are, waiting for your arrival. I go through all your tiny outfits and dream about the day when we will meet in the outside world. I know you already, my baby. I know you are strong and stubborn. Each kick and flutter announces, "Hey Mom. Here I am!" Our bond is strong now, but it will be even stronger when I can show you my love and we can build our relationship, day by day.

I have been very frightened about having you by myself, but over these months I have grown to cherish your every movement and have anticipated the day we touch, skin on skin.

You are and always will be my angel. I thank God that you are a part of my life.

Love,
Mother

I smiled as I folded the stationery into the envelope and sealed it. I reached down on the floor beside my bed and picked up the keepsake box I'd created for my little daughter-to-be. I placed the envelope in the box, then closed it. When the lid snapped shut, it was as if I closed away all my fears, too. All that remained were thoughts of Loreena joining me soon.

Twenty days later, Loreena entered the world. I didn't sleep at all for the entire twenty-four hours I stayed in the hospital. I couldn't tear my eyes away from the tiny creature who had changed my existence. My daughter, my little angel, was perfect. I didn't want to miss anything.

Today, it's hard to remember those fears I had. They've disappeared, replaced by the feeling that being Loreena's mom is the most natural thing in the world.

My daughter is already a year old. She's outgrown the tiny outfits and booties I first dressed her in, and I've put them away in her keepsake box, along with presents people have given her for "when she's older."

Each time I tuck another treasure in the box, I see the envelope addressed in my handwriting to Loreena. I envision the day years from now when my daughter is able to read and will open that envelope and see the words of love I wrote—on the day I was finally ready to be a mom.

Karie L. Hansen

"I'd like to order a large pizza topped with sausage, black olives, pickles, chocolate-covered raisins, popcorn, peppermints, coconut marshmallows, beef chow mein, licorice, lobster, maple syrup and fried catfish. And on the other half, I want . . ."

It Just Isn't Fair

I'd wanted a child for so long. I'd endured the diabetes testing and the pelvic exams. I'd cried during my ultrasound when I saw my son for the first time, and I'd laughed through the baby shower my sisters had given me. I was thrilled with my pregnancy, but now, as I prepared the bedroom down the hall for my new son, try as I might, I couldn't shake the thought: *It just isn't fair.*

As I got closer to motherhood, thoughts of my own mother came more and more frequently. My mother had died of cancer when I was thirteen. In my memory, she had been the very best mother in the whole world—patient, kind and loving. She had enjoyed her children, caring for us and meeting our every need the way only a mother can.

Her death at the age of forty-one had been no beautiful, poignant *Love Story* death; she'd fought hard for her life and the struggle had consumed the last year of her time with us. After she died, I missed her with a bottomless ache in my soul that never went away. When I graduated from high school I pushed away thoughts of my mother. I tried to ignore how unfair it felt that she wasn't there to see me get my diploma. At my wedding, I deliberately closed the emotional door to memories of Mom. But now, as I waited for our son, I found I couldn't stop thinking about my mother.

Growing up, I'd found substitutes as best I could. My father kept his family together, trying hard to make up for Mom's death. My five sisters and I made a tight-knit, loving unit, and we all mothered one another.

Then God gave me a second mother in my wonderful mother-in-law, Ethel. In the early years of my marriage Ethel never intruded but also never failed to give good advice when she felt it justified. Ethel died three years before I got pregnant, and although her death was more peaceful and less painful than my mother's, I still missed her terribly. As my baby grew inside me, I felt keenly the fact that I had no mother to help me.

I'm ashamed to admit I felt jealous of other pregnant women who had mothers. I saw them together shopping for maternity clothes while I went, alone, to buy my own. They were there cooing over cribs and cradles when my husband and I shopped for the perfect bed for our baby. Even in our Lamaze class there was a mother-daughter team, huffing and puffing right alongside the counting husbands and the eagerly attending ladies.

I had this little fantasy that I'd let my mind play: my mother and I, enjoying lunch together at a restaurant while she told me wise stories about the wiles and ways of babies. I could picture myself, listening intently and laughing at tales of her own mothering. But of course, it was just a fantasy. *It just wasn't fair.*

I knew I could never forget my mothers; their faces are etched in my memory. But I wanted my son to somehow "know" his grandmothers, so a few months before our baby arrived, Tom and I decided to hang a picture of each of our mothers on the wall. In my mother-in-law's picture, taken when she was a lively, vibrant young woman, Ethel looks a lot like her son—complete with the slightest suggestion of faint lines under her eyes, a hereditary trick of the skin that my husband shares. It's a distinctive feature, and I noticed it in Ethel the first time I met her.

My own mother's picture looks down at me with the large, beautiful and smiling brown eyes I remember so vividly from my childhood. I'd found comfort in those eyes when I hurt myself. I'd loved the way she smiled and how her eyes lit up with laughter when she felt delighted. And despite the stress and strain of raising six children, with a husband in Vietnam, there had always been deep peace in her eyes.

For me, labor lasted thirty-three hours and ended in an emergency C-section. The doctor whispered the word "brain damage" into the phone while she summoned the high-risk pediatrician, and I knew from the way the nurse frowned at the monitor and from her honest answers to our questions that my baby was in trouble.

It was a far cry from the delivery I'd planned, the one where my husband and I would participate joyously in the miracle of birth. I was sure that I'd cry the first time I heard the baby cry out, and I knew my husband would, too. But I wasn't awake to see my baby born. Right before the general anesthesia put me to sleep, my last conscious thoughts were prayers for his safety.

When I woke up from the delivery, my husband and my sister were with me. My first thought, even before I could open my eyes, was for the baby. I'll never forget my sister's voice saying, "He's beautiful—and he's huge!" In spite of the doctor's fears, Ben was healthy, hearty and weighed nearly ten pounds. Finally they brought my son to me. I was groggy and in pain from the staples on my incision, but I couldn't wait to meet him.

I took the heavy bundle they handed me—they didn't

tell me he'd be so heavy! Someone put a pillow on my belly so I could hold him more easily, and I did what I'm sure every new parent does—I held his hand and counted his fingers, amazed at the tiny, perfect little fingernails. He made a face when I did that, his eyes still closed in sleep. I watched him breathe, watched the way his barrel chest went in and out, in and out. I savored the bowed, pudgy little legs and the perfect roundness of his head. I held him while he slept, breathing in that unforgettable fragrance of new baby. An hour later, he stirred and woke. I watched as his eyes opened, held my breath as he looked at me for the first time.

Considering that his grandmothers were absent, I'm proud to say that up until then I'd done pretty well. I'd felt too full of joy and thanksgiving at Ben's safe arrival to feel the "just isn't fair" feeling. And, when my son opened his eyes, *It just isn't fair* ended for good.

You see, my son has my mother's eyes—big, deep brown, and full of sparkle and life. And there's a funny little skin fold under his eyes—just like his father, just like Ethel.

When I see my two mothers smile at me from my son's face, I no longer have any thoughts about "fairness." I just know that I have been blessed with a beautiful son whose smile gives me back both of my mothers every day of his life.

Nancy L. Rusk

5

ON ADOPTION

Of all the rights of women, the greatest is to be a mother.

Lin Yutano

The Question

Joyfully, our adoption process was nearing the finale! In the beginning, I had supplied, verified and simplified every question and every fill-in-the-blank. But even then, amidst the facts and figures, one lone and very specific uncertainty tugged at my heart. I thought about it when we attended our first welcoming seminar. I tried not to be obvious as I searched the faces of the other prospective parents—were they feeling the same uncertainty?

Finally, we received the long-awaited "call," and the next day a tiny baby was placed into my arms. That one nagging little fear was overshadowed by the sheer joy of holding my newborn son and naming him Eric. I considered it once again in the courtroom the day the paperwork became final. He was six months old, able to coo and giggle, oblivious to legalities or titles. Yet all the while I wondered. Where and when and how would he ask me the inevitable question: Are you my real mother?

I knew there were books and pamphlets explaining all the "right" answers to be given at all the "appropriate" age levels. I told myself I would read the scholarly information and wait my turn to recite the correct reply.

So I read and reread, but the security never came with the knowledge. Now I knew *what* to say, but would I say it right, say it so he could understand? What if the question came on the freeway while the two of us maneuvered in and out of traffic? Would I pull the car to the side? Would I ask that he wait till we got home and we'd talk? After all, a question so important could hardly be addressed between Thirty-second and Thirty-fourth Street.

Maybe he would ask me in the playroom of a golden-arched restaurant or as we exited his favorite movie. *I would be prepared,* I told myself. I would briefly, very briefly touch on conception and then even more briefly on pregnancy and then deal with the who and why of what came after that.

Would there ever be words that could explain it all? How could I make him understand that he grew in one woman's womb and another woman's heart? How could he know the anguish his birth mother felt on placement day as she held him one last time or the breathless joy I felt the second he was placed in the warmth of my arms?

One night, as I was preparing dinner, tired from the day's lack of accomplishment and frustrated by the lateness of the hour, a small-framed three-year-old boy came and stood beside me as I stirred the mashed potatoes.

"Mommy," he said. "I have a question for you."

"Uh-hum," I mumbled out of habit.

"Mommy," he tugged at my shirt. "Mommy, I said I have a question."

"Okay, okay." I stopped and turned to see two bright eyes staring up at me. I knew something was wrong. He blinked, trying to hold back the tears, but they fell nevertheless. I bent down to him, forgetting the potatoes and the day. What mattered more than anything was the little boy before me. I held his chin in the cup of my hand and asked him softly. "What's wrong? What is so important to ask me that it would make you cry?"

No sooner had the last word left my lips than I knew. We were here. The moment had arrived, and I was as unprepared as the minute it had first crossed my thoughts.

"Mommy, Sarah says you aren't my real mommy. I told her she was wrong. She was wrong, right, Mommy?"

All the days of guessing and planning and memorizing, and I was speechless. I pulled him closer to me and wrapped my arms tightly around his little body. My son. My precious son. I wiped away the tears continuing to fall against his cheek. Then with a calmness I'd never before possessed, I held out my hand.

"Sweetheart, do you see Mommy's hand?"

"Uh huh," he replied as he bobbed his head up and down.

"Well," I slowly said, "Go ahead and touch it. Touch my hand." His tiny fingers stroked across my palm.

"Do I feel real to you?" I asked.

"You do!" he said as a smile broke across his face. He ran his fingers along my arms and then against my face and through my hair.

"Then I am your real mother, and my love for you is real. But there is another lady who loves you and is very real, too. She loved you so much she gave you life and let you grow inside her until it was time for you to be born and join Mommy and Daddy. She's called your birth mother, and one day we'll get to meet her.

"How does that sound?" I asked. I wasn't sure who the question was for, him or me.

He grabbed my neck and began to cover my cheek with kisses. I pulled him closer, the tears rolling down my cheeks. And then before I was ready to let go, he pulled away and off he ran to the living room, ready to play once more.

It had happened. I had seen tears that needed to be wiped away, and they had left with the stroke of my hand. I had seen a little boy who needed to be hugged, and I had given him the warmest, softest hug I could give. The question had been asked. And I had answered.

I knew, in another time and another place, there would be other, harder questions but for now, I knew . . . I had done well.

Mary Chavoustie

Race Against Time

The back legs on the chair almost lifted off the floor as Clarin leaned closer to the television screen—closer to the image that tugged at her heart.

"Anna," the voice said in a Russian accent. The voice said something more, and the little girl obeyed: She danced a little, sang a little. Then the tape stopped. "She only has a few months," the woman beside Clarin said. "A few months before she's lost for good . . . "

We can't let that happen, Clarin thought. *But can we stop it in time?*

Just weeks earlier, Clarin and her husband Paul hadn't even heard of the little Russian girl. Their life was full raising six kids. The oldest, Josh, was leaving for college. The youngest, Stephen, still needed his boo-boos kissed. In between, there were pleas to borrow the car from Allyson and Brian, seventeen and sixteen, and pleas for privacy from Kristal and Alex, thirteen and ten.

Then one day, Clarin's friend Michelle, who'd adopted a Russian boy, told Clarin about Anna.

"She's a loving girl—and blind," Michelle said, as the couples sat around in the May sun.

Blind? Clarin's heart ached. Anna had been in the orphanage since birth. And though she'd been well cared for, it was still far from being a real home. And if they didn't find a home for her by the time she turned seven in November, "they'll transfer her to a home for invalids. And those places are awful—the neglect, the abuse. . . . " Michelle sighed.

Later that evening, Clarin couldn't stop thinking about Anna. Years before, hearing heartbreaking stories about orphans in other countries, the couple had considered foreign adoption. But as their own children came along, those plans had faded—until now.

"What if we adopted Anna?" she said, taking Paul's hand.

He'd been thinking the same thing. But how could they afford it on Paul's salary as a teacher, and Clarin a stay-at-home mom? She felt her heart sink, but the thought came, *what if one of my kids had to live in that dark, distant world?* And in just a few months' time, that world would turn more frightening—and cruel.

But this wasn't a decision she and Paul could make alone. "It will affect your lives, too," Clarin explained to the kids. "Search your hearts."

It would mean sharing everything with one more. But this little girl had nothing. Before long, the children had an answer: "Bring her home."

And now as they sat in the adoption agency, watching the videotape of a little girl auditioning for someone to want her, Clarin knew just how important this mission was.

Many in the invalid homes die from illness, Clarin learned. And if Anna does survive there, Clarin was told, she'll wish she hadn't.

Clarin wiped her tears away. *God,* she prayed, *we have to rescue her. Help us find a way.*

Deciding to adopt Anna was easy. Bringing her home however, would be anything but. The cost of adopting her could be more than twenty thousand dollars! But Michelle and her husband (the friends who had already adopted a Russian boy) were spreading the word that Clarin and Paul needed help.

So as Paul and the kids did odd jobs to raise money, donations poured into the adoption agency. Friends stopped by, too. "For Anna," they'd say handing her an envelope.

The family was grateful. But by summer's end, they only had a quarter of what they'd need. *What more can we do?* Clarin asked herself. Anna's life depended on them.

Meanwhile, Clarin and Paul rushed to complete the required mountain of paperwork, while Paul also studied Russian and taught it to the kids.

And one night, Clarin, Paul and all the children sat around a tape recorder. "Anna, this is Mama," Clarin said, first in English, then in Russian. "This is Papa," Paul began. *"Syestra* Kristal," Kristal said, beaming. "Sister." One by one, each of them introduced themselves. Then they sang a song they'd made up, "Hello, hello, we're glad you came to join our family. . . ."

They sent the tape to Orphanage No. 40, where Clarin pictured a little girl listening to it again and again, repeating the new words and the names belonging to the new voices.

Back in the United States, more donations poured in. But by October, they were still thousands of dollars short.

"You can have my frequent flier miles," neighbors said. "Let me know if you need a loan," friends urged.

In the face of such generosity, Clarin wept with gratitude. Even the Russian government waived some fees.

Finally, they reached the required amount. "We did it!" they cried. "Anna, we're on our way!"

In nervous excitement, they flew to St. Petersburg, where Clarin and Paul sat in the waiting area at the orphanage, their hearts beating wildly. The door opened.

Tears sprang to Clarin's eyes as a beautiful little girl entered, her arms extended, searching. "Mama! Papa!" she called.

In an instant, Clarin and Paul had taken her into their arms. Anna traced her fingers over their hair and faces. "Hello, hello," she hummed the tune she'd heard on the cassette tape.

"Mama and Papa are finally here, Anna," Clarin whispered. "We're your home now and forever."

At home, Anna's new brothers and sisters introduced themselves. Allyson scooped Anna up in a warm hug and the little girl wrapped her arms and legs around her big sister. "*Sistonka*, my sister," she cried happily. All the other children took turns hugging her. Brian, who had drilled himself with Russian flash cards, managed to say in Russian, "Hello, my name is Brian." Minutes later, Anna was skipping gaily down the hall with them.

Today, Anna is thriving. Russian words are slowly being replaced with English ones. And the two Clarin hears most these days are, "by myself."

Kristal, who shares her room with Anna, has taught her to play with dolls and have little tea parties. If five-year-old Stephen cries, she will dash over to "love him better." Often, she will sing Russian folk songs in a lilting voice and get lots of hugs when she bows at the end.

In fact, the little Russian girl has adjusted to her new family so quickly that for Clarin, there is only one explanation: Although she was born half a world away, Anna belongs with them.

Marilyn Neibergall
Excerpted from Woman's World

George and Gracie's Babies

Adopting babies was a popular thing to do among show business people in the 1930s. I was agreeable; Gracie wanted to have children and I wanted to make Gracie happy. But we just kept putting it off. We were on the road too much, the apartment wasn't big enough, we had a picture coming up, there was always something. Then one afternoon we had lunch with another actor and he brought along his adopted daughter. The kid did all the right things—she smiled at Gracie and laughed at my cigar. As soon as we got home, we called The Cradle, a Catholic foundling home in Evanston, Illinois.

Months passed before we heard from The Cradle. Finally, they called and told us that we could have a baby if we came to Evanston immediately. Gracie and her friend Mary were on a train to Chicago three hours later. I stayed in New York.

They showed Gracie three babies to select from. How do you pick out a kid? How do you know which one is going to be tall and attractive and smart? How do you know which one is going to have a good disposition? How do you know which one is going to laugh at her father's jokes? The answer is, you don't, you can't. It's exactly the same chance you take as having a child naturally.

Gracie picked the smallest baby, a tiny five-week-old with great big blue eyes, and named her Sandra Jean. Sandra Jean Burns.

The Cradle offered to provide a nurse to accompany Gracie and Mary back to New York, but Gracie figured two grown women should be able to take care of one small baby. And the two of them felt very confident—until the baby sneezed. That's when Gracie realized they were outnumbered. Neither one of them knew what to do, so Gracie covered the baby's body with her fur coat. Sometime during the night, the coat slipped down and covered the baby's head. When Gracie woke up and saw that, she thought she'd smothered her daughter. Making a lopsided cake was one thing, but smothering your daughter a few hours after you've had her? She grabbed the coat and watched helplessly to see if the baby was breathing. The baby was fine—it was Gracie who was having trouble breathing. So she sat up in the compartment the rest of the trip just watching her daughter breathe.

I didn't get to pace up and down in a waiting room; I had Grand Central Station. Believe me, I was as nervous as any expectant father has ever been, and I knew exactly when my baby was due. The train pulled in on time. That was one of the rare occasions when a train conductor delivered a baby.

The first night we had Sandy at home Gracie asked me if I wanted to change the baby. "Nah," I said, "let's try this one out first." That was about as close as I ever came to actually eating a cigar. I guess Gracie was a little sensitive. But what did I know about changing a baby's diapers?

The thing about the baby that surprised me most was how much space something so small could take up. Our second bedroom, which had been my den, became her nursery. The kitchen was the operations center—that's where we kept her bottles, her milk, her formula, her jars of baby food, the piles of clean diapers and some of the toys that overflowed from my former den. I don't know, maybe there were some babies who had more toys than Sandy did. Santa Claus's kids, for instance.

As it turned out, Sandy was such a delight that we decided she should have a brother.

Gracie picked out our son Ronnie because he needed her most. Now, that sounds like a line written by a Hollywood press agent, but it's true. The other babies they showed her were all chubby and healthy, and she knew there was a long list of people waiting to adopt chubby, healthy babies. Ronnie's crib was off by itself in a corner; maybe that's what first attracted Gracie's attention to him. She went over and looked at him. "He was so small," she told me when she finally brought him home, "and he followed me with his eyes when I moved, and I knew I had to take him."

He was premature, a nurse told Gracie, and for several weeks doctors didn't know if he was going to survive.

Since I'm telling the truth, I have to admit that Ronnie was an ugly baby. People say all babies look like Winston Churchill; Ronnie made Winston Churchill look handsome. Ronnie looked like a wrinkled little man with a funny-shaped head. "What do you think, Nattie?"

I thought that if I was smart, I'd keep my mouth shut. "Look, you know I don't mind responsibility," I said, "but, Googie, why'd you pick a sick kid?"

"I just fell in love with his eyes. I know he's not well, but we can make him well. It's the same chance we would have taken if we'd had him, isn't it?"

Ronnie had a tough first year. For a long time he couldn't gain any weight, and his skin was so sensitive that we could only bathe him in oil and we had to wrap him in cotton. Gracie and our nurse spent a lot of time in doctors' offices. Gracie fussed over him like I worked on our scripts. But Ronnie was a smart kid, and once he figured out how to grow, he didn't stop until he was almost 6' 2" tall and much better looking than Winston Churchill.

Gracie had been right.

George Burns

After the Tears

"I'm sorry, Mrs. Coe. The test was negative."

Not that I was surprised. I felt it coming. I'd known I wasn't pregnant for the last week and a half.

What did I do to deserve this?

Sobs broke from my husband first. I was numb. We held each other, but there was no comfort. It had been our last *in vitro* fertilization attempt, the last we would ever try. We'd spent the last seven years hoping for a baby, undergoing every procedure known to reproductive gynecology—hoping, hoping.

I'd gone home and put on a record—a song wailing about how God sometimes just doesn't come through. Intermittently, I cried. But mostly I was angry and scared. I was at the end of my rope, faith-wise, hope-wise. *God, sometimes you just don't come through.*

Adoption, I sighed in resignation. There was a meeting for prospective adoptive parents, and Tom wanted to go. He was getting over the infertility issue; he wanted to move forward. Okay, I'd go. I didn't want to go, but I'd listen. I would try to keep an open mind.

Six couples stared across a conference table at each

other. Five minutes into the meeting, the woman across from me was sobbing. Finally, I broke down, too. This agency had judged me hopelessly unable to give birth, only able to become a mother by taking someone else's child. I was officially unfixable. This was the pain I'd just begun to face.

The next Sunday was Mother's Day, and all the kids at church were invited up front for a children's homily. The priest told them what blessings they were to their parents. *But what about us? Why didn't we get these blessings? What did we ever, ever, do to deserve this?*

We went for counseling. We met with a woman who had suffered multiple miscarriages, who could now say, "If those children had lived, I would never have had these other children." We looked into the face of someone who had survived this, someone to whom this all finally made sense.

So we'd adopt. But the agency hadn't placed any babies in the last year. We'd have to advertise and find a baby ourselves. We'd have to get out there on the front lines and leave ourselves open to even more pain, even more disappointment. Worst of all, if someone did agree to give us her baby, she could change her mind, and there would be nothing we could do about it—except grieve again, and ask, why us?

I took a deep breath, and asked a group of women, some I hardly knew, to pray for me. It was something I'd never done before. And I waited.

Then one day while I was hanging around the house, thinking that for once I was actually happy, finally coming out of the funk I'd been in for years, the phone rang. A young woman wanted to give us a baby.

For the next few days, we were in a daze. We were going to become parents. An ultrasound was done. It was a perfect little girl, the doctor said.

Although I knew it was unreasonable, there was a part of me that grieved yet a little more. I had always wanted twins, a boy and a girl the same age. I thought maybe I would get them through all the fertility drugs I had taken. And somehow, I had always thought my first child would be a boy. But I convinced myself that a daughter would be wonderful. Truly a miracle—though not what I had expected or secretly hoped.

Then the most unlikely of unlikelies happened. We got another phone call. Another woman wanted to give us a baby—a boy, born just that morning. We walked into a hospital, and he was placed into my arms. "This is your mommy and your daddy."

The papers were signed within hours. We appeared before a judge, and it was done. We were parents.

But what about the other baby? The girl? We decided to take her, too. Her birth mother was as dazed and joyous as we were. A brother the same age for our little girl! And so, exactly one month later, at another hospital, we were handed another baby—parents again.

As inexperienced parents of two tiny babies, the next few months were harder than we ever imagined. We agonized whether we had done the right thing, whether we had taken on too much. But one day, as I held my beautiful infant son on my knee, he leaned over to smile at his little sister. She had only begun smiling herself in the past few days. But he kept smiling, egging her on, until she burst into a big smile at him. They gazed smiling at each other, held in each of my arms, joyous to be exactly where they were. I felt tears of pure joy fill my eyes. I, too, was exactly where I wanted to be.

Today, a door opens to a nursery school classroom. Two blond heads look up and burst into grins. "Mommy! Mommy!" Two pairs of legs come running toward me. I kneel, my arms open wide.

What did I do to deserve this?

Cynthia Coe

Love by Choice

Solemn brown eyes stared at me through inch-long eyelashes casting spiky shadows on the tiny Native American face. The thickness of his diapers made his legs look short and bowed. At seven months, he walked everywhere. The curiosity of this alert child held my attention. He hesitated at the top of the stairs to my living room.

"This is David," his mother said, pushing him further into the room.

Now that my children were all in school, baby-sitting was not on my agenda. But my heart overruled my head, and I agreed to baby-sit for a few days until David's mother could find someone else.

David's sense of security rested in the pacifier hanging around his neck attached to a somewhat soiled string. Once in awhile he popped it in his mouth.

As I talked with his mother, he examined everything with his eyes. I spoke his name in an effort to get acquainted. He looked straight at me but stayed his distance. He was not to be swayed at this early stage.

His mother left us together for the afternoon. He didn't cry or show signs of anxiety but stood his ground in the middle of the living room.

When my daughter, Linda, returned from school, he looked her over, but he did not venture toward her. As she smiled and picked him up, in went the pacifier. She walked quietly to the overstuffed chair. He lay in her arms sucking furiously on the pacifier. Linda cooed and talked to him, tenderly brushing his hair away from his forehead. "I like him, Mom," she said softly, her eyes never leaving his face. The bonding began. And slowly, one by one, David accepted each of us.

As the days turned into weeks, this precocious child stole our affections and captured our attention without any effort on his part. Our only son enjoyed having another boy in the family, even though my son was twelve years older.

Forgotten sounds of babyhood rang throughout the house. Little did we realize then just how much we would be involved in David's life. I could not distance myself from those soul-searching eyes and the smooth way he leaped into my heart. My baby-sitting went from a few days to several months.

One evening the telephone rang. The voice on the other end was tense. "I won't be needing you to baby-sit anymore." Then I heard a sudden burst of tears, followed by a rush of words that I couldn't understand.

It was David's mother. "What in the world is the matter?" I asked.

"I just can't handle David anymore. I am going to give him up to the state."

"If I thought you meant that, we'd take him in a heartbeat." My impulsive but sincere words seemed to quiet her down. I convinced her to bring David as usual, and we would talk. I passed the episode off in my mind as an emotional bout of fatigue and frustration.

The next morning the doorbell rang at 6:00 A.M. There stood a disheveled mother, carrying David on her hip, still in his pajamas. He was covered with hives, whining and sucking vigorously on his pacifier. Without hesitation she asked, "Did you really mean it when you said you would take David?"

"Well, I don't know. Do you think it's what you want?"

"I just can't take care of him," she said, obviously exhausted. "He is so hard to handle. He cries all night."

"Honey, you're really going to have to think about this. You just don't give up your baby because he keeps you up at night."

"But I am so tired," she moaned.

"Well, let's both think about it for awhile. I thought you were just upset last night. In the meantime, I will talk to my husband."

After that, she started leaving David for longer and longer periods. Her attitude changed almost overnight ... from a concerned mother to an emotional bundle of nerves. One day she gave me a choice. Either I take him or she would turn him over to the state. She had made her decision. I had a week to make mine.

Advice came from all sides. "Don't you think you have enough responsibility?"

"You're probably too old and have too many children."

"Can you really afford another child? You've already got four kids."

Even our pastor and our doctor threw cold water on the idea. And our lawyer didn't encourage such an adventure either. "Let's get the paperwork going and see what happens," he said. "But I don't think any judge is going to go for this."

Within two weeks the court date was set. By now we knew we wanted David—utterly and completely. When the day arrived, I was anxious. So much rested on one man's decision. I hardly heard my lawyer's kind advice as we entered the judge's chambers. "This judge is tough. He might ask a lot of personal questions. Just answer honestly."

The judge greeted us with a warm handshake and began to thumb through the papers before him. Looking over his dark-rimmed glasses, he said, "Do you think you can handle another child?"

"Easily," I chuckled, a little nervously. "He's already been with us for over a year."

He pursed his lips, reading the information in front of him and asked, "Are you concerned about his ethnic background?"

"Judge, to me he is just a baby who needs a family."

The judge rubbed his chin, thinking through my impulsive answers. Then he leaned forward, and after gazing at us intently for a moment, he spoke. "These papers seem to be in order. I think this will be a good move for David."

"You mean we get to keep him, Judge?"

"He's yours." Just like that. Suddenly, the judge grinned from ear to ear and offered his hand in congratulations. My husband sat with his mouth open, and I giggled like a schoolgirl.

Today, over thirty years later, I can still feel the giddy joy of knowing that David was ours. I have never regretted—not even for an instant—the decision to take David into our family. People have told me they thought that David was lucky. Maybe so, but we were lucky, too. For when we left the judge's chambers those many years ago, our lives had expanded—emotionally and officially—to include another child. All at once we had *five* children to love, four by birth and one by choice.

Shirley Pease

6

MOTHERS AND DAUGHTERS

Mothers are really the true spiritual teachers.

Oprah Winfrey

"You're not supposed to start turning into me until
you're much older, Susie."

Mothers and Daughters

"You won't forget to bring the potato masher, will you?"
I said to my mother on the phone after telling her I had to
have a mastectomy. Even at eighty-two, and three thousand miles away on the long-distance line, she knew what
I meant: soupy mashed potatoes.

This was what she had made for every illness or mishap
of my childhood—served in a soup bowl with a nice round
spoon. But I had been lucky as a child and was rarely sick.
Most often the potato medicine soothed disappointment
or nourished a mild cold. This time I was seriously ill.

Arriving on the midnight plane from Virginia, Mom
looked fresh as a daisy when she walked through the front
door of my house in California the day after I came home
from the hospital. I could barely keep my eyes open, but
the last thing I saw before I fell asleep was Mom unzipping
her carefully packed suitcase and taking out her sixty-
year-old potato masher. The one she received as a shower
gift, the one with the worn wooden handle and the years
of memories.

She was mashing potatoes in my kitchen the day I told
her tearfully that I would have to undergo chemotherapy.

She put the masher down and looked me squarely in the eye. "I'll stay with you, however long it takes," she told me. "There is nothing more important I have to do in my life than help you get well." I had always thought I was the stubborn one in my family, but in the five months that followed I saw that I came by my trait honestly.

Mom had decided that I would not predecease her. She simply would not have it. She took me on daily walks even when I couldn't get any farther than our driveway. She crushed the pills I had to take and put them in jam, because even in middle age, with a grown daughter of my own, I couldn't swallow pills any better than when I was a child.

When my hair started to fall out, she bought me cute hats. She gave me warm ginger ale in a crystal wineglass to calm my tummy and sat up with me on sleepless nights. She served me tea in china cups.

When I was down, she was up. When she was down, I must have been asleep. She never let me see it. And, in the end, I got well. I went back to my writing.

I have discovered that Mother's Day doesn't happen some Sunday in May, but on every day you are lucky enough to have a mother around to love you.

Patricia Bunin

Stranded on an Island

When she was little she clung to me and said, "You're my best friend in the whole wide world."

She used to cry when I went away, for a night, for a weekend. "Why can't you take me?" she would ask.

And I would explain, "Because this party is for grown-ups. Because this is a business trip. Because you'd be bored."

"No, I wouldn't, Mommy. I'd never be bored around you."

Such absolute, unconditional love.

"Someday you'll go away and leave me," I would tell her. "You'll spend a night at a friend's, and then maybe a weekend and pretty soon you'll be going off for weeks at a time and before you know it you'll be traveling all over the world and then you'll move to Japan and you won't miss me at all."

"I'd never move to Japan without you," she would say, laughing. The idea of growing up and living in Japan always chased away her tears. It was something said offhandedly to divert sorrow, but it became a tradition. Whenever she would grumble about my leaving, I would tease her about her leaving me to go to Japan.

She's only fourteen now, and she hasn't left yet. Not physically, anyway. But mentally she's prepared to go, though she doesn't know it and I didn't know it either until the other day.

She came home from school with a homework assignment: Choose six people, dead or alive, real or fictional, with whom you would choose to be stuck on a deserted island. Her English class had just finished reading *Lord of the Flies*, a story about a group of stranded children on just such an island.

I never thought for a minute that I wouldn't make the list. It didn't cross my mind. Didn't she say I was her best friend in the whole world? Didn't she know I would love her and take care of her better than anyone ever could?

And yet that night, when she recited the names of the people she would take, there was no mention of me. There was the fictional Mafatu, a boy from *Call It Courage* who had survived life on an abandoned island. "He would know what to do," she said. "I'd take him because he's been through this before." And there was Mary Poppins, "because she's nice and magical and could whisk us to places off the island if we got bored," she said.

And she chose her brother, Robbie, "because I love him, and he'd know how to make a boat," and John McLean, her godfather, "because he knows how to fix everything," and TV character Doogie Howser "because he's a doctor and young and won't die soon," and Anne of Green Gables "because she's smart and imaginative and funny."

"But what about me? I can be smart and imaginative and funny, too," I said.

"Anne of Green Gables is young and can have babies, Mom. She's more useful."

I'm old, and I'm not useful. That's what she was trying to say. I immediately began to sulk.

"You're not serious, Mom, are you? This isn't real, you know. I'm not going to live on an island. I'm not going anywhere."

"Oh, yes you are," I wanted to say. "You just don't know it yet."

I moped around for a while, a little in jest but a little in earnest, too. I understood why she didn't choose me. It wouldn't have been a wise choice. What do I know about survival? I consider it a crisis when the electricity goes out during a storm. Her selections were all sensible.

The thing is, I would have chosen her. I wouldn't have been sensible. I wouldn't have thought about what each person could contribute. I would have thought only about who I would most like to be with.

"If I could have picked only one person, Mom, I would have picked you," she reassured me the next day. But that's only because when she asked me to make her a grilled cheese sandwich, I suggested that Anne of Green Gables make it, and when she said she needed a ride to the mall, I hinted that Mary Poppins should take her.

"You know, Mom, you're being very immature," she told me.

I know I am. Very immature. But that's because our roles have suddenly reversed. The little girl who clung to me and called me her best friend clings no more. Instead I am the one watching her move on and asking, "Why can't you take me?"

Beverly Beckham

Mum and the Volkswagen

I didn't know how to tell her I was buying an old Volkswagen convertible—Mum, who had survived the Great Depression, and whose number-one edict was, "Save every penny you can, you never know when you might need it." I was sure owning a convertible in the North, let alone a second car, would seem most excessive by her standards.

When my mother's health had failed dramatically, I'd moved in to tend to her during her final years. I became the parochial Catholic child again. I didn't want to do anything to hurt my mother or anything that might provoke her disapproval. Spending money "frivolously" on a VW convertible that I didn't need but only wanted—she would certainly purse her lips, at least mentally.

But this time, I just didn't care. A friend had found a bargain and I wanted this car. I hadn't figured out how I'd tell her, but somehow I would live with the consequences. I was forty-one years old. I had the right to spend my money the way I chose. Why did I still need the approval of the woman I called "Mum"? Why at my age could I still not challenge her or cause her disappointment? I had no answers, but I was buying the car and that was that. And I did.

I drove home in my little VW with the top down and parked it squarely in the drive. I stepped into the house gingerly and said, "Come on, Mum, I did something extravagant, and you're going to love it!" Inside I was churning. I helped her out of her chair, put my arm around her frail little body, supporting her for balance as we walked to the door.

"Oh my Lord . . . ," she paused.

Here it comes, I thought, steeling myself.

"What a cute little jalopy! Can we go for a ride?" She spoke breathlessly, her failing heart unable to cope with the burden of her obvious excitement.

I was smooth. I behaved as if all along I just knew she'd be thrilled by it. Inside I couldn't believe my ears. *Can we go for a ride?* Whose wee voice was that? Not my mother's— it couldn't have been. But outside I calmly said, "Let's bundle you up. It'll be chilly with the air blowing on you," and we retreated inside.

She was hooked after the first mile. "Oh, doesn't this make you feel young?"

In my mind's eye, I saw her: a truly beautiful young woman, not a fragile, ailing seventy-six-year-old. It was easy for me to respond to her, "Young we are, Mum. Young we are."

That first week I purchased a heated lap blanket that plugged into the lighter. I would bundle Mum up and toss the blanket over her, and we'd be off. It became quite a ritual. As we backed from the driveway, her words were always the same, not because her mind was fading but out of sheer fun.

"What a great contraption this is," she'd say with a smile in her voice.

My reply was always the same, "You mean the blanket?"

"No silly, this baby car. It makes me feel so alive."

Oftentimes when the weather was dreary or it appeared too chilly, I would head us toward the every-season car and she'd say, "Can't we take the baby car?"

My response was always, "Sure, why not?"

Climbing into that little rig enriched the last two years of our lives together. We would exchange our ritual words, and then we would take off, not always going far and not always talking much, but always together in the kindred knowledge of shared pleasure. We would crank up the tunes and laugh together like a couple of teenagers. When autumn approached, she was as sad as I was when the New England weather would change and it was time to store the VW.

Now my first and last ride of the convertible season is always taken alone. I drop the ragtop and head out hearing her words in the air beside me: "What a great contraption this is. . . ."

The summer months begin and end with only her spirit along for the ride, sharing my joy and freedom of the open air. I head for the same destination spring and fall, year after year. A pink rose rides in the passenger seat where my Mum once did. When I arrive and open the door, I feel an odd sense of loneliness combined with an overwhelming love that time has not diminished. We chat for a while and when I leave, the pink rose rests gently at her headstone.

Driving off, my words are whispered into the wind, and they are always the same, "I miss you, Mum."

Dorothy Raymond Gilchrest

The Heart Remembers

There never was a child so lovely but his mother was glad to get him asleep.

Ralph Waldo Emerson

"The mother she remembers is the mother she will become."

These words filled my head on the morning I became a mother for the first time. And as they placed Kaley in my arms, a warm, wriggling bundle with wide eyes, I'd vowed to myself that I was going to be the very best mother, the kind of mother that I did remember: loving, patient, ever-calm and placid. My whole life had pulsed with love, and as I stroked my baby's tiny head, felt her turn her face to nuzzle my finger, I vowed to her, "You will know only love, little one. Only that."

I remembered the quote again two weeks later, at 3:00 A.M. as I paced in circles with my screaming, colicky newborn in my arms. At that moment, however, the words were hardly a comfort. After all, what baby would want to remember me as I was then—sleep-deprived, anxious, patience worn as sharp and thin as a razor blade.

And despite my earlier vow, I sure wasn't feeling love. I wasn't feeling much of anything. I was numb, weak with fatigue, trying to do everything by myself even though my husband and mother were asleep just down the hall. I shushed Kaley and cradled her closer, but she just kicked and flailed and wailed even louder. Suddenly I couldn't stop the tears. I sank to the floor in the darkened living room, lay her in my lap and sobbed into my hands.

I don't know how long I stayed that way, but even though it seemed like hours, it couldn't have been more than a few minutes. Through a haze of tears, I saw the light go in the hallway, silhouetting the figure of my mother as she shrugged into her housecoat. Soon I felt her hand on my shoulder.

"Give me that baby," she said.

I didn't argue. Defeated, I just handed the screaming bundle over and crawled to the sofa, where I curled into a tight ball.

My mother murmured into Kaley's ear, and with an ease borne of decades of practice, shifted her to her shoulder. Eventually the crying turned to sniffles, the sniffles to hiccups, and in half an hour, I heard only muffled baby snores.

I felt relief but no real peace. What kind of mother couldn't calm her own child? What kind of mother didn't even want to try? I watched Mama ease into the rocking chair, watched her start the slow rhythm that I knew had lulled me to sleep on countless nights, and all I felt was a sense of desperate, exhausted failure.

"I'm a terrible mother," I muttered.

"No, you're not."

"You don't understand." Fresh tears thickened at the corner of my eyes. "Right now, I don't even like her. My own baby."

My mom laughed softly. "Well, she hasn't been very

likable today, now has she? But you stayed with her through it all. You've bounced her, rocked her, walked her. And when none of that worked, you just held her and kept her close."

I sat up and wrapped my arms tightly around my knees. "But all I feel inside is frustration and anger and impatience. What kind of mother is that?"

My mom didn't reply immediately. She just looked down at the sleeping baby in her arms. But her face grew thoughtful, and when she spoke, her voice had a faraway, wistful quality. "I remember all those," she said softly. "Especially the last one. After you were born, I used to pray for patience. Cried and begged for it." She looked at me, a half-smile on her face. "Still haven't gotten it yet."

I couldn't believe what I was hearing. "But, Mama, that's the thing I remember most about you. No matter what, you never lost your cool. You somehow managed to keep everything going all at once."

She had. No matter how many brownies needed baking at the last minute, no matter how many science project posters needed coloring, my mother always came through. Always calm. Always serene. As a nurse, she worked irregular hours, but at every play and every recital I was in, even if she didn't make the opening curtain, I could always count on seeing a familiar figure in white slipping into the darkened auditorium.

This was the mother I remembered, the mother who made every moment matter. The mother who never behaved the way I felt right then.

"I could always count on you," I said. "Always."

But to my surprise, she rolled her eyes. "That may be the way you remember it, but all I remember is being pulled in seven directions at once. You and your brother, your father, the people at work. They all needed me, but I never had enough time to be there for everybody."

"But you *were* always there!"

She shook her head. "Not like I wanted to be, not as often or for as long. And so I prayed for patience, so that I could make the best of the time we did have. But you know what they say. God doesn't send you patience. He just sends you moments that make you practice being patient, over and over again."

She looked down at Kaley. "Moments like this one."

I watched the two of them, and then suddenly I understood: Memories don't rest in our brains, which are apt to record the details wrong anyway, but in our hearts. My mom and I didn't recall my childhood in exactly the same way, but we did share the one thing that did matter.

We both remembered the love.

I moved from the sofa and sat at the foot of the rocking chair. We stayed that way for a while—my mother, my daughter and I. And even though the crying started again at sunrise, for that golden, still moment, as I sat at my mother's feet and lay my hand on the soft hair of my daughter, I breathed a silent "thank you."

If Kaley somehow remembers that night, I hope she will recall only the instinctive love that kept me by her side through it all.

Tina Whittle

Step on a Crack,
Bring Your Mother Back

"Step on a crack, break your mother's back," my best friend Franny laughed. She stomped her detested new white bucks on every scar on the cement, giggling. From that call to attention, our walk to school became dangerous. I marveled at her risky rebelliousness as I tiptoed my Mary Janes around the sprung concrete of those New York City sidewalks. I come from a superstitious tribe. A broken Mom was a big threat, something I could never—would never—wish on my mother.

These days my mother lives on the Pacific side of the continent in a small group home. Several of the other residents, like my mother, have Alzheimer's disease.

It was no surprise to me when my mother was diagnosed with Alzheimer's. Over a period of years her optimistic eyes began to dim and the mental agility of this eternal student began to disappear. The process was slow and subtle; at first she made jokes about her forgetfulness, but gradually the benign humor vanished, to be replaced by a more severe helplessness. At the memory disorder clinic of a nearby teaching hospital, they described the prognosis; they recommended to me the books I could read that would help. They were kind and caring. The rest of my mother's life, though, seemed a frightening pathway, cracked and distorted by the unpredictable course of a debilitating disease.

"Does she still know you?" This was the first question people asked when I mentioned my mother's disability. Not understanding the slow course of the disease, they always pictured the worst and were surprised and reassured when I told them that my mother did indeed still recognize me. In fact, I told them, her humor surfaced frequently, like when she coyly introduced me as *her* mother. Her vocabulary was often startlingly original and, with great effort, she still had pockets of usable memory.

A better question emerged: Did I still know her? Who was that woman who looked like my mother but whose eyes could not belie her bewilderment? She was a woman of independence who had lived alone for more than twenty years after my father's death. Unprepared for her sudden widowhood, she learned over the years to manage well on her own, physically, financially and socially. She was determined to survive the poverty of her first-generation immigrant upbringing and, finally, in her later years, she came to enjoy a freedom she wasn't raised to expect.

Alzheimer's, a thief in slow motion, stole that freedom and left a woman who could no longer remember her personal history or how many years ago her husband had died. She couldn't recall where her money was or how much it amounted to. Her supposedly golden years were spent living in a house she never called home and enduring a sense of disorientation that she did not understand.

One morning, her arm threaded in mine, we strolled out of her group house for our walk around town. The sidewalk in front of the house was slowly giving way to a mighty cedar tree that dwarfed the Victorian structure.

Suddenly, my boot wedged in a deep crevice in the walkway, and I was pitched forward. My mother reacted instantly, making her arm rigid and yanking me upright. I regained my composure and smiled at her gratefully.

"Are you okay?" she asked with concern. I looked at her, and the thrill of recognition gave me goosebumps. My old Mom, the Mom that I had always known, was smiling at me, her eyes clear, bright with the light of purpose, not a trace of confusion evident.

For a brief moment, my mind flashed back to another time, many, many years ago, when I had seen my mother smile at me in just that way. It was a rainy winter's day in Queens, New York. The weather had been stormy all week and our '54 Plymouth didn't like the rain any more than we did. It stalled just after we picked up my father's shirts at the cleaners. As we sat together in the car, patiently awaiting the tow truck, my mother took my rainboots off and tickled my feet under her coat. We laughed and talked as a car pulled up and parked behind us on the downward incline of a slight hill. A woman in a red kerchief and dark coat sprinted to a shop across the street. Something in the rearview mirror caught my mother's attention. In a flash, she thrust open the car door and swooped me out into the street as the car behind us rolled from its parking spot and slammed our Plymouth into the car parked in front. But we were safe. I huddled against her in the rain, peering up with surprise. She hugged me closer and smiled with relief.

"Are you okay?"

She needn't have asked. Of course I was. I was in my mother's arms.

Those same arms now wrapped around me after my stumble on the sidewalk, and that same smile reassured me.

"I love you so much," she said as she kissed me. "I don't want anything to happen to you." I had heard her say this many times in my life but not recently. I felt overjoyed to have her back.

We continued on down the street where we had walked several times a week since I moved her closer to me. "I haven't been on this street in years," she announced. As she turned to me for confirmation, something she does often given the erratic universe of her mind, I saw that my real mother had slipped away again.

Nothing in my life could have prepared me for the complicated task of caring for a parent with Alzheimer's. Our tender relationship has become an act of balancing familiarity with strangeness. It is one thing to grieve for a parent gone; it is quite another to have to learn to love one you still have but no longer know.

Even though I see my mother often, I miss her very much. I keep looking forward to the next time I might stumble across her endearing old self, feel her love wrap around me and, if only for a moment, keep me shielded from the pain of losing her.

Sandra Rockman

My Mother's Face in the Mirror

"You look just like your mommy."

I couldn't have been more than three or four years old the first time I heard someone say it. I'll never forget the feeling of pride as it welled up inside my tiny chest at the mere notion that someone thought I resembled my mommy.

After that, for a while, I stood a little taller.

Gentle. Soft. Kind. Loving. Beautiful. These are my earliest recollections of my mother. Yet as I grew older, I grew less elated about looking like her.

I must have heard it a million times: "You look just like your mom." By the time I was eight, I equated my mom with a stifling barrier standing between the "me" I was forced to be and the "me" I wanted to be. I began to hate those six words.

By the time I was ready to cross the threshold into puberty, when someone mentioned the likeness, I wanted to scream, "Nooooo! I don't look like her! I look like ME!"

When I moved away from home, our relationship could only be called turbulent. Over the next thirty years, our lone commonality was the certainty of our differences; at the crux of those differences were evidence of the generation gap, as well as some of the world's most "significant" troubles.

For example, in the 1960s, while I was gaga over Tom Jones, Mom clung to her conviction that Bing Crosby was the greatest singer the world had ever known. In the seventies, when women's roles were evolving from traditional housewives into independent entities responsible for their own livelihood and happiness, Mom and I were at odds over what she considered my cavalier interest in finding a man to "take care of me." In the eighties, when I financed three trips to Europe, she admonished me for squandering "a small fortune" on travel expenses instead of investing it in a retirement plan. And finally in the early 1990s, we bickered constantly over the proper way to raise my new son.

"That baby needs to be on a schedule!" she'd insist.

"He's hungry now," I'd respond defensively.

Throughout those years, if she said, "Black," I'd say, "White."

If I said, "Black," she'd say, "White."

And so it went.

Our relationship revolved around superficial issues. Too bad we dealt with them like children. Bickering, nitpicking and competing.

Never in all those years did the thought occur to me— and I'm sure it didn't occur to Mom, either—that a time was approaching when we would be forced to cast aside our differences and respond to one another with mutual respect and to demonstrate the love undeniably ingrained deep in our hearts.

That time came when she was diagnosed with cancer, a deadly variety at an advanced stage. Then everything changed. There would be no more bickering. No more nitpicking. No more competition. There wasn't time. And I realized there had never been time.

Posted at her hospital bedside during her last five months, I watched her grow weaker and sicker as layer upon layer of the protective coating that shielded her most private vulnerabilities was stripped away. I came to understand what an incredibly messy ordeal dying is— chemotherapy, dialysis, being poked and prodded, bleeding, swelling, deteriorating and even suffering from dementia caused by improperly prescribed medications. Yet through it all, my mother maintained her pride and her dignity—two very important qualities I had arrogantly overlooked in all those years of squabbling.

As the clock measuring her life approached the twelve o'clock hour, we made our peace and I rediscovered the beauty, gentleness and kindness of the woman I was so proud to resemble so long ago.

"Mom, I'm here," I had said to her upon my arrival around noon of the day before she died. I am certain, even though a veil of pain-numbing medications shrouded her senses, she knew I was there. She nodded ever so slightly.

But then she stopped responding.

I stayed at her bedside all that night. Except for her arduous breathing, the monotonous gurgling of her oxygen filter and the sporadic beeping of the machines to which she was attached, the hospital room was still. The half-lit fluorescent wall fixture above the bed emitted a surreal illumination that was relaxing in spite of the critical urgency of the moment. I was propped up in a chair next to the bed, alternating between nodding off and waking up every few minutes. When I checked the clock, it registered five o'clock. Mom's breathing was labored and shallow, but no different than it had been for hours. I meant to stay alert, but I couldn't help drifting off again.

At forty minutes past five, shortly before sunrise on Valentine's Day, I awoke. The machines were still beeping, the oxygen was gurgling, but from Mom came only silence. And that's how she slipped away. Quietly, while I slept.

I like to think that as she shed the tired, worn-out shell lying in the bed, she felt whole again. And free of pain. And that before she crossed over to the other side, she took a last look at me and saw the traces of herself that she was leaving behind.

I like to think she knew that my feelings for her had come full circle.

Four years have passed, and I still miss her so. She visits me sometimes in my dreams and assures me she is still nearby. It's immensely comforting. But I have found that when I want to see her, I don't have to wait for sleep. I can simply turn to the closest mirror. The reflection looking back at me may be mine . . . but the face is my mother's.

I see that, and I stand a little taller.

Janis Thornton

"You'll have to be strong, Mrs. Whatney.
I'm afraid it's puberty."

Leaving Home

It's always been my feeling that God lends you your children until they're about eighteen years old. If you haven't made your points with them by then, it's too late.

Betty Ford

"I'm not going to cry," I told my husband, Chuck, as we left the parent-orientation session held several months before our daughter would attend college in the fall.

Maybe those *other* mothers were going to cry after dropping off *their* kids at the dorm, but not me. I looked around the auditorium at the other mothers, wondering which ones were going to be crybabies. I thought, *I won't clutch a box of tissues when the time comes to say good-bye to Sarah. I'm from sturdier stock than that. Why snivel and sob just because my little girl is growing up?*

We'd spent the afternoon listening to parents of upperclassmen talk about how our lives were going to change when our children left home for college. One seasoned mother warned that we would cry all the way home.

I elbowed Chuck. "That's ridiculous," I said. "Why are

they making such a big deal out of this?" Being a mother has always been important to me, but—for crying out loud—it isn't the only thing! I have a job, I have friends, I have a life!

Sarah and I spent the summer snipping at each other. I hated the way she talked about how she couldn't wait to leave—as if her life at home with us had been some kind of hostage standoff. She hated the way I nagged her about cleaning up her room and putting her dishes in the sink, the way I grumbled when I needed to use the phone and she was tying up the line, the way I questioned her whereabouts when she went out with her friends. After all, she was eighteen. She didn't need to check in with her mom every five minutes.

In August, I ran into my friend, Pat, at the library. Pat remembered the weeks before her daughter left home for college the previous year.

"We fought all summer long," she said. "I think it was our way of getting used to the idea of living apart. When you're arguing all the time and angry, then you don't feel so bad about her leaving."

"And," I responded thoughtfully, "she doesn't feel so bad about leaving when she's mad at Mom."

On moving day, we helped her unpack and store her belongings in the dorm room. I tucked the extra-long twin sheets onto Sarah's mattress while Chuck assembled a storage shelf for her closet. After lunch, we said good-bye, hugged at the curb, and then Chuck and I drove away.

The woman at the parent-orientation session was wrong, I thought. *This isn't so bad.*

Two days later I walked by her bedroom. The door was open, her bed was made and all the clutter of her childhood, of her teenage years, was missing. Suddenly, it dawned on me: She's gone.

Later, as I was vacuuming in the living room, I thought I

heard someone say, "Mom," and I turned off the vacuum cleaner to listen for footsteps coming through the door, to answer a child's call. Then I realized I was alone in the house. Sarah was gone, and nothing would ever be the same.

I longed to hear her voice. I wanted to know what she was doing. I wanted her to sit on the edge of my bed at night like she used to and tell me about her day, her classes, her teachers, her friends, the boys she liked, the boys who liked her. . . .

"What's wrong?" Chuck asked when he came home. I was chopping vegetables for stir-fry. He peered into my face. "Are you crying?"

"It's just the onions," I sniffed as a tear snaked down my cheek.

After dinner I said, "Let's call her. Maybe she's expecting us to call."

"It's only been two days," Chuck said. "Let's give her at least a week to settle in."

He was right, of course. I didn't want to turn into some kind of Stalker Mom. I remembered what it was like to be eighteen and away from home for the first time. She was meeting new friends, learning new ideas, forming new bonds. I had to give her the space—the distance—she needed.

Then the phone rang.

"Hi, Mom," Sarah said. "Could you send me some pictures to put on my bulletin board? And a few stuffed animals?"

She wanted her teddy bear. She wanted a photo of her father and me—and one of her younger brother. She loved being at school, but she missed us, too. And then she started telling me about her day, her classes, her teachers, her friends, the boys she liked, the boys who liked her. . . .

Beth Copeland Vargo

BABY BLUES® By Jerry Scott & Rick Kirkman

The Mailbox

"You're a wonderful mother," I wrote on the Mother's Day card with the picture of sunflowers, garden gloves and watering can. "You were always home for me after school, with warm cookies and milk. You led our 4-H club and worked in PTA. Best of all, now you're my friend, sharing with me a love of beauty, puzzlement at the mysteries of men and respect for children."

I walked out the gravel driveway to the mailbox, opened the metal door and slid in the card. As I shut the door and pulled up the red flag, I remembered another mailbox from long ago. . . .

As a child I spent hours in a small playhouse in the back yard. I decked it out with curtains strung on twine, a window box planted with marigolds, and a mailbox made from a coffee can.

The can was nailed to the outside wall of the playhouse, next to the window. It was painted with green house paint and fitted with a small board inside to create a flat horizontal surface.

One languid summer day I ran into the house and found my mother mopping the kitchen floor.

"Mama," I asked, "could you bring me some mail?"

She straightened up and held the mop in one hand, massaging the small of her back with the other. She smiled, and her eyes softened as she looked at me, her suntanned, pigtailed sprite.

"Well, yes, I think I can, after I finish this floor," she said. "You go back to the playhouse and wait awhile. I'll be there."

So I ran outside, letting the screen door slam behind me. I skipped down the narrow brick path to the clothesline and under it to the playhouse beside the dwarf apple tree. I busied myself with little-girl housekeeping: washing my doll dishes, tidying the bed, sweeping the floor with the toy cornstraw broom.

Then I heard steps on the brick path.

"Mail time," Mama called in a high voice. Then I heard the thunk of envelopes firmly striking the inside of the coffee can.

I waited to give her time to walk back to the house, then rushed out of the playhouse and reached into the can to grab my treasure. Shuffling through it, I found three envelopes, a catalog and a small package. What a haul!

I sat on the grass that sloped down to the garden to open it.

Naturally, I went for the package first. Tearing away the brown grocery sack paper, I lifted the lid from a tiny box. Wow! Two sticks of Juicy Fruit gum; a square of waxed paper wrapped around a handful of chocolate chips, raisins and miniature marshmallows; and a new Pink Pearl eraser. I munched on the snack mixture while I explored the rest of my mail.

Thumbing through the seed catalog, I enjoyed the brightly colored flower pictures. Then I spread the envelopes out in my hand. Each was addressed to "Patty, Playhouse, Back Yard, Oregon" and posted with an S & H

Green Stamp. I slipped my finger under the flap of one and ripped it open. It held a flyer from a car insurance company. In the next I found an advertisement for magazine subscriptions with a hundred tiny stamps to stick onto the order form. From the last envelope I pulled a page of notepaper.

"How are you doing?" I read in my mother's perfect printing. "It's been beautiful weather here, though a little hot for me. I've been canning beans. We have a lovely, large garden, as usual. Do come visit us. You know you are always welcome. Love, Mama."

She signed it in "writing" with swirls at the beginning of the "M" and at the end of the "a."

That was probably forty years ago.

I thought Mama and I had become close friends only recently. But remembering the mailbox, I realized I was wrong. The mother who took the time from her mopping and canning to gather up some junk mail and trinkets to put into a package, write a personal note and deliver it all in true play-acting style was my special companion even back then. Mama was always my friend.

Patty Duncan

I'm Right Here with You, Honey

When I was a girl, if I'd had a difficult school day, my mother would call me into her bedroom shortly after I returned home. She'd be sitting on her bed, patting it and smiling at me until I sat down. She'd offer me a Hershey's Almond Joy bar from her secret cache (in her bottom-left lingerie drawer) and tell me that when I wanted to talk, she'd be there to listen. "I'm right here with you, Honey," she'd say.

And she was. Through grade school, high school, college, and into my twenties and thirties. Even when she was dying from ovarian cancer. I remember asking her in a moment of fear, "If there's a hereafter, will you find a way to stay in touch with me?"

She laughed and said, "What if you go first? I'll agree if you agree."

"Okay," I said, humoring her while still looking for reassurance. "Whoever goes first will contact the one left behind, but without scaring them, like turning on the lights without warning."

"Fine," she said. "But if you decide to turn on the lights for me, remember to turn them off before you float out of the room. You know how your father hates it when anyone leaves the lights on."

Three days after she died, I reflected on that conversation while I sat at my computer, writing in my journal. I smiled as I remembered her wacky sense of humor and then cried knowing I'd never hear her laugh again. My thoughts drifted. The next words I typed were a question, "Where are you, Mom?" As I sat there, the strangest thing happened: I heard my mother's voice inside my head, and felt her presence as if she were standing right next to me. I was scared, but equally curious, so I typed what she said as fast I could: "I'm right here with you, Honey. We have a book to write together. Whenever you're ready to write, I'm prepared to help."

When her voice faded back to my own thoughts, I sat there dumbfounded. I wasn't sure what to think; overwhelmed, I decided that I just missed her a lot and this was my mind's way of comforting me.

A year after Mom died, I moved from Milwaukee to San Diego. With the moving and rebuilding of my speaking business on the West Coast, I didn't write in my journal as often and forgot about the book idea until I woke up from a dream in the middle of a summer night two years later. In the dream, Mom and I were sitting at her kitchen table. She said to me, "It's time to start writing the book. It will be a book of questions that daughters will ask their mothers to help them know their mothers better and to help them make healthier choices so they don't end up like me. I will help you write it." Startled and equally excited by the clarity of her message, I wrote down the dream. As I fell back asleep, I shook my head, thinking how preposterous it all sounded. I'd heard countless stories of how near-impossible it is for an unknown first-time author to find a publisher. Now add to that a *real* ghostwriter. No one would take me seriously—except my mother!

My first phone call of the morning was from my friend Laurie, whom I hadn't talked with for quite a while—who also just happened to be a literary agent. *What a wild coincidence!* I thought. When she asked, "What's new?" I told her about the dream.

Laurie said, "I think it's a great idea. I've been trying to record my mother's history with her all summer. I could use that book. If you write the proposal, I'd love to sell it."

I hung up the phone and burst into tears. I was thrilled that Laurie believed in me enough to suggest I write a book, but I wasn't sure it was a book I could write. My mother wasn't alive, and I wasn't even a mother. Who would take me seriously? "Mom!" I cried out in frustration.

"Write the book," I heard back in my mind.

My mother's idea continued to nudge me; I continued to question it while encountering a far bigger challenge than writing a book. After my annual fall checkup, my gynecologist told me I had cervical cancer and would need a hysterectomy. I was forty-three years old. I thought about dying. I thought about my mother's ovarian cancer. I thought about my mother's hysterectomy when she was only thirty-eight.

Why didn't I think to ask her about that? Why didn't we ever talk about it? If only I'd known more . . .

What irony, I thought, *I need this book I'm supposed to write!*

As I recovered from surgery with no sign of cancer, I felt a new appreciation for my mother and her health challenges that previously I had dismissed—her headaches, her mood swings, her fears about being ill. Now I had them all. I began incorporating my experience and insights into my speaking engagements. Women seemed to identify even more strongly with what I was saying about making healthier choices. I continued to share more memories of love and healing between my mother and me. One story in particular, "Squeeze My Hand and I'll Tell You That I Love You," seemed to touch women in a special way. I heard my mother's voice gently encouraging me, "Write the story down."

I wrote the story and sent it to *Chicken Soup for the Mother's Soul.* After submitting it, tired of being all talk and little action, I made an agreement with my mother's spirit and said, "If this story is accepted in *Chicken Soup,* I'll write the book you've been telling me to write. But if it isn't accepted, I'm letting this idea go and moving on with my life." I thought this was a good compromise. I'd been told that *Chicken Soup for the Soul* books receive thousands of submissions, so I knew the odds were not in my favor; it would take a miracle for my story to be published.

To my great surprise, nine months later, that miracle arrived. On April 11, 1997, while sitting at my office desk, I received a phone call from the *Chicken Soup for the Soul* office—my story had been accepted! Now, this alone was enough to send chills up and down my spine, but what was even more amazing was when I looked at my calendar. That day, April 11, was the sixth anniversary of my mother's death! I glanced at the framed photo sitting next to my computer of Mom smiling. I realized then that writing "our" book was not an option—it was a calling.

It's been three years since "Squeeze My Hand and I'll Tell You That I Love You" was published in *Chicken Soup for the Mother's Soul.* Many more challenges, gifts, divine guidance and miracles have arrived, including the publication by a major publisher of our book, *My Mother, My Friend: The Ten Most Important Things to Talk About with Your Mother.*

I have come to believe that on a spiritual level *My Mother, My Friend* completes a contract I made with my mother to help me and all women respect, appreciate and trust ourselves and our mothers, and to remember that their guidance is always with us—in life or in death. What a blessing.

Mary Marcdante

7

ON WISDOM

The walks and talks we have with our two-year-olds in red boots have a great deal to do with the values they will cherish as adults.

Edith F. Hunter

DENNIS THE MENACE

"How do you expect me to hear you
when I wasn't even listening?"

Close Your Mouth, Open Your Arms

*Children require guidance and sympathy far
more than instruction.*

Anne Sullivan

My friend called with disturbing news: Her unmarried
daughter was pregnant.

My friend recounted the terrible scene when her
daughter finally told her and her husband. There had been
accusations and recriminations, variations on the theme of
"How could you do this to us?" My heart ached for them
all: the parents who felt betrayed and the daughter who
had gotten in over her head. Could I be of any help to
bridge the gap?

I was so upset about the situation that I did what I often
do when I can't think straight: I called my mother. She
reminded me of something I heard her say often through
the years. I immediately wrote a note to my friend, sharing Mom's advice: When a kid's in trouble, close your
mouth and open your arms.

I tried to follow that advice while my own were growing up. With five children in six years, I didn't always

succeed, of course. I have a big mouth and little patience.

I remember when Kim, my oldest, was four and knocked over a lamp in her bedroom. Once I saw that she wasn't cut, I launched into a tirade about how this lamp was an antique, that it had been in our family for three generations, that she should be more careful, and how did this happen—then I saw the fear on her face. Her eyes were wide, her lips trembling. She was backing away from me. I remembered Mom's words. I stopped in mid-sentence and held out my arms.

Kim flew into them, saying "Sorry . . . Sorry," between sobs. We sat on her bed, hugging and rocking, for a long time. I felt awful for scaring her and for letting her think even for a nanosecond that that lamp was more valuable to me than she was.

"I'm sorry, too, Kim," I said when she calmed enough to hear me. "People are more important than lamps. I'm glad you weren't cut."

Fortunately, she forgave me. There are no lifelong scars from the lamp incident. But it taught me that it's better to hold my tongue than try to retract words spoken in anger, fear, disappointment or frustration.

When my children were teens—all five at the same time—they gave me many more opportunities to practice Mom's wisdom: trouble with friends, being "in," not having a date for the prom, traffic tickets, science experiments that bombed, and getting bombed. I'll freely confess that my mother's advice wasn't the first thing that came to mind when a teacher or principal called. After fetching the offender from school, the conversation in the car was sometimes loud and one-sided.

Yet on the occasions when I remembered Mom's technique, I didn't have to retract biting sarcasm or apologize for false assumptions or rescind unrealistic punishments. It's amazing how much more of the story, and the motivation, you get when you're hugging a child, even a child in an adult body. When I held my tongue, I also heard about their fears, anger, guilt and repentance. They didn't get defensive because I wasn't accusing. They could admit they were wrong, knowing they were loved anyway. We could work on "what do you think we should do now" instead of getting stuck in "how did we get here."

My children are grown now, most with families of their own. One came to me a few months back. "Mom, I did a stupid thing. . . ."

After a hug, we sat at my kitchen table. I listened and nodded for nearly an hour, while this wonderful child sifted though the dilemma. When we stood up, I got a bear hug that nearly collapsed my lungs.

"Thanks, Mom. I knew you'd help me solve this."

It's amazing how smart I sound when I close my mouth and open my arms.

Diane C. Perrone

The Potato Puppy

My four-year-old son, Shane, had been asking for a puppy for over a month, but his daddy kept saying, "No dogs! A dog will dig up the garden and chase the ducks and kill our rabbits. No dog, and that's final!"

Each night Shane prayed for a puppy, and each morning he was disappointed when there was no puppy waiting outside.

I was peeling potatoes for dinner, and he was sitting on the floor at my feet asking for the thousandth time, "Why won't Daddy let me have a puppy?"

"Because they are a lot of trouble. Don't cry. Maybe Daddy will change his mind someday," I encouraged him.

"No, he won't, and I'll never have a puppy in a million years," Shane wailed.

I looked into his dirty, tear-streaked face. How could we deny him his one wish? So I said the words that were first spoken by Eve, "I know a way to make Daddy change his mind."

"Really?" Shane wiped away his tears and sniffed.

I handed him a potato.

"Take this and carry it with you until it turns into a

puppy," I whispered. "Never let it out of your sight for one minute. Keep it with you all the time, and on the third day, tie a string around it and drag it around the yard and see what happens!"

Shane grabbed the potato with both hands. "Mama, how do you make a potato into a puppy?" He turned it over and over in his little hands.

"Shh! It's a secret!" I whispered and sent him on his way.

"Lord, you know what a woman must do to keep peace in her home!" I prayed.

Shane faithfully carried his potato around for two days; he slept with it, bathed with it and talked to it.

On the third day I said to my husband, "We really should get a pet for Shane."

"What makes you think he needs a pet?" My husband leaned against the doorway.

"Well, he's been carrying a potato around with him for days. He calls it Wally and says it is his pet. He sleeps with it on his pillow, and right now he has a string tied to it and he's dragging it around the yard," I said.

"A potato?" my husband asked and looked out the window and watched Shane taking his potato for a walk.

"It will break his heart when the potato gets mushy and rots," I said and started getting out food for lunch. "Besides, every time I try to peel potatoes for dinner, Shane cries because he says I'm killing Wally's family."

"A *potato?*" my husband asked. "My son has a pet *potato?*"

"Well," I said shrugging, "you said he couldn't have a puppy. He was so disappointed, in his mind, he decided he had to have a pet. . . . "

"That's crazy!" my husband said.

"Maybe you're right, but explain to me why he is dragging that potato around the yard on a string," I said.

My husband watched our son for a few more minutes.

"I'll bring home a puppy tonight. I'll stop by the animal

shelter after work. I guess a puppy can't be that much trouble," he sighed. "It's better than a potato."

That night Shane's daddy brought home a wiggling puppy and a pregnant white cat that he took pity on while he was at the shelter.

Everyone was happy. My husband thought he'd saved his son from a nervous breakdown. Shane had a puppy, a cat and five kittens and believed his mother had magic powers that could change a potato into a puppy. And I was happy because I got my potato back and cooked it for dinner.

Everything was perfect until one evening when I was cooking dinner, Shane tugged on my dress and asked, "Mama, do you think I could have a pony for my birthday?"

I looked into his sweet little face and said, "Well, first we have to take a watermelon. . . ."

Linda Stafford

A Forgiving Heart

This morning, I was in a hurry to get home after running some errands. As I made the right turn into my neighborhood, which is slightly obscured by shrubs, a small boy in a bright yellow T-shirt flashed across the street in front of my car. He stood on the pedals of his red bike, legs pumping, oblivious to me—or any other danger—secure in a boy's invincible immortality.

He passed inches, literally, from my front bumper. I slammed on my brakes, a meaningless physical reflex since he was already long gone. I was shaking, and it took a minute to catch my breath. In one terrible instant, that boy's life surely could have ended. His parents would have been in pain forever, and my own life would have been a nightmare.

I continued down the street, recalling the image of the boy's face. Magnified by my fright, I could clearly picture his eyes wide with a dazzling mix of bravado and fear, a bright haughty smile lit by yet another triumph over the dull world of adult concern. He was so startlingly energetic, so fearless that my shock at very nearly killing him was almost immediately replaced by anger bordering on fury.

Churning with rage—at his carelessness, not mine—I went home. The agitation my near-miss brought upon me troubled me most of the day. Then, at twilight, I remembered Mikey.

Growing up, Mike Roberts was my best buddy. My father was a doctor in a small Ohio River town, and my parents and Mike's parents were close friends. In fact, his house was one vacant lot away from my father's clinic.

Mikey, as we all called him, was adventurous and daring. His mother, Judy, was easy on us kids and made the best peanut butter cookies in the universe. They never locked their doors, and I had the run of their house.

One Friday, my mother planned to go to Cincinnati to shop and told me I should spend the day at the Roberts's house. Judy was expecting me. I was not to eat too many cookies or ride my bike in the road.

When my mother left that morning, I set off on my bike to the Roberts's house. I was about fifty yards from the turn that led to Mikey's street when I heard a sound that I can still hear sometimes in dreams. It was the fierce squeal of tires when you put on the brakes really hard. It seemed to last for a very long time, although I am sure, in retrospect, that the noise died quickly. And then there was the harsh sound of metal crushing. In a flash, I took off on my bike and rounded the corner at full speed.

There was a truck in the road, turned almost sideways. Beyond the front fender was Mikey's red Schwinn, folded so that it seemed to be just half a bike, two tires now flattened against each other.

Mikey was lying on the grass, a great hulk of a man bent over him. I got off my bike, dropped it, and ran to where my friend lay, silent and still on a carpet of leaves. At that instant, the front door of his house opened and his mother came out. I don't think I have ever seen anyone run so fast. At the same time, a gurney appeared from my father's clinic followed by my dad and an orderly.

Instantly, there was quite a crowd. Judy knelt at Mikey's head and passed her hand gently over his forehead. My father told Judy not to move her son and bent to examine him. The truck driver sat down heavily a few feet away. He must have weighed over two hundred pounds. He had great round shoulders and a thick neck that had deep circles of wrinkles that shone with sweat. He had on blue coveralls and a red plaid shirt.

Now he sat on the grass like some stunned bull. His head rested on his drawn-up knees and his shoulders shook, but I don't think he was crying.

I stared at the man, trying to make him feel how mad I was. *He had probably not been paying attention,* I thought. Not an unfamiliar failing among the adults I knew. They often seemed careless to me, and this one had hurt my friend. I wanted to hurt him back in some terrible way.

In a few minutes, Mikey was awake and crying. My father had him immobilized on a stretcher board and loaded onto the gurney. Judy held Mikey's hand, and they all moved away into the clinic's emergency entrance. I was left alone with the trucker who was now sitting with his head bowed on his crossed arms. His body was still shaking like he had a chill.

We sat in silence for what seemed a long time. Then Judy came out of the clinic's front entrance and walked over to us. She said that Mikey would be fine. It was only his arm. It could have been much worse.

I thought she surely would slap the driver or at least give him a severe talking to. But what she actually did astonished me. She told him to come with her into her house. "And you, too," she said to me.

She asked the driver his name and told him to sit by the fireplace and she would get some coffee. He raised his hand to wave her off but she brought coffee anyway, and milk and cookies for me. Stan, the driver, couldn't eat or drink. He sat in the blue armchair, filling it completely. From time to time, he would shake and Judy would put her arm around his shoulder and talk to him in her wonderful gentle voice, "It's not your fault. You weren't speeding. Mikey takes stupid risks, and I am so sorry about that. I'm just grateful he wasn't hurt badly. And I don't blame you. You shouldn't blame yourself, either."

I listened to her incredulously. *How could she say such things to the man who'd nearly killed her son, my friend? What was the matter with her?* Before long, she got the driver sort of put back together—at least that's how it looked to me—and he got up to leave.

As he reached the door he turned to her and said, "I have a boy, too. I know what it took for you to help me."

Then, to add one more astonishment to the day, Judy stood on tiptoe and kissed him on the cheek.

I had never been able to understand how Judy could offer ease and comfort to a man who had very nearly killed her child . . . until today, when I turned the corner into my familiar neighborhood and came within inches of what surely would have been a terrible and irreversible act.

Still trying to shake the dread that had occupied my mind all day, I thought of Mikey's mother and that day in a long-ago autumn. And although there was no one there to comfort me, to tell me that I had not been at fault, that bad things do happen no matter how careful you are, the memory of that day reached across time to help me.

That one mother's empathy, like all other gifts of goodness, had never left the world, and it could be called upon to console and heal. And would continue to do so . . . perhaps forever.

W. W. Meade

A Sweet Lesson

The mother's heart is the child's schoolroom.

Henry Ward Beecher

My father loved honeybees. When a wild honeybee came buzzing around, Dad would stop whatever he was doing and wait for the bee to get its fill of nectar. As soon as it was full, it would take off as straight as an arrow to its hive in the woods. Our father would then set off after it. Even if he lost sight of it, he could approximate where it would end up because honeybees don't waver from a straight beeline when they go home.

Whenever Dad found a hollow tree with a swarm of bees in it, he'd visit the landowner and get permission to cut the tree. Dad always gave the owner all the honey in exchange for the bees. That was how he built up a large apiary, which eventually provided a major portion of our family income.

A hive of honeybees could die of starvation during the winter if its supply of honey gave out before the flowers were in bloom. Beekeepers routinely helped their bees survive the cold months by feeding them syrup made from sugar and water.

During World War I, our nation had a severe sugar shortage. The government rationed sugar, along with many other things. This created a great demand for honey as a substitute. Because of this need for honey, beekeepers were given an extra ration of sugar to keep their bees alive through the winter. We kept our government allotment in a barrel in our summer kitchen. We kids knew that it was to be used strictly for feeding the bees.

Because of these shortages our country suffered during World War I, it was often difficult for mothers to cook good meals for their families. It was especially a struggle when company came to visit.

One day we received word that some favorite relatives, who lived several miles away, would be coming to visit the next day. We were so excited. Mom started to plan the dinner she would prepare for their visit. Wistfully she said, "Oh, how I wish I could bake a cake!" She prided herself on her beautiful cakes. However, our small ration of sugar for the family had already been consumed, so cake baking was impossible.

Of course we children wanted that cake as badly as she did! We begged her to take enough sugar from Dad's bee ration to make it. We argued that there was no way the government would know about it. Finally, she gave in. She went outside to the barrel of sugar in the summer kitchen and used it to make her delicious yellow cake recipe. It took skill to bake a perfect cake in a wood-fired oven, but our mother could do it. When she finished decorating it with her special meringue icing, we were so proud to serve it to our guests.

A few days later it was time for our family of seven to receive our monthly allotment of sugar. Dad went to the grocery store to buy it. The grocer put it in a tiny brown bag and tied it securely. When Dad got home he sat it on our table.

Mom looked at that package for a moment. Then she got out the utensil she'd used for measuring the sugar for the cake. As we children looked on in awe and disbelief, she measured out exactly the same amount that she'd used. Then we solemnly followed behind her as she went out to the bee sugar barrel and poured it in.

The scanty amount left at the bottom of the small paper bag was meager for a family of seven, but still it had to suffice for our month's family ration. Quite a sobering thought for a small child who loved sweets. Mom made no fuss over it. No fanfare. She didn't preach to us about honesty. It was just a natural action on her part, in keeping with the integrity with which my father and she lived their lives.

I'm ninety-two years old now. It's been a long time since I was a small child standing on tiptoes peering over my mother's kitchen table. Many things have changed in my lifetime. I still make a cake when company comes to visit, but I bake from a mix now because I can't stand up as long as I used to. I no longer have to use a wood stove. There is certainly no shortage of sugar in our country.

But some things should never change. And so I have told this story about my mother's unconditional honesty many times to my children and grandchildren and even to my great-grandchildren. Mom was like those honeybees my dad loved to follow. You could always count on her making an honest path through life, a beeline straight as an arrow. Because of that, she quietly shaped four generations of our family's conscience.

Mildred Bonzo

Sunglasses

We have a picture of him somewhere, a brokenhearted five-year-old, slumped on a bench at Disney World, eyes fighting back tears, lips so tense you can almost see them quivering, his felt Mickey Mouse ears cocked to one side.

Or maybe we don't have a picture, except in our minds. And yet it's the same image my husband and I share: A sunny day, white light glinting off the windows on Main Street, reflecting off dozens of chrome carriages with chrome wheels, light and heat shimmering everywhere and our two children clamoring for sunglasses, "Please, Mommy? Please, Daddy? Pleeeze!"

We ducked into a shop and Rob picked out Donald Duck glasses, blue and white plastic things that slid down his nose and made him look far more like Scrooge McDuck than Donald Duck. But we didn't tell him this. He loved those glasses. Lauren, three and already into fashion, chose pink Minnie Mouse glasses because she was dressed in pink that day.

They wore them out of the dark store into the day, up Main Street, through the castle and into Fantasyland. During "Peter Pan's Flight" they took them off and clutched them in their hands, and they did the same in "Pirates of the Caribbean." On "Mr. Toad's Wild Ride" they had them on, I know, because we have a picture of them smiling and waving.

Somehow, somewhere, after that, maybe when he was getting off that ride, maybe when he stopped to tie his sneaker or fix his Mickey ears, or maybe when we were having lunch, the Donald Duck glasses disappeared. And Robbie, who was five and loved those glasses, cried.

"If you had loved them you would have taken better care of them," is what we said to him. Or something like that. Imagine. But we were young and new at this parenting thing, and weren't we supposed to teach him to take care of what was his? Wasn't it our duty to make sure that he knew that money didn't grow on trees?

What did those sunglasses cost? A dollar? Two dollars? What harm would it have done to wipe his tears and say, "Come on, we'll get you another pair. I know you didn't mean to lose them." Would he have grown up to be a bad person? Would he have been corrupted in some unforeseeable way?

Lauren said, "You can have mine, Robbie." But he didn't want hers. They were pink and for girls. And his were blue and for boys. And they were gone, and he had loved them and he was miserable.

If I had it to do over, I'd have marched back down Main Street and bought a brand-new pair of Donald Duck glasses and pretended that I found them on the ground. I would have yelled, "Hey, look what I have!" And he would have leaped up and come running and laughed and thrown his arms around me and put on those glasses and this would be the memory of that day.

You live and you learn.

A few months ago we were in Orlando, not exactly at the scene of the crime, but close enough. Our son, long an adult, was there on business and we flew down to meet him, and in the flurry of rental cars and restaurants and going here and there, guess what? He lost his sunglasses.

We didn't scold him, didn't even think about saying, if you really liked them you would have taken better care of them, because people lose things all the time. Instead we did what most adults do for other adults: We helped him figure out where he could have lost them and—what do you know—he found them in a meeting room he'd been in the day before.

He was grinning when he walked to the car, his steps light and quick, his sunglasses hiding his eyes, nothing of the five-year-old left in him to see.

Except I saw.

He was my first child, and the first has it the hardest, because you're new at this and you go by the book and you don't want to mess up and be too soft, but you mess up anyway, because what do you know?

I know that as parents we have an obligation to teach our children. But I also know that everything doesn't have to be a lesson. That sometimes, lost sunglasses are just what they are: lost sunglasses and nothing more.

Beverly Beckham

Song of the Spirit

There is a tribe in East Africa in which the art of true intimacy is fostered even before birth.

In this tribe, the birth date of a child is not counted from the day of its physical birth nor even from the day of conception. For this tribe the birth date is the first time the child is a thought in its mother's mind. Aware of her intention to conceive a child with a particular father, the mother then goes off to sit alone under a tree and listens until she can hear the song of the child she hopes to conceive.

Once she has heard it, she returns to her village and teaches it to the father so that they can sing it together, inviting the child to join them. After the child is conceived, she sings it to the baby in her womb. Then she teaches it to the old women and midwives of the village, so that throughout the labor and at the miraculous moment of birth itself, the child is greeted with its song.

After the birth, all the villagers learn the song of their new member and sing it to the child when it falls or hurts itself. It is sung in times of triumph, or in rituals and initiations. This song becomes a part of the marriage ceremony when the child is grown, and at the end of life, his or her loved ones will gather around the deathbed and sing this song for the last time.

Jack Kornfield
From A Path with Heart
Submitted by Lianne Mercer

Silence

One laugh of a child will make the holiest day more sacred still.

Robert G. Ingersoll

The noise is almost deafening. Scampering about the living room, my son gathers his blocks. They clack against one another as he carefully constructs a skyscraper. "Vroooooom! Vrooo-vrooooom!" I hear his car imitation, and I can envision what is about to happen. Crash! Brandon squeals with delight. His car just had a head-on collision with a skyscraper.

"All broken, Momma!" he hollers. "Momma, come! All broken!"

"Just a second!" I call out to him.

"Just a second! Just a second!" he screeches back like a parrot.

"Momma! Come, Momma!" His cries are persistent. And very, very loud.

"Just sit down and be quiet!" I call to him impatiently.

Then I freeze. I have just said the words that I swore would never pass through my lips.

Brandon is undaunted and keeps hollering, but I hardly hear him now. I'm remembering my promise to myself, and its reason.

Our first son was Matthew, and he was born with a heart defect. Because we didn't know how much time we would have together, we lived every day as if it were our last. Nothing got in the way of playing with Matthew. Dusting, laundry, chores—all went undone as I cherished my moments with my son.

I was a proud stay-at-home mother; I could think of no job that equaled it. It wasn't a prestigious title, and money was tight, but nothing beat getting my paycheck in the form of first steps, first words, smiles, and hugs and kisses. I used to receive my pay in a bland white envelope. How could that compare with the feeling I got when I held my son, a warm and full sensation, starting from deep within and rising like the sun bursting forth? This was my calling. I savored my time with Matthew and thrilled at the new baby that was already squirming in my belly.

When I was six months pregnant with baby number two—the now-boisterous Brandon playing in the next room—we traveled to Switzerland from our home in Germany to have Matthew's surgery. We had painstakingly researched to find the world's best surgeon for the job, and his work on Matthew was exceptional.

But complications arose. Matthew died. Deafening silence filled the next three months.

My ears strained in the empty house for Matthew crying "Momma!" I woke in the middle of the night expecting his cries, a scream at the top of his lungs, anything! But all that greeted me was oppressive silence.

Never will I tell a child of mine to sit down and be quiet, I vowed. *Never.*

Brandon broke the silence two days before Christmas, emerging from my womb kicking and squalling. He carries inside himself a perfectly healthy heart and the energy and excitement of ten children.

And he never gives up. He's standing at our child safety gate now, still calling, "Momma!" I go to him, and he holds out his arms, smiling. "Big hug, Momma." I wrap him in my arms and hold him tightly. Another paycheck.

As I put him down he pulls on my pants leg and says, "Come! Come, Momma. Sit down, Momma," luring me to his play. The living room is strewn with toy cars and blocks. I turn toward the kitchen and see the dishes piled high, three baskets of clean clothes ready for folding. "Sit down, now!" Brandon commands, his eyes sparkling with excitement.

"What's the magic word?" I ask.

"Please!" he cries. I sit on the floor. Playing cars can be awfully fun, and I'll have plenty of time to clean the house when Brandon is eighteen.

We vrroooom and screech. We are very, very loud.

Call my name all you want, Son. Run around. Fill our life and home with the pitter-patter of little feet and the wonderful music of a child's laughter. Just remember, when you are grown with children of your own, don't tell your children to sit down and be quiet.

Silence is not always golden.

Debbie Gilmore

Calm Mother

I love people. I love my family, my children . . .
but inside myself is a place where I live all alone
and that's where you renew your springs that
never dry up.

Pearl S. Buck

As a teenager growing up in the sixties, I knew what I wanted
to do with my life and what I didn't want to do. I wanted to
travel and see the world. I didn't want to be a mother.

Both desires were a rebellion against my own childhood. I grew up on the flat prairie land of the Midwest and
thus yearned to see mountains, clouds and trees. My own
parents never treated me well, so I grew up not liking anybody, except for my kind, loving grandmothers.

Every hot, cloudless prairie summer, my family would
travel to the tree-lined city to visit both of my grandmothers. Around their own mothers, my parents treated
me well. How I loved my grandmothers! Best of all, they
loved me back.

Achieving my teenage goals would be easy: After
getting a college degree, I planned to travel to the city of

my choice and get a job. After two or three years when I began to get bored, I would move on to another ideal city. If I found my true love along the way, I would get married and settle down, but I wouldn't have children.

In my twenties, I graduated from college and went to live in my chosen city. So far, so good. Then, one summer I decided to visit the hot, flat prairie town where I grew up. It was fun to chatter away with the adults I had known as a child. For once, I was being treated like an adult among other adults.

One of the couples I visited asked me if I would baby-sit for their five little boys. I had never baby-sat for anyone before. *How hard can it be?* I thought to myself and accepted.

I found out it could be very hard. I didn't know that five boys, aged two to twelve, could be so loud and energetic. They also got very physical, and amazed as I was, I did not try to control them. This made the situation even worse. Just as the parents walked in through the front door, the little two-year-old boy, who was very wound up, hurled himself onto me trying to greet his parents. Without thinking, I turned around and hit him. The whole family froze in shock. I looked bewildered at everybody until the father asked quietly, "Why did you hit my son?"

"He hit me first," I answered, feeling completely justified.

"It was an accident," he replied.

"It was?"

Violence in my own childhood had been intentional and frequent, never accidental. This new concept had never even occurred to me. I turned toward the little boy and asked, "Did you mean to hit me?"

Still whimpering, he shook his head earnestly, the tears falling down his flushed cheeks. My hardened heart cracked.

"I'm sorry."

The tension relieved, they quickly forgave me and we embraced. Their warmth and forgiveness affected me deeply. I saw that simply not having children wouldn't solve the deeper problems inside me. The abuse I'd experienced as a child had turned me into a violent adult. I couldn't ignore it anymore, but I honestly didn't know what to do. I didn't want to tell anyone, for fear of ruining what few friendships I had. After all, I had almost lost one friendship with a loving family—with one unthinking blow.

The following spring I visited my older brother, who had recently married. He and his wife and child lived on an Indian reservation. I attended church with my family, and found it interesting to be in the minority, one of the few whites among so many Native Americans. During my visit, I befriended an Indian grandmother.

One day, right after church ended, the grandmother and I were standing together and she remarked, "White man's babies are so noisy." Looking around the room at all the contented Indian babies and then at the crying, whimpering white babies, I realized the truth in her words! My nephew was no exception.

"Why is that?" I asked her in astonishment.

She answered by describing the tradition of her tribe. When a young girl started menstruating, she left the tribe for one day to spend time alone in the wilderness and meditate about what kind of woman she would be when she grew up. Of course, her father followed discreetly to ensure her safety.

Each following month, at the appropriate time, she would spend another day by herself and meditate. As she grew, she meditated about what kind of young man she wanted to attract. After engagement, she meditated about what kind of wife she would be. After her marriage, she meditated about what kind of mother she would be, and so on. Thus, each woman took time each month to be alone and meditate about where her life was going, what kind of person she was becoming and what to do about her problems. The grandmother ended her narrative by saying, "Calm mother makes calm baby."

Listening to her, I felt a surge of warmth and love inside me. I knew I had finally discovered the answer to my curse of violence. I followed her advice exactly, only I meditated once a week to make up for the lost years.

First, I meditated on how to be a better worker at my job and how to be a better friend. In the stillness, answers came. I needed to stop taking offense so easily in both situations. I needed to stop thinking and saying "I" so much and start asking about the other person more.

As I was dating, I meditated about each boyfriend and our relationship. Did I give more than I took? Did we laugh easily? Was I a good listener? Did I like him when I wasn't in love with him?

Eventually, I found my true love. After our marriage, I continued the frequent meditations. The process of two becoming one seemed to bring out issues I thought I had resolved sufficiently when I was single. The questions kept coming. However, I stayed calm and stuck with the plan, meditating week by week, month by month.

It's worked! Our marriage has continued happily, and now we have five wonderful children. All of these "white man's babies" have mostly been calm, and the violence of my childhood has remained a thing of the past.

How grateful I am that an old Indian grandmother whose name I never knew managed to change my life and the lives of my children for the better with her simple wisdom: Calm mother makes calm baby.

Holly Danneman

8

MIRACLES

In the presence of love, miracles happen.

Robert Schuller

The Miracle Baby

Faith is being sure of what we hope for and certain of what we do not see.

Hebrews 11:1

He was born six and a half weeks prematurely on a hot, August day in 1967 and was quickly whisked away to a waiting incubator. At a mere four pounds, eleven ounces, and looking like a partially inflated doll, he was still the most beautiful baby she had ever seen.

The baby's father, Dr. Carter,* tried to tell his wife, Donna, not to expect too much—their baby was severely jaundiced. More than anything in the world, he had wanted to tell her their little baby was just fine, especially after three miscarriages, and all the sadness they'd felt and tears they shed. But their baby wasn't fine.

In spite of all his medical training and experience, Dr. Carter choked on the words. But he knew he'd have to tell her that the baby they had wanted so badly for years was probably not going to live—maybe forty-eight hours at

*Names have been changed throughout the story to protect privacy.

the most. He had to prepare her for what was to come.

She immediately named the baby Jeffrey, after her husband. As the baby's jaundice grew worse, fellow physicians came by to console them. They shook their heads and tried their best to offer some encouragement. But they knew the odds were not good. Even if he lived, unless little Jeffrey's liver began functioning soon, the jaundice would produce permanent brain damage.

Donna told everyone he was going to be all right. She knew her baby was going to live. The nurses felt sorry for her since her baby was probably going to die anyway, and so they let her hold him. When she touched his tiny, fragile body and whispered that he was going to grow up to be a strong, healthy man, little Jeffrey smiled. She told the nurses what had happened, and they looked at her sadly and said that babies have involuntary smiles and she needed rest. They did not have the heart to tell her more.

The extended family discussed burial arrangements with her husband and the parish priest. They finally came in to speak with Donna. She started crying and asked everyone to leave the hospital room. Her baby was not going to be buried. He was going to go home, jaundiced or not. She would not even think of burial!

At sixty-two hours, the baby's blood count was checked again. The jaundice was considerably better! Little Jeffrey began eating every two hours. Donna asked to hold him as much as possible, and she talked to him. Since he didn't need oxygen, the nurses humored her. At the next check, the count had dropped another two points. Donna began planning his homecoming party.

Jeffrey did go home almost three weeks after birth. That, however, was not the end of the story.

Six weeks later, at his first checkup, the pediatrician told Donna he thought the baby was possibly blind or had eye damage. She said this was nonsense since he followed her with his eyes. After a few tests, it proved to be a false scare. Yet, the first year, the baby did not do much. He had routine checkups, but Donna knew he seemed far behind in his development. Had he suffered severe brain damage from the jaundice?

At thirteen months Jeffrey suddenly had a small seizure. They rushed him to the hospital, and he was diagnosed with a possible brain tumor. After several tests and X rays the neurologist said Jeffrey was hydrocephalic (water on the brain), and they would have to operate immediately to put a permanent shunt inside his head. At this time, a shunt operation was still rather experimental. It was the only procedure known to keep these children alive.

Once again, Donna did not fully accept the diagnosis. If he was hydrocephalic, why did it just now develop? Her friends told her she was in denial. She'd better listen to the doctors.

Of course, she would do whatever was necessary to help her son, but she also made her own plan of action. Three days before the operation, she called everyone she knew in several states and asked them to pray at 7:00 P.M. each night before the operation. She asked them to ask others to join them if they could.

When the operation day arrived, she felt calm. Friends in seven states had been praying for their son. Later, to her astonishment she learned that her friends had called people, who then called other people, and that ultimately hundreds of people had been gathered to pray at 7:00 P.M. on three successive nights. Even a group of people in Israel were among those praying! And all for a tiny child none of them even knew!

The operation started very early. Donna and her husband paced the floors of the hospital. After what seemed only a short time, the neurosurgeon came running out, wildly waving X rays. He was grinning from ear to ear.

"It's a miracle! We didn't have to do anything. We did the last test through the baby's soft spot, and there was nothing there. He is not hydrocephalic!"

They all started to cry and laugh at the same time. The neurosurgeon said he did not know what to think. He had no explanation for it.

So Jeffrey came home once again to a jubilant crowd of friends and family. All the people who prayed for him were notified of the results and thanked for their prayers. He never had another seizure again.

Still, according to everyone else's timetable, his development was very slow. At Jeffrey's three-year pediatric checkup, the doctor looked sternly at Donna and asked if she and her husband had given thought to institutionalizing him. Donna was stunned. *Institutionalize him? How could anyone do that?* She refused, and it was never discussed again.

Instead, Donna set up the family basement playroom like a Montessori school. Jeffrey wasn't really learning language so she worked with him by engaging learning techniques that involved all his senses—sight, smell, touch, taste and hearing. Donna believed Jeffrey was normal and just didn't follow other people's timetables.

She taught him colors using M&Ms. He quickly learned the names of colors and of other things, too. And, while not speaking much more than a few words here and there until he was three and a half years old, his first full sentence was "Pass the ketchup!" He progressed quickly when he learned anything new—not little by little as his sister did, but in giant spurts, all-at-once kind of steps. This became a pattern in his life.

When Jeffrey was four, Donna wanted him to go to real preschool just like his sister. The first year he played with the water fountain—all year. He turned the water off and on, endlessly. The teachers said it was a waste of money to send him to school. He would be better off in "special school." They said he was "slow," and one teacher in exasperation said that Jeffrey was retarded and she ought to know—she'd been teaching for twenty-five years!

Donna remained firm. Would they mind as long as she was paying for it, to keep him another year? They reluctantly agreed but only if he was not allowed to play with the water fountain. She agreed to the terms.

The next fall he began preschool again. This time he began building intricate architectural structures. He also began examining all the plastic dinosaurs and knew their names, classifying them by types. He found new interests in doing the math blocks, talking and asking question after question after question. He was more social and didn't play with the water fountain. The teachers couldn't believe it. He actually seemed bright!

However, at his pediatric checkup, his new doctor said he thought Jeffrey needed testing. He felt he had developmental delays. After testing, the pediatrician, who is now distinguished nationally in his field, said Jeffrey was autistic. Donna decided she'd had enough! Since birth, Jeffrey had been "diagnosed" as possibly (1) blind, (2) hydrocephalic, (3) epileptic, (4) retarded and now finally (5) autistic. If she and her husband had listened to experts, well-meaning friends and even some family members, Jeffrey would be in an institution. Donna was polite but said that she did not think Jeffrey was autistic at all. He was in preschool and was going to start first grade on time.

Other than being very uncoordinated and not having well-developed motor skills, Jeffrey's elementary years were not unusual. His learning ability was completely on track. He became an Eagle Scout, an honor student, a presidential scholar in his senior year, won two academic scholarships for college and was in all gifted classes. His SAT scores shocked everyone.

But even this is not the end of the story.

After graduating from college with honors, Jeffrey was encouraged to go to medical school. Donna always told him she had faith that his life had a special purpose and that he was here to help people. After graduating medical school, Jeffrey was accepted at a prestigious clinic for his residency program.

One day, while he was doing a rotation in the emergency room, an older man burst in. He was suicidal and, as a last-ditch effort, one of his friends had brought him in to talk to someone. Jeffrey saw him and asked about his life. The man told him about how sad he was about his recent divorce and being downsized out of a job he had held for years. He felt hopeless, that his life was over and nothing he had done had mattered. Jeffrey talked to him a while and, after giving him some tests, gave him a prescription that would help him for the next few days. Jeffrey also got him approved for a caseworker to follow him up for the next month.

Suddenly the patient looked at the doctor's badge and said, "Jeffrey Carter? Is your mom's name Donna?"

Jeffrey answered, "Why, yes. How did you know?"

"You're the miracle baby! You're the miracle baby!" the man cried excitedly. "I prayed for you when you were in the hospital, and now you're a doctor!"

Jeffrey confirmed that he had been born in Minnesota and now he'd returned "home" to complete his medical training.

The old man smiled and just gazed at his new doctor as if examining every inch. Then he told Jeffrey the story.

"Were you really one of the people who prayed for me?" Jeffrey asked him.

"Oh yes, three nights a week at 7:00 P.M. for years. We were only supposed to do it until the operation, but some of us just kept going for a while."

"You prayed for me all that time?"

As the man nodded, tears began to form in his eyes. Jeffrey reached out to embrace his patient—a man who only hours before had thought of taking his own life because he had lost all faith.

"Thank you, for praying for me . . . for caring about me. You see, I'm here because of you."

Faith had come full circle for both men.

Ronna Rowlette

The Message

My mother had battled breast cancer and won. She had been cancer-free for five years when she went into the hospital to have exploratory surgery. After the operation, her doctor took me aside and told me that not only had the cancer returned, but there was nothing he could do. "Three months," the doctor told me sadly.

I wondered how my mother would take the news, but as each day passed, I realized the doctors hadn't let her in on the miserable secret. Did they really expect me, her son, to have to break it to her? I didn't see how I could.

Three days passed with no word spoken. I watched as she packed up her things, ready to leave the hospital after recovering from her surgery. She was cheerful, telling me her plans for the next week, when something she saw in my face stopped her.

"Mom," I managed to say, "haven't they . . . haven't they told you?"

"Told me what?" she said.

I couldn't answer, but I didn't have to. The tears coursing down my face told her everything.

We held each other as I explained what I knew.

We had always been close, but after that day, I opened up to my mother in a way I never thought possible. I returned to New York, to my job as a hairstylist and the life I'd created there, but we talked long and often on the phone—not just as mother and son, but as friends.

Not long after, I took a month off and spent it with her, talking about anything and everything—her life and mine, politics, philosophy, religion. She was disappointed that I hadn't kept to the faith in which I'd been raised. She tried to convince me of God's existence, but although I didn't argue, nothing she said persuaded me that she was right. I suppose I was an agnostic: I just didn't know.

When I left, I wasn't sure if I would ever see her again, but in a certain way it didn't matter. Although we didn't agree on everything, we were complete with one another.

The day before I left, my mother presented me with a beautiful cross, one of her most valued possessions.

My mother had always been a deeply religious person. And although she rarely mentioned it, as a young woman she had entered the convent and spent two years as a nun. When her family urgently needed her to help with the family business, she made the difficult decision to leave the convent and go home.

Eventually, she married and I, her only child, was born. The cross she gave me that day was the one she received when she became a nun. It was exquisitely made, and as I took it in my hand, I could feel the love she gave to me along with it.

Within a month, the call I'd been dreading came. My mother had slipped into a coma. The doctors felt she didn't have much time left, so I hurried to the airport to catch the next flight home. As the plane took off, I looked out my window, watching the sky color with the setting sun. All at once, I was overcome with grief.

This heaviness stayed with me for the entire flight.

When I arrived at the hospital, I was informed that I was too late. My mother had died while I was on the plane—at the exact time the sadness had overwhelmed me.

After my mother's funeral, I returned to New York. I missed my mother but was grateful that nothing had been left unsaid. She was gone, leaving an empty spot in me. *That's how life is,* I thought wistfully. *When it's over, it's over. You're dead, and that's the end.*

One day, three months after my mother died, a client came into the salon for her appointment. This particular woman had been coming to me for almost a year, but she was not a client with whom I was friendly. She was a high-powered businesswoman with a reserved air of cool politeness. We didn't talk about our lives. In fact, I had been surprised when, at her last appointment, she let it slip that she had been diagnosed with breast cancer.

Today, she didn't mention her illness and neither did I. I put her under the hair dryer and turned to walk away.

"Thomas," she said, lifting the dryer hood. "I hesitate to tell you this because I know this is going to sound strange. I have this very strong feeling that I'm supposed to tell you that Anita? . . . Marie? . . . Mary? . . . Anita Mary is okay. She said to tell you everything is all right."

I was floored. My jaw dropped. How could she know? For although my mother's name was Joyce, the name she'd taken as a nun—the name inscribed on the cross my mother had given me—was Sister Anita Mary. Nobody knew that but the other nuns and me.

In an instant, my whole view of reality turned upside-down. Mom had chosen a woman with breast cancer to tell me, in a way that could leave no doubt, that death is not the end and that the spirit survives.

Thomas Brown

For Love of Logan

*Jesus said to them, "Go and tell John what you
hear and see: the blind regain their sight, the
lame walk, lepers are cleansed, the deaf hear,
the dead are raised. . . ."*

Matthew 11:4–5

Tami grew up in a small Indiana town, married shortly
after her high school graduation and had her first baby,
Jaclyn, a few years later. It was a routine pregnancy and
delivery, with no trouble at all. She and husband Todd
settled into a peaceful life on their farm, enjoying parenthood and planning a larger family. There was no warning
of what was to come.

Tami became pregnant again seven years later. Everything seemed normal until her sixth month, when an
ultrasound revealed problems. The doctor gently broke
the news: The child, a girl, would die either during the
next few months or shortly after birth.

Tami and Todd were heartbroken. They named their
unborn daughter Megan and hoped she knew how much
they loved her. Eventually Tami gave birth, but there was

little to celebrate, for baby Megan was stillborn.

Tests on Tami and Todd showed nothing amiss, however, and eventually Tami became pregnant again. But now she was nervous, afraid to get her hopes up. And although Tami had grown up as a Southern Baptist, she hadn't been to church in years. But gradually, as this pregnancy progressed, Tami found herself talking to her Heavenly Father. "God, please give me a healthy baby," she asked each day, Megan's death still fresh in her mind. Even if she and God had not been close for a while, he surely wouldn't ask her to go through another loss like that, would he?

Time passed, and despite her worry, Tami had no problems. The doctor monitored her carefully. The baby—a boy whom they had already named Logan—looked vital and completely normal.

One morning, a few days before her due date, Tami was admitted to the hospital. Labor began, and everything seemed fine. Baby Logan was closely monitored, and his heart was healthy and strong. Todd and Tami's sister, Ruthie, were with her, and as things progressed, the grandparents assembled in the waiting room. It would be a joyous event—not like the last time, they all assured each other. Logan was almost here!

By late afternoon, Tami was taken to the delivery room. She was almost to the end now, and as the nurses cheered her on, she pushed and pushed. "One more!" a nurse shouted. "He's almost here!" Tami pushed again. But Logan's heart rate had suddenly slowed. And as the doctor took him from the womb, there was no heartbeat at all. He wasn't breathing.

The doctor quickly carried the lifeless infant to the warmer on the other side of the room and gave him oxygen. "Come on, Logan!" the doctor murmured. "Wake up. . . ." Another nurse started chest compressions.

There was no cry, no heartbeat or pulse. The baby's eyes remained closed, his limbs limp, his color an unhealthy gray.

"Logan?" Tami asked. "Todd, why isn't he crying?"

Todd stood in shock, watching nurses running here and there. No one was saying anything, and the silence was horrible. Ruthie realized something terrible was happening and hurriedly left the room.

Within seconds, it seemed, an emergency room physician raced in, followed by Tami's pediatrician. A respiratory therapist passed Tami, then an X-ray technician. "What is going on?" Tami screamed, beginning to sob. Tears streamed down Todd's cheeks.

The doctor came to Tami's side and explained that everything possible was being done. To Tami, it was all a horrible nightmare. She had thought everything was under control, and now she realized that nothing was. Only God could help Logan now. "Dear God," she whispered through her tears, "please don't do this. I don't think I can handle it. Please save Logan, please."

Medical personnel continued to work over the baby, but Logan never showed any signs of life. A half-hour later, the neonatal specialists agreed to discontinue all resuscitation efforts. Logan was pronounced dead.

Unobtrusively, a nurse baptized Logan. Another weighed him, cleaned him, wrapped him in warm blankets, put a little stocking cap on his dark head and laid him in Tami's arms for a last good-bye. She held him close, searching his perfect little face. "Logan, don't go—I need you," she whispered. But her son's eyes were closed, his body completely limp. *Dear God, please.* She had to let go, to accept the inevitable, but somehow, she couldn't stop praying.

The doctors stood by Tami's bed, unable to explain what had happened. They wouldn't know unless they did an autopsy. Tami blinked back tears. Perhaps an autopsy would save another family the suffering she was enduring. "All right," she agreed. "But I want to hold him for a while."

Someone brought a consent form, and still holding Logan, Tami reached over and signed it.

Then all the relatives in the waiting room streamed in, murmuring words of encouragement, mingling their tears with Tami's and Todd's.

Todd cuddled Logan, then passed him to Ruthie. The nurse took some photographs. Occasionally the baby's body moved slightly, and the first time it happened, the nurse went out to the front desk and alerted the doctor who explained that it was just a spasm or a reaction to the medication the baby had received.

Forty-five more minutes passed. It was time, everyone knew, to turn Logan's body over to the hospital. Tami's stepmother was holding him, and she bent over him to say a last good-bye. Once again, his little body went into a spasm.

Tami's stepmother looked, and looked again. "He—he's gasping!" she cried. "Look, his leg moved!"

"It's just a spasm, like the nurse said," Tami answered.

"I don't think so—I think he's breathing," Grandma exclaimed. "Ruthie, get a nurse!"

Ruthie did. The nurse came quickly and put her fingertips on the baby's chest. Then she reached for a stethoscope and listened. "Wait right here!" she shouted, as she ran out of the room.

The doctor was still filling out forms when the excited nurse approached. "Logan has a heartbeat!" When the doctor reached the room, the baby was turning pink.

Astonished, the doctor took the baby from the grandmother. His little chest was rising and falling rapidly. "He *is* alive!" the doctor cried. "Let's take him to the nursery!" Nurse and physician ran with the infant out of the room.

Tami began to weep. It was just a cruel joke. For some reason Logan's little body was still reacting to treatment, and everyone thought . . . but such things were impossible! Her son had been dead for an hour and eighteen minutes—no one could come back to life after all that time.

And yet, she had asked God for a miracle, hadn't she?

Medical personnel began reappearing with bulletins for Tami and Todd. The neonatologists had returned, dumbfounded. They were currently examining Logan in the nursery. Despite the impossibility of it, Logan was breathing on his own and appeared healthy. He had been placed in an oxygen tent, and tests were proceeding.

Of course, there were undertones that were not mentioned, at least not at this joyful, exultant moment. A baby clinically dead for over an hour would no doubt have severe brain damage, as well as nonfunctioning optic nerves, tissue damage, seizures, the list could be endless. But for now, everyone was in a state of awe. It was, as the doctor described it later, like seeing the shadow of God passing by.

Baby Logan was transferred to another hospital and remained there for five weeks. He slept for the first two, due to medication reducing the possibility of seizures, then gradually began to awaken. Although brain-damaged babies often don't suck, he nursed immediately. Tests showed that his eyes and hearing were completely normal. Today he is progressing a bit more slowly than the average baby, but the doctors are "cautiously optimistic" that Logan's future is bright.

What happened to this very special baby? No one really knows. So far, there has been no medical explanation, only theories suggesting that Logan may have experienced the same kind of situation as a drowning victim—when systems shut down for a time, then spontaneously revive.

However, Logan had never actually *been* alive after birth. Not one, but *all* of the physicians there, including the neonatologists, agreed: Logan was dead, and then he was resurrected.

The "how" is hard enough to answer, the "why" almost impossible. Tami knows that the mystery of her baby's death and life has touched many. Perhaps that is a reason in itself. "Maybe God wanted to show us that miracles do happen, to say, 'I'm still here and I still raise people from the dead,'" Tami says. She doesn't believe it's her job to ask why, but just to keep telling others, and keep saying thank you.

She and Todd are very willing to carry out that heavenly assignment. What else can one do with such a wonder?

Joan Wester Anderson
Condensed from Where Wonders Prevail

Smokey

My daughter had her parenting cut out for her. Only two days after my grandsons Josh and Jarod, identical twins, were born, my daughter brought them home from the hospital. The babies weighed only about four pounds each, and my daughter had dressed them in Cabbage Patch nightgowns, the only clothes she could find to fit them.

For the next five days, we all pitched in. The household revolved around these two tiny creatures. They ate every two hours, and we spent virtually the entire day in some stage of feeding them: making bottles, emptying bottles, cleaning bottles, changing diapers, preparing more bottles. After the twins had sucked down the last of their 8:00 P.M. bottles and we had changed them and tucked them into bed, we would head to the kitchen for a cup of coffee and a much-needed break. What we needed was a full-time, paid staff. What we had was Smokey, the family cat.

Smokey had been fascinated with the twins since the day they came home. He spent more time at their side than we did, watching them curiously or napping near their beds. We watched him cautiously at first, making sure he didn't hurt the babies, but though he never left their side, he never got too close to them. He seemed a loyal caretaker.

One evening, though, we briefly doubted our trust. We were unwinding in the kitchen when Smokey let out a blood-curdling howl, like an animal killing its prey. We raced into the twins' room, and the sight that greeted us filled us with terror. Smokey was almost sitting on Josh, the smaller twin, butting the baby's little body with his head and literally rolling him around the crib. As we ran to save Josh from what we thought was serious injury or worse, Smokey suddenly lay down and started softly mewing, almost moaning. That's when we discovered that little Josh wasn't breathing.

I immediately started CPR while someone else called 911, and an ambulance raced Josh to the hospital. It turned out that both boys were highly allergic to milk. Their bodies had reached their limit in milk intake, and because Josh was smaller, he had gotten sick sooner. Mercifully, Josh had not been without oxygen for very long. Smokey had realized that Josh had stopped breathing and alerted us just in time. Josh would be fine. In fact, the doctor said Smokey had definitely saved Josh's life.

Over the following months, the family settled into an amiable routine. Then late one night, Smokey jumped into bed with my daughter and son-in-law and started to bite and scratch them. More annoyed than puzzled at the cat's strange behavior, they got up to shut him into the bathroom for the night. But Smokey dodged their grasp and darted upstairs to the twins' older brother John's room. When my daughter followed in the chase, she found John so ill that he couldn't move or call for help. "My chest," was all he could say. When he underwent emergency heart surgery, the doctors found that his aorta was almost totally blocked.

Smokey, the hero-cat, now holds a special place in our

family. He may have been content to be your typical family pet when the house was half-empty, but as it filled up with children, he decided he better promote himself to a mothering position. When it comes to raising a houseful of kids, Smokey figures it doesn't hurt to have some extra help.

B. A. Sutkus

A Visit from Mom

Several of us were standing around the nurses' station in the surgical intensive care unit (ICU) where we worked, when I asked the question. "Working in ICU, have you ever felt like someone else was in the room when there was no one else there you could see?"

Another smiled and added, "Or smelled perfume in the room of a patient who was dying when no one else had been in there?"

And another, "Or have you passed by someone in the hallway, turned around and there was no one there?"

We all looked at each other and laughed. "I thought I was the only one," I said.

Explanations were offered. Maybe it was because we had to spend so much time around people who were straddling the threshold between life and death—or maybe it was just stress.

"I think it's real," one of the nurses said soberly, "and has something to do with the kind of love that doesn't end when life does." She went on to tell this story:

A man in his early twenties was admitted to the ICU after a large piece of machinery at work had crushed his foot. He needed immediate surgery, and she quickly began to prepare him for the operating room. She had just started to go through her preoperative procedures when an anxious woman entered the ICU, asking about the young man.

"Is he all right?" the woman asked.

"He's stable and sleeping quietly," the nurse replied.

"Is he in pain?" the woman cried.

"No," the nurse reassured her. "They gave him some very strong medication in the emergency room when he first arrived."

"Is he going to be okay?" the woman asked, her face still creased with worry.

"He's young and healthy, and he should recover wonderfully after the surgery," the nurse assured her.

The woman looked somewhat relieved but asked to see him. "I'm his mother," she explained.

The nurse gave the woman a sympathetic look. "I understand your anxiety, but I have to prepare him for surgery. If you give me five minutes, I promise to let you see him before he is taken to the operating room."

"But he's all right?" the mother repeated. "He's going to be all right?"

"He's going to require a lot of physical therapy, but he looks like a hard worker and I'm sure he will do great."

Relief filled the woman's face. "Thank you so much for taking such good care of my son," she said. "I'll wait outside."

When the nurse had finished her duties, she walked down to the waiting room as promised to get the mother. No one was there. She checked the bathrooms and the vending machines, but still there was no sign of the woman who had been so anxious to see her son. The nurse was about to have the woman paged when a group of the man's coworkers walked up to ask about their friend.

"You can go in and see him for just a few minutes," the nurse replied. "I have to find his mother."

"Ma'am, he doesn't have a mother," one of the men said, looking at her strangely.

"But a woman was here who said she was his mother. I just talked to her," the nurse insisted.

"You don't understand," another coworker said. "His mother died a few years ago. All he has is a cousin. We called him and told him what happened, but we didn't call anyone else."

The nurse was baffled but went back to her work. A little while later, while the young man was in surgery, his cousin arrived and asked about him. The nurse updated him, and then, as he turned to leave, she called:

"By the way, a woman came by and asked about him. She said she was his mother."

The cousin stood motionless for a moment. "What did this woman look like?" he finally asked, and as the nurse described the lady, he slowly shook his head and smiled in disbelief and wonder. "Thank you," was all he said, and left.

When the nurse asked her coworkers later about the woman who had come into the ICU, no one remembered seeing her at all. She never showed up again.

For a minute, we were all silent, reflecting on the nurse's story. Was it possible? Who can really say? All I know is that from my experience as a nurse, I no longer doubt that love goes beyond death. Or that a mother looks out for her children for as long as she lives—and longer.

Patricia A. Walters-Fischer

Triumph in the Sky

Dallas grew up around airplanes. As a two-year-old he sat on his pilot-father's lap, wearing earphones and "flying." While other teenage boys saved for automobiles, young Dallas bought a plane instead. So when he became senior flight captain for a mining company in Casper, Wyoming, he was right where he wanted to be.

One spring, some years ago, Dallas received an unusual assignment. One of the company's engineers, Michael, and his wife, Sandi, had an eight-month-old baby needing a liver transplant. Little Benjamin had already gone through several unsuccessful surgeries designed to buy him some "growing time" until a donor liver could be found.

Now a transplant was Benjamin's only remaining chance for life, and he was on waiting lists at hospitals in Omaha and Pittsburgh, places specializing in infant transplants. Through the donations of charitable foundations and friends, the cost of the transplant had been covered. Everything was in place—except the journey itself. Because Michael and Sandi lived in such a remote area, it was doubtful they could get an immediate commercial flight to any medical center, especially within the short window of time necessary for surgery to proceed (usually seven to eight hours after a donor organ became available). Nor could the weather be counted upon; when they had taken Benjamin to Denver for an evaluation a few months earlier, they had almost missed their flight due to heavy snow.

Benjamin's parents began wearing pagers, waiting for a call from one of the hospitals. If one came, the mining company had authorized their flight department to use a company aircraft—or to do anything else necessary—to get parents and baby where they needed to go.

Dallas seldom flew east of the Mississippi. But it didn't matter; surgery would surely take place in Omaha, since it was so much closer. However, more than six months passed with no liver available for Benjamin. Dallas had almost forgotten about the family when, as he worked in his garage late on a fall afternoon, the phone rang.

"There's a liver for Benjamin in Pittsburgh," an emotional Michael told him. "Can we get there?"

"I'll meet you at the airport right away." Dallas hung up. Pittsburgh! So much farther than he'd expected, and he didn't have the necessary charts. Maybe the company jet could get them there in time. However, when Dallas phoned his flight scheduler, he discovered that the jet was in use, and the only plane available was a small turboprop. It was not nearly fast enough, and would require a stop for refueling, using up more valuable time.

Worse, the weather forecasts looked ominous. Not only would he be flying into strong head winds, there were thunderstorms over Chicago, and snow predicted for Pittsburgh.

The whole venture was starting to unravel. He couldn't start out on a journey he knew he couldn't finish. . . .

Dallas thought of his own two toddlers. How would he feel if *their* lives depended on others?

No, he wouldn't give up before he'd even tried. He frowned, deep in thought. Maybe he could *start* with the turboprop, and transfer parents and child to a faster plane somewhere along the route.

Dallas made a few phone calls from home, trying to locate a charter jet, but he had no luck. He would try again en route. He headed to the airport, and soon the airplane—with its precious three-passenger cargo—lifted into the sky.

The parents were too absorbed in the immediate situation to realize how concerned their pilot was. At first, Sandi hadn't been able to locate Michael. Then there had been the frantic rush to line up a flight on top of dealing with a cranky, hungry Benjamin, who couldn't eat before the surgery. Exhausted, Sandi prayed as she had done from the beginning of her baby's ordeal: "Lord, I can't put Ben through much more. If you're going to take him, do. I put him completely in Your hands." Then she fell into a much-needed sleep.

In the cockpit, however, things were not as calm. Dallas and the copilot couldn't find a charter jet for a transfer. Then Michael mentioned that Pittsburgh had informed him that Benjamin needed to be at the hospital within six hours; otherwise, the liver would go to another child. Six hours! Factoring in the time that had been lost trying to locate Michael, it all seemed even more impossible.

Worst of all were the head winds. Although the plane was flying through the air at about 270 miles per hour, the head winds had slowed its progress considerably.

They had lifted off a little after 5:00 P.M. (7:00 P.M. in Pittsburgh), and thus had less than five hours to complete a journey that, according to the pilot's calculations, would take at least seven. There was no way they could do it. Not without a miracle. Dallas put the plane on autopilot, leaned back and closed his eyes. "Father, we need help," he prayed quietly. "This child needs to get to the hospital in time."

Almost immediately, the plane began to shake. Pilot and copilot watched the ground speed indicator in disbelief. It had started to climb. Up, up it went, from 270 to an amazing 390 miles per hour, before the quivering stopped. The silence was broken by the voice of the Denver air traffic controller. "You've really picked up speed. Everything okay?"

"Great!" Dallas answered, still astonished at the wind's sudden and complete turnaround.

Pilots of larger aircraft were noticing the phenomenon, too. "What's going on?" they radioed one another. "Things are crazy tonight!" Such sudden, strong wind shifts did occur, Dallas knew, but they were extremely rare. And the chance of him being in the perfect place at the exact moment when they did was even rarer.

But there were still obstacles ahead, especially the cold front expected in Chicago. When cold air slipped under the warm air, thunderstorms would result, and the little plane would lose precious time detouring around them. Now, as they approached, they could see the front, like a gray wedge lying in the star-studded sky. Yet their radar reported no storm activity. "Father," Dallas murmured again, "You're in charge, and You know what we need."

The front got closer, closer . . . but, unbelievably, as they approached it, it had become only a thin mist, wafting gently away into the darkness. No thunderstorms. No lengthy bypass needed after all.

The plane continued its placid journey. Just two hundred miles left until Pittsburgh. By now Dallas should have stopped for refueling. However, the unusual tailwind had pushed the plane along so fast that plenty of fuel remained. They would land at Allegheny County Airport, which was closer to the hospital, rather than the congested Pittsburgh airport, but because of this, new concerns surfaced. Since the Allegheny control tower closed at midnight, there wouldn't be anyone on the ground to direct the pilots where to park the plane and tell the parents where to meet the ambulance. Finding these things could eat up priceless moments. And was it snowing in Pittsburgh? If visibility was limited, Dallas would need to make a time-consuming instrument approach to the airport, or even change airport destinations.

But once again, all the decisions seemed to have been made for them. Dallas's radio crackled with an updated weather report. Pittsburgh was clear, unrestricted. There had been no snow, after all. "Oh, and by the way," the controller casually added, "the tower is staying open until you arrive. And your ambulance is standing by at your destination."

Finally the little plane taxied to a stop and its passengers tumbled out, running toward the flashing red lights of the ambulance. "Good-bye, and thanks!" Sandi turned and waved to Dallas.

Little Ben received a new liver in Pittsburgh, and was home and healthy by Christmas. When he was two and a half, and the family had moved to the Midwest, he received an unexpected letter from Dallas. "I thought I'd wait until you were completely recovered to let you know what a special flight you were on . . . ," the letter began.

Only then did Sandi and Michael realize just what had taken place. And as Benjamin grows, they plan to tell him more about the night his Heavenly Father, some Pittsburgh surgeons and a faith-filled pilot gave him a miracle. They will explain that the plane was too small, the weather too rough, the fuel too limited . . . yet somehow, a seven-hour journey took only four and a half.

For nothing is impossible with God.

Joan Wester Anderson
Condensed from Where Wonders Prevail

9

SPECIAL MOMENTS

The quality of your life is measured by the little things.

Barbara Braham

A Doll from Santa

Alice's mother died when she was five years old. Although her nine brother and sisters were loving and caring, they were no replacement for a mother's love.

The year was 1925, and life was hard. Alice, who grew up to be my mother, told me that her family was too poor to even afford to give her a doll.

In the aftermath of her loss, Alice vowed to care for others. First, her father, then her husband, later her three children and then her grandchildren were the main focus of her life. She felt that she could make up for her sad childhood through her dedication to her own family, but an unfilled void seemed to remain.

In December 1982, I had a job at a local bank. One afternoon, we were decorating the tree in the bank lobby and singing carols, getting ready for the Christmas season. One of my customers approached me with a sample of her handiwork: beautiful handmade dolls. She was taking orders for Christmas. I decided to get one for my daughter, Katie, who was almost five years old. Then I had an idea. I asked my customer if she could make me a special doll for my mother—one with gray hair and spectacles: a grandmother doll.

The doll maker felt that this idea was certainly unique and took it on as a creative challenge. So I placed my Christmas order: two dolls, one blonde and one gray-haired for Christmas morning!

Things really started to fall into place when a friend had told me that his dad—who played Santa Claus at various charitable functions in my area—would be willing to make a visit on Christmas morning to our home to deliver my Katie her presents! Knowing that my parents would be there as well, I began to get ready for what would turn out to be one of the most memorable days of my mother's life.

Christmas Day arrived and at the planned time, so did Santa Claus. I had prepared the presents for Santa to deliver, along with one for my mother tucked into the bottom of Santa's bag. Katie was surprised and elated that Santa had come to see her at her own house, the happiest I had ever seen her in her young life.

My mother was enjoying watching her granddaughter's reaction to the visit from this special guest. As Santa turned to leave he looked once more into his knapsack and retrieved one more gift. As he asked who Alice was, my mother, taken aback by her name being called, indicated that she in fact was Alice. Santa handed her the gift, which was accompanied by a message card that read:

For Alice:

I was cleaning out my sleigh before my trip this year and came across this package that was supposed to be delivered on December 25, 1925. The present inside has aged, but I felt that you might still wish to have it. Many apologies for the lateness of the gift.
Love,
Santa Claus

My mother's reaction was one of the most profound and deeply emotional scenes I have ever witnessed. She couldn't speak but only clasped the doll she had waited fifty-seven years to receive as tears of joy coursed down her cheeks. That doll, given by "Santa," made my mother the happiest "child" alive.

Alice Ferguson

Altar Boys

When they were young, life with my two sons was what would tactfully be called "challenging." For years, broken bones, stitches, notes from the school principal, torn jeans and numerous unusual pets hidden under their beds were part of our daily family life. But sometimes I would get a comforting glimpse of the fine young men Kevin and Eric would one day become, and suddenly the world would seem right.

One such glimpse came when Kevin and Eric befriended a new boy in the neighborhood. My sons were about ten and twelve that year, and Danny was somewhere in between. Danny was an intense child, thin and slightly built. But he couldn't run and jump and climb like the rest of the neighborhood children. Danny spent his days in a wheelchair.

Although there were dozens of children for blocks around, only Kevin and Eric took the time to meet Danny and spend time playing with him. Usually, they would go around the corner to his house. And once in a while, they would help Danny navigate the streets and sidewalks and bring him to our home.

As the boys' friendship with Danny blossomed, I was gratified to see that they accepted and loved Danny without seeing him as physically limited. More than that, they realized that Danny both needed and deserved to experience, as much as possible, all the things "normal" children could enjoy.

One Saturday, several months after Danny moved into the neighborhood, Kevin and Eric asked if he could spend the night with us. My husband and I said that was fine, and we reminded them that we would attend church as usual the next morning. Danny was invited to sleep over, and to accompany us to church.

That night, the three boys had a great time playing games and watching television. When it was time for bed, my husband carried Danny upstairs to the boys' room, and we made certain he was comfortable for the night.

Dealing with a child in a wheelchair was a new and very humbling experience for us. Suddenly, a few scraped knees and broken arms seemed to be blessings—products of having healthy, active children. They were reasons to give thanks, rather than the purple hearts of parenthood we'd thought them to be.

The next day, with help from all of us, Danny was soon dressed and ready for church. Kevin and Eric helped Danny into the backseat of the station wagon, and we loaded the wheelchair into the cargo area. Once at the church, we unloaded everybody, and the boys happily wheeled Danny off to meet their friends.

At the time, our church had a rather pleasant tradition of letting the children in the congregation take turns each week being unofficial acolytes. Invariably, the children were excited when they were chosen to walk down the center aisle of the church carrying a long brass taper used to light the candles. We adults always enjoyed seeing how seriously the youngsters took their job, how slowly and tentatively they climbed the stairs to the altar and solemnly touched each candle, ever-so-lightly, until it caught flame.

After church school, we were preparing to enter the sanctuary when the minister approached us. Kevin and Eric had asked him if Danny could light the candles this week.

Concerned about the logistics of Danny navigating the stairs, the minister had tried to persuade them otherwise and had pointed out the obstacles. But my sons had insisted that Danny perform the honor, he said, and had assured him that they had figured out a plan. Wisely, the minister had given consent and left the situation in the boys' hands.

As the opening music began, I turned in my seat to see how my two unpredictable sons would make this miracle happen. Kevin and Eric stood behind the wheelchair, beaming from ear to ear. In front of them sat Danny, proudly and nervously holding the long brass rod that would set the candles blazing. Slowly walking to the music, the boys pushed the wheelchair down the aisle. Soon, all heads were turned to follow their progress. The entire congregation had just became aware of the challenge ahead: the series of steps Danny would have to climb to reach the altar.

As the wheelchair neared the altar, every breath in the room suspended. We had no idea how they were going to pull this off. Did they plan to carry that heavy wheelchair up those stairs? Would they try to pick him up and carry him? Was this fast becoming a disaster?

Kevin and Eric rolled Danny's chair to the foot of the steps and stopped. Every eye was riveted on the three boys and the wheelchair at the front of the church.

Slowly, and with a dignity beyond their years, Kevin and Eric ascended the stairs while Danny remained in his chair. Each boy grasped a candlestick and carried it back down the stairs. Reaching Danny's wheelchair, they leaned forward and offered the altar candles to their waiting friend.

Danny proudly raised the golden wand and gently lit each candle. Kevin and Eric carefully guarded the flames with cupped palms as they carried the candles back up the stairs and placed them back on the altar. Then they returned to Danny and rotated his chair to face the congregation. Slowly, they wheeled him back down the aisle.

Danny's face was a joyous thing to see. His grin blazed through the sanctuary and lit the very rafters of the church, sending a thrill through every heart. He was visibly elated and held the brass candle lighter as though it were a royal scepter. A soft glow seemed to surround the three boys as they walked to the rear of the church. I noticed it took a few minutes before the minister could trust his voice to begin the service.

I've often been proud of my sons, but seldom have I been so touched. I had to blink a bit to see their smiling faces as they passed my pew on their way to the rear of the church. But then, my eyes weren't the only ones in the congregation blurred by tears from the pageant of love we had just witnessed.

Marcy Goodfleisch

A Real Home

Her world had shattered with the divorce.

Bills, house payments, health insurance. Her part-time job provided little income and fewer benefits. With no financial support, she had finally lost the house.

At wit's end, Karen managed to rent a cramped camper at the local RV park for herself and five-year-old Joshua. It was only a little better than living out of their car, and she wished with all her heart that she could provide more for her child.

After their evening ritual of giggling over a table game and reading stories, Karen sent her son outside to play until bedtime while she agonized over the checkbook. She glanced out the window when she heard voices.

"Say, Josh, don't you wish you had a real home?" asked the campground manager.

Karen tensed and held her breath as she leaned nearer the open window. Then a smile spread across her face when she heard Joshua's response.

"We already have a real home," he said. "It's just that we don't have a house to put it in."

Carol McAdoo Rehme

"I have to warn you, there is some nudity in this book."

Rites of Passage

For some time, my fourteen-year-old son Tyler had been acting more responsibly: doing his chores without having to be told, keeping his room organized, keeping his word. I knew he was making his transition into manhood.

Memories of other turning points flooded my mind. I remembered breathing in Tyler's scent as a baby, and then one day noticing that scent had shifted, changed—my baby had become a little boy. Then I recalled the day the training wheels came off his bicycle. Another time, I'd watched wistfully as he had thrown out all of his toys, only saving a stuffed gorilla that my mother had given him when she was alive. Now another, bigger change was brewing. So, with tears welling up inside, I began to plan a rite-of-passage day for my son.

Tyler's special day began with breakfast at a restaurant. It was just Tyler, his father, stepmother, stepfather and me—no other children. He seemed so happy being with us all together for the first time by himself.

After breakfast, we all went to a heavily wooded park outside of town. I gave him a special journal created just for the day. In the weeks before the ceremony, I had written numerous questions in the journal for him to think about and answer. Questions like: Who was his hero and why? When did he feel the deepest connection to God? What gift in his life had been his favorite and why?

He had chosen several adults who were important in his life, and I had arranged for each of them to come and walk with him for about an hour over the course of the day. The adults were told that this was Tyler's time to "pick their brain," and they were asked to be as open and candid as they comfortably could.

His school principal, whom Tyler had invited to walk with him, shared his favorite prayer—the St. Francis prayer—with Tyler. This had special meaning for my son as it is the same prayer my mother read every morning of her life. She and Tyler were very close, and later he told me it almost felt as if she were there reading it to him.

As dusk began to settle, family and friends gathered for a ceremony on a dock by a lake. A brief rain had freshened the air, which held a fall chill. A tape of Indian flute music played as we sat around a dancing fire. During the ceremony, Tyler shared his intentions about his responsibility to the planet, guests publicly blessed him and we, his parents, made a verbal commitment that—from that moment on—we would hold him as a man in our hearts.

The guests had been instructed to bring nonmonetary gifts to share with Tyler. He received a box of "What I Love About Tyler" notes filled out by the guests, an acorn of a mighty oak tree, handmade pouches and more. One man read a poem aloud that he had written about his father.

During the ceremony and in the weeks following, numerous people came up to me and said, "I would be a different person today if my parents had given me the gift of a rite-of-passage ceremony." Never in my wildest dreams as a mother could I have anticipated the feelings and sacredness that my son and I experienced that day.

Things are different in our house now; there is a deeper, richer feeling of respect for each other. Frequently, before I speak to Tyler, I ask myself, "How would I say this to a man?" And Tyler seems less self-absorbed and more sensitive to how others feel.

This was clearly demonstrated several months later, when our family was planning a fun outing. It was a cold rainy day, and everyone wanted to go to play games at the arcade—except for me. I had made some feeble attempts to recommend something different, but their enthusiasm won out. I did not have the energy to stick up for myself that day.

We were walking out the door when Tyler, now a head taller than I was, came over and put his arm around my shoulders and said, "I can see that you don't really want to go to the arcade. Let's sit down and decide on something we ALL want to do. 'Cause I'm not going anywhere unless you're happy, too."

I was so surprised, I burst into tears, but they were tears of happiness. It felt wonderful to be cared for and to know that my son would be a loving husband and father to his own family someday. Yes, Tyler had become a man—a good man.

Kathryn Kvols

Cool Dude Earring

A number of years back, my six-year-old son and I had gone shopping at one of those giant discount toy stores with toys piled to the ceiling. We had just come around the corner of an aisle when I saw a young, longhaired bearded man in a wheelchair. He must have been in some terrible accident because both his legs were missing and his face was badly scarred. Just then my six-year-old saw him, too, and said in a loud voice, "Look at that man, Momma!"

I did the normal mother thing and tried to shush my son, telling him it was not polite to point; but my son gave a hard tug, broke free from my hand and went running down the aisle to the man in the wheelchair. He stood right in front of him and said in a loud voice, "What a cool dude earring, man! Where did you get such a neat earring?"

The young man broke into a grin that lit up his face. He was so taken aback by the compliment that he just glowed with happiness, and the two of them stood there talking awhile about his earring and other "cool stuff." It made a lifelong impression on me.

For I had seen only a horribly scarred man in a wheelchair, but my six-year-old saw a man with a cool dude
earring.

The Editors of Conari Press
From the book, More Random Acts of Kindness

Children Speak to God

The following letters express that part of a child's world reserved for special thoughts and wishes. Some letters are disarmingly wise, others naïve; some are knowing, some simple. Many are weighted with seriousness; others are lit with smiles. All of them are addressed to God with much hope and trust.

Dear GOD,

In school they told us what you do. Who does it when you are on vacation?

—Jane

Dear GOD,

Is it true my father won't get in Heaven if he uses his bowling words in the house?

—Anita

Dear GOD,

Did you mean for the giraffe to look like that or was it an accident?

—Norma

Dear GOD,

Instead of letting people die and having to make new ones, why don't you just keep the ones you have now?

—Jane

Dear GOD,

Who draws the lines around the countries?

—Nan

Dear GOD,

Did you really mean "do unto others as they do unto you"? Because if you did, then I'm going to fix my brother!

—Darla

Dear GOD,

Thank you for the baby brother, but what I prayed for was a puppy.

—Joyce

Dear GOD,

Please send me a pony. I never asked for anything before, you can look it up.

—Bruce

Dear GOD,

If you watch me in church Sunday, I'll show you my new shoes.

—Mickey

Dear GOD,

We read Thomas Edison made light. But in school they said you did it. So I bet he stoled your idea.

Sincerely, Donna

Dear GOD,

I bet it is very hard for you to love all of everybody in the whole world. There are only four people in our family and I can never do it.

—Nan

Compiled by Stuart Hample and Eric Marshall

A Red Rose for Richard

"Mom, why do just the girls get flowers?" my son asked in the car. We were driving home from the first performance of his fifth-grade musical, a coveted rite of passage for the elementary students who were graduating to middle school.

I thought back to earlier that evening, how I had beamed at my son from the second row as he spoke his lines from memory perfectly and how, after the performance, I had hurried backstage. For once, Richard didn't shun my open affection: a big bear hug. Yet he was distracted by the bouquets of roses and carnations lavished on all the girls and the female teachers. Somehow, the tradition seemed a little unfair to him—he wouldn't mind getting a few flowers himself.

"I don't really know why it's that way," I answered him.

As we continued the drive home and the excitement of the evening wore off, I settled into a habitual train of thought: fretting. As an overloaded single mother, I often felt I wasn't up to meeting my son's needs. The musical's final performance—the most important one—was scheduled for a morning, and I absolutely could not get off work that day. My job was sixteen miles away, and I had back-to-back meetings and scheduled appointments.

When I kissed Richard good-bye on the morning of the final performance, I told him for what must have been the hundredth time: "I wish I could be there today, Honey."

He smiled. "It's okay, Mom. I understand. Honest!"

He was trying to be stoic, and I tried to convince myself that it was okay. After all, I had been able to see two of his performances—that should be enough. I was trying my best. So why didn't I feel good about it? My resentment at having to be at work that morning must have shown; my assistant and secretary figured out why I was so glum. "We'll help you reschedule your appointments," they offered. "We'll make it work."

And before I knew what was happening, I was speeding down the road toward the school. As I zipped past a grocery store, with only five minutes to spare, I impulsively pulled into the parking lot. I ran inside the store, quickly reemerging with a single red rose.

When I finally arrived inside the school, the gym was packed to standing room only. Friends in the last row scooted aside to make room for one more. Just as I squeezed into the seat, the lights dimmed and the curtains opened. There was Richard, center stage. I was sure he did not know that I was in the audience.

When the curtain opened the last time to reveal the entire cast, I quickly located my son on a middle row of risers. He looked out over the audience, not seeming to focus. Then suddenly, his gaze turned in my direction. His whole face lit up, and he smiled so radiantly that the women sitting on either side of me gasped, then excitedly exclaimed in unison, "He sees you! He sees you!"

Afterwards, I pushed my way up through the crowd to meet Richard in the wings, my heart still thumping from the loving intensity of that beaming smile, and thrust forward the red rose. Richard didn't say much, but I thought he was pleased. By the time I got back to work, I felt peaceful. Maybe I wasn't doing such a bad job of parenting after all.

A year passed, a difficult, tiring year that pushed out of my mind any sense of peace and accomplishment as Richard's mother. I finished my master's degree by commuting to a graduate program 160 miles away, yet the new career I had anticipated didn't materialize. I plodded along in the same position, burned out and overwhelmed with responsibility. My plate was too full, and I knew it, and I feared the one thing I cared about most, my son, was suffering because of it. Was I giving my son everything he needed?

One evening, I rushed from work to a meeting at Richard's school, arriving fifteen minutes late. I still hadn't quite figured out what the meeting was about when it adjourned. As I stood up to leave, Richard's resource teacher gently touched me on the arm, urging me to stay.

"I think you should have this," she said. "Normally we don't allow parents to review the completed testing, but this is what Richard wrote for the essay component. I'm a mother, and I know that if my son wrote this, I'd want to take it home." She handed me an essay with Richard's name on it:

The Best Day I Ever Had
by Richard Irwin-Miller

The best day I ever had in school was in the fifth grade. We worked for months on a musical. We did the musical seven times. The last time was my favorite. It was a performance during school. I really wanted my mom to come to see it and

*to bring me a rose, but she said she had to go to work, so I
didn't ask her. In the musical, there were three acts. I was in
the first one. Then I had to go backstage and wait until the
end, come back out with everyone and sing a song. Well, I finished my act. Then I came out to do the last song and saw my
mother. I was very happy. At the end of the last song, she
came up and gave me a red rose.*

My tears threatened to spill over the page. I wanted to
give my son everything, and what I actually had to offer
him was far less than that: stolen moments, rushed meals,
brief hugs and kisses at bedtime, a single rose. But I loved
Richard, and he loved me, and that made it all more than
enough. That made it the best.

Earle Irwin

Mother's Christmas Stocking

My sister Trudy and I snuggled close and giggled at our predicament. We were too big to fit *under* the Christmas tree, especially with all the piles of presents, so we slept *around* the Christmas tree instead. Actually we were more in the middle of our mobile home's modest living room floor. But it was tradition—we just had to sleep under the tree on Christmas Eve—even if we were ten and twelve. My eight-year-old brother, Ashley, was already asleep. He had pretended to be too grown-up to be excited about sleeping on the living room floor. And being the lowest in the pecking order, he had been assigned the spot farthest from the tree—squashed between an older sister and the coffee table that was pushed to the side to make more room.

Trudy was the most likely to have her head between brightly wrapped boxes with fragrant cedar boughs scratching against her cheek. I was happy to be protected on both sides by warm bodies, and of course Breanna, our three-year-old baby sister, was given the safest and most comfortable spot of all. Breanna was sleeping soundly, curled on the couch hugging an oversized teddy bear.

Trudy and I lay whispering to each other, discussing what we expected to get in our stockings the next morning and guessing what was in each of our already well-shaken packages. We gazed at the four flannel stockings hanging limply by the fireplace, and we realized that one was missing. *Weren't there five people in our family? How come Mommy didn't have a stocking?*

She had told us that when she was a little girl her family didn't hang stockings on Christmas Eve because they were a "no-nonsense family." We were glad our family was a "nonsense" family, and we figured Mommy deserved to be a part of the tradition she had created for us. It was then that an idea hatched between us that would forever change the way we would see Christmas and, more importantly, giving.

Quickly Trudy woke Breanna, and I hurried to wake Ashley. Trudy piled our pillows to one side and smoothed out the quilt for us to have our conference. Her enthusiasm sparked our own. Amidst smothered giggles and excited exclamations of "Oh—yes," and "That would be perfect," we planned Mother's stocking. For several minutes we scattered to go on a treasure hunt through our possessions, returning with only our very best. Now began the task of assessing their potential significance to Mother.

Breanna brought her candy box. We picked through the half-sucked peppermint sticks and found a handful of unwrapped Santa chocolates and a mammoth fruit-striped candy cane. Trudy suggested we write explanations on Post-It notes and stick one on each gift. I wrote in neat, rounded letters, "For your sweet cravings," and pressed it on Breanna's carefully wrapped, but crinkled, package of chocolates. We put this into the toe of an old, oversized, red wool sock Ashley found in the coat closet and stuck the candy cane inside so that the neck hooked over the side.

Ashley brought two of his favorite toy cars and told us they were for when Mommy's car broke down. Now she would always have two extras. Trudy wrote the explanation for him.

I brought a package of cabbage seeds and wrote around the packet edge, "So you will always have fresh seeds of Inspiration." I put the packet in a small terra-cotta pot that I had painted at school and slid it into the red stocking on top of the toy cars.

Trudy crafted a little creature out of a round river rock the size of a hazelnut. She painted face features, glued wiggly eyes, wrapped it in a miniature plaid blanket and wrote a set of tiny adoption papers for "Herman Periwinkle." That was so Mommy would always have a baby, because she often complained that her real baby was growing up too fast.

After adding a few loose coins, pretty bird feathers and a small peach-scented sachet for good measure, we hung Mom's sock on the highest nail and left Trudy's stocking on top of the wood box. Then we stepped back to admire the lumpy sock—only one thing was missing. Trudy climbed back up on the wood box and safety-pinned a note to the outside of the sock that said, "To: Mother Santa Claus—From: The T.A.A.B. Elves." She was proud of her acronym for our names, and we were all so excited we could hardly sleep.

In the morning, we rushed right past our now-bulging stockings, straight into Mom's bedroom. In our excitement we forgot to knock and tumbled, yelling "Merry Christmas!" onto her bed. Mother was sitting up against the headboard, her treasures spread about her, and tears running down her face. She was holding Herman Periwinkle. When she looked up at us, she smiled her biggest smile and formed the words "Thank you," though they were too soft to be audible.

We clambered over each other to get to her, and she kissed us all and hugged us, laughing and crying at the same time. It was so unlike her usual calm manner. But we understood. It was her first-ever Christmas stocking.

Amberley Howe

THE FAMILY CIRCUS   By Bil Keane

"Could you keep your eyes shut, and wrap this, Mommy? It's for you from me."

10

LETTING GO

To live in hearts we leave behind is not to die.

Thomas Campbell

The Girl Who Loved Cats and Flowers

Those who love deeply never grow old; they may die of old age, but they die young.

Arthur Wing Pinero

Early in the autumn of 1984, my mother—for no apparent reason—began writing down the story of her life. An energetic woman in her seventies, she laughingly referred to it as "my book" and her desire to put down her thoughts and memories became something of a minor obsession.

Once she turned down a dinner invitation, telling me she had to work on her book. I laughed and asked her where the fire was.

The fire, as it turned out, was inside her. She finished her book in early December. Three days after Christmas, her cancer was discovered, and three months later she was dead.

From my mother's book: *I have loved family, friends, nature, animals, music and many other things. It will be hard to say goodbye to those I love and to the beauty in the world.*

I read these words for the first time surrounded by

packing crates in my mother's apartment, a month after her death. I tried to picture her face as I read the words, but the memories of the last two months as she lay dying were too painful. I closed her book wondering if I would ever feel healed enough to open it again.

On a rainy Sunday afternoon one year from the day my mother entered the hospital, I suddenly knew the time had come to remember and honor her life—and her death. I knew also that it was time to make my peace, if I could, with the loss of the most important influence in my life.

For a month I pored over the notebook I had kept during her hospitalization and, of course, my mother's book. When I was finished, I realized that my mother was no longer lost to me; in some new and different way I had regained her.

From my notes, dated January 21, 1985: *My mother continues to amaze me. Despite what is happening to her body—the disease is cutting off one function after another, a new loss every day—she continues to appreciate nature and the small bits of life she can observe from Room 235. There is a large magnolia framed by her window, and she enjoys watching the birds busily flying in and out of it.*

Her pain is awesome; she can no longer sit up. Today is her grandson's birthday, and somehow she managed to write a note to him. One day I will tell him of the unimaginable amount of effort his grandmother put into writing this note.

One warm day in February—a day when the smell of the earth seemed to rise up to meet you, promising all sorts of things—I cracked open the window in her room. The soft, scented air spilled in, causing my mother to open her eyes and ask, "Is the grass beginning to grow?"

It was a joke between us. I closed my eyes and a memory ran across the years to meet me: *I am five years old and have crept out of the house in the middle of a summer night to watch the grass and flowers in our garden grow. Suddenly my mother is at my side. Instead of sending me back to bed, she joins me. I have never been up so late before, and the sense of adventure is high. We sit there together in white, wooden lawn chairs, listening to the cicadas making whirring noises in the trees.*

"Look," she says, pointing to a shooting star, its light piercing the bruised blue sky. But I am looking at the light in her eyes and her long, black hair, which is a spill of ink against the approaching dawn. Later I fall asleep with my head in her lap.

I remember the day my mother asked that I write a last message from her to each member of the family. "It will make them feel better," she told me.

I wrote through my tears, aware that while my mother had accepted her impending death, I hadn't. I was still trying to figure out how to get her on her feet again, to get her home. She saw my struggle and, as usual, waited for me to catch up with her.

I recall with extreme clarity the night I broke through my denial of her condition.

From my notes—January 26, 1985: *The radiation treatments, combined with the painkillers, are finally beginning to give her some relief. Slowly I am giving up hope that my mother will ever be the way she was. I think she is going to die.*

Over the next few days, my mother wanted to talk about her life, to hold the past like a globe and spin it around until all her memories were allowed to come into full view.

And so we began our long, final conversation, adding pieces to the puzzle of memory until, finally, a picture of a life emerged from the stories that spilled out. And as we talked, and the picture of my mother's life grew stronger, so did she. Not in any physical way, of course, but in a way that had to do with her being a *person* and not just a *patient.*

From my mother's book: *I haven't forgotten what it's like to be young—all the hopes and anxieties and the overwhelming sensation that everything you do is going to advance or wreck your life. No in-betweens when you're young.*

My ambition was to go on the stage. My sister and I took danc-ing lessons and practiced the intricate steps holding on to the back of a chair. In those days I thought I'd be a famous actress! It was all a dream, of course.

Lying in the hospital, my mother had other dreams. One morning she awoke, convinced she had just seen a man fall from the roof. All that day her thoughts were of falling. Would I catch her when she fell?

"Don't be afraid," I reassured her. "Of course I'll catch you. For all those years when I was growing up, you caught me. Now it's my turn."

Her face relaxed under the oxygen mask, and she closed her eyes. *For as long as I can,* I thought, *I will catch you.* But I knew there would come a time—and soon—when I would have to let go.

And so would she.

On a particularly beautiful winter day, five days before she died, we watched in silence as the afternoon light glanced off the side of a red-brick building opposite her window. The wind was tossing the branches of a young beech tree while the sun silvered the promising red buds that already swelled with life at the tip of each branch.

"Close the curtains," she said, looking away sadly from the beauty that seemed both insolent and innocent in its indifference to her suffering. She closed her eyes, retreat-ing from the play of light and life that was not her world anymore.

Without knowing why, I began taking home her clothes that night.

From my notes, March 1, 1985: *She is very weak and her breathing is irregular. But her spirit is still connected to the world. When I held the pot of jonquils close to her, she said delightedly, "Oh, that's so pretty! Isn't it wonderful how life goes on?"*

*She wanted to talk about the family, especially her grand-
children. "Don't let anything happen to their characters," she told
me over and over again.*

That next-to-last day of my mother's life, one of her
grandsons showed up at her bedside. She had been hearing music for the last few days, she told him. A choir
singing. "Do you hear it?"

Her grandson gently lowered his head next to hers, listening in silence. Then he straightened up. "I think I hear
it, too," he said evenly, his eyes filled with the life-light
that was fading from hers.

For the rest of the afternoon, she wavered between con-
sciousness and disorientation. As it grew dark outside, my
mother stared out of the window into the blackness.

"What are you looking at?" I asked her.

"Nothing," she replied.

"Well," I said, "look at *me*."

More than anything else, I wanted her last conscious
moments to be spent looking at the face of someone who
loved her.

The summer after my mother died, when the first
brilliant-yellow lily appeared, I ran into the house to telephone my mother with the news. Then I remembered.
Even now, I keep thinking of things I ought to tell her,
things I want to ask her. She had a way of giving perspective to my life; of reminding me that I was building my life
on the foundation of those who had come before me and
that it was my duty to give that past to my children for
their future.

From my mother's book: *When I turned seventy someone
asked me how it felt to have arrived at such an age. Well, even
though my body isn't the same, I am still the same. I will always
be the girl who loved cats and flowers and raced home from school
to practice my dancing lessons. Inside I am still that person.*

I miss that person.

Alice Steinbach

Missing Pa

To love is to receive a glimpse of heaven.

Karen Sunde

One day my four-year-old son, Sam, told me that he'd seen his baby-sitter crying because she'd broken up with her boyfriend. "She was sad," he explained to me. He sat back in his car seat and sighed. "I've never been sad," Sam added. "Not ever."

It was true. Sam's life was happy—in no small part because of his relationship with my father. Pa Hood was more than a grandfather to him. As Sam eagerly told everyone—they were best buddies.

Once Sam and I watched the movie *Anne of Green Gables.* In the scene when Anne wishes aloud for a bosom friend, Sam sat up and declared, "That's me and Pa—bosom friends forever and ever."

My father described their relationship the same way. When I went out of town one night a week to teach, it was Pa in his red pickup truck who'd meet Sam at school and take him back to his house. There they'd play pirates and knights and Robin Hood.

They even dressed alike: pocket T-shirts, baseball caps and jeans. They had special restaurants they frequented, playgrounds where they were regulars, and toy stores where Pa allowed Sam to race up and down the aisles on motorized cars.

Sam had even memorized my father's phone number and called him every morning and night. "Pa," he would ask, clutching the phone, "can I call you ten hundred more times?" Pa always said yes and answered the phone every time with equal delight.

Then my father became ill. In the months that he was in the hospital with lung cancer, I worried about how Sam would react to Pa's condition: the bruises from the needles, the oxygen tubes, his weakened body. When I explained to Sam that seeing Pa so sick might scare him, Sam was surprised. "He's my Pa," he said. "He could never scare me."

Later I watched adults approach my father's hospital bed with trepidation, unsure of what to say or do. But Sam, undaunted by the medical apparatus and the changes in Pa's appearance, knew exactly what was right: hugs and jokes, as always.

"Are you coming home soon?" he'd ask.

"I'm trying," Pa would tell him.

When my dad died, everything changed for Sam and me. Not wanting to confront the questions and feelings my father's death raised, I kept my overwhelming sadness at bay. When well-meaning people asked how I was doing, I'd give them a short answer and swiftly change the subject.

Sam was different, however. For him, wondering aloud was the best way to understand.

"So," he'd say, settling in his car seat, "Pa's in space, right?" Or, pointing at a stained-glass window in church, he'd ask, "Is one of those angels Pa?"

"Where's heaven?" Sam asked right after my father died.

"No one knows exactly," I said. "Lots of people think it's in the sky."

"No," Sam said, shaking his head, "it's very far away. Near Cambodia."

"When you die," he asked on another afternoon, "you disappear, right? And when you faint, you only disappear a little. Right?"

I thought his questions were good. The part I had trouble with was what he always did afterward: He'd look me right in the eye with more hope than I could stand and wait for my approval or correction or wisdom. But in this matter, my fear and ignorance were so large that I'd grow dumb in the face of his innocence.

Remembering Sam's approach to my father's illness, I began to watch his approach to grief. At night, he'd press his face against his bedroom window and cry, calling out into the darkness, "Pa, I love you! Sweet dreams!" Then, after his tears stopped, he'd climb into bed, somehow satisfied, and sleep. I, however, would wander the house all night, not knowing how to mourn.

One day in the supermarket parking lot, I caught sight of a red truck like my father's. For an instant I forgot he had died. My heart leapt as I thought, *Dad's here!*

Then I remembered and succumbed to an onslaught of tears. Sam climbed onto my lap and jammed himself between me and the steering wheel.

"You miss Pa, don't you?" he asked.

I managed to nod.

"Me, too. But you have to believe he's with us, Mommy," he said. "You have to believe that, or what will we ever do?"

Too young to attach to a particular ideology, Sam was simply dealing with grief and loss by believing that death does not really separate us from those we love. I couldn't show him heaven on a map or explain the course a soul might travel. But he'd found his own way to cope.

Recently while I was cooking dinner, Sam sat by himself at the kitchen table, quietly coloring in his Spiderman coloring book.

"I love you, too," he said.

I laughed and turned to face him, saying, "You only say, 'I love you, too' after someone says 'I love you' first."

"I know," Sam said. "Pa just said, 'I love you, Sam,' and I said, 'I love you, too.'" He kept coloring.

"Pa just talked to you?" I asked.

"Oh, Mommy," Sam said, "he tells me he loves me every day. He tells you, too. You're just not listening."

Again, I have begun to take Sam's lead. I have begun to listen.

Ann Hood

The Pencil Box

I was deep in thought at my office, preparing a lecture to be given that evening at a college across town, when the phone rang. A woman I had never met introduced herself and said that she was the mother of a seven-year-old and that she was dying. She said that her therapist had advised her that discussing her pending death with her son would be too traumatic for him, but somehow that didn't feel right to her.

Knowing that I worked with grieving children, she asked my advice. I told her that our heart is often smarter than our brain and that I thought she knew what would be best for her son. I also invited her to attend the lecture that night since I was speaking about how children cope with death. She said she would be there.

I wondered later if I would recognize her at the lecture, but my question was answered when I saw a frail woman being half-carried into the room by two adults. I talked about the fact that children usually sense the truth long before they are told and that they often wait until they feel adults are ready to talk about it before sharing their concerns and questions. I said that children usually can handle truth better than denial, even though the denial is intended to protect them from pain. I said that respecting children meant including them in the family sadness, not shutting them out.

She had heard enough. At the break, she hobbled to the podium and through her tears she said, "I knew it in my heart. I just knew I should tell him." She said that she would tell him that night.

The next morning I received another phone call from her. She could hardly talk, but I managed to hear the story through her choked voice. She had awakened him when they got home the night before and quietly said, "Derek, I have something to tell you."

He quickly interrupted her, saying, "Oh, Mommy, is it now that you are going to tell me that you are dying?"

She held him close, and they both sobbed while she said, "Yes."

After a few minutes, the little boy wanted down. He said that he had something for her that he had been saving. In the back of one of his drawers was a dirty pencil box. Inside the box was a letter written in simple scrawl. It said, "Good-bye, Mom. I will always love you."

How long he had been waiting to hear the truth, I don't know. I do know that two days later the young mother died. In her casket was placed a dirty pencil box and a letter.

Doris Sanford

Cards for Mom

I'd lost my dad three years earlier, and my mom was visiting for what I suspected would be the last time. We still were hoping that there'd be a rally. We thought she might be able to beat brain cancer the way she'd beaten lung cancer, but we weren't nearly as confident.

My "white tornado" of a mother—so named because the cleaning product ad reminded us of her whirlwind energy—was suddenly weak. She was becoming accepting instead of being the defiant warrior we'd observed during her first battle with cancer. I recognized the signs of impending death because I'd too recently been through it with Dad.

Mom pulled a box from her suitcase just before she left and she handed it to me, asking me not to open it for a few months. I knew what that meant, and I braved out the next few hours with her, only cracking as she drove away. The tears seemed to flow from then until Christmas Eve. The call that she was gone came just as we were leaving to drive the seven hours to be by her side. I'd seen her many times since she'd left the box for me. We'd talked about everything but what was really happening.

The week of Christmas passed in a blur. My sisters and I all tried to salvage the holiday for our children even as we were coming to terms with the fact that we no longer would be able to lean on the strength of our parents.

I'd been home from the funeral for several weeks before I even remembered the box . . . a few more weeks before I could bring myself to open it. I steeled myself with a cup of tea (the panacea used by all Scottish girls) and sat cross-legged on the floor to open the battered blue file box that my mother had left to me.

To my surprise, the box was full of greeting cards. My mother, the same one who'd incurred my wrath as a teenager for indiscriminately throwing out my treasures, had saved every single card we'd ever sent to her. The card on top was a recent one, a get-well card from her time in the hospice, received while she'd been fighting her first cancer. It was from my sister. Inside my mother had written her own note to us about how much it had meant to her that we'd been there for her and with her. Her spidery writing reached out to me from the card and made me cry.

I dug to the middle of the box and came up with an anniversary card from another sister who had been sixteen when it was sent. My heart skipped as I saw that there was another note written from Mom inside, in a bolder hand: "Hen, I'm looking at you and Terry and feeling so proud of what a beautiful woman you're becoming. Seeing you with your first boyfriend makes me look forward to the day when I'm sending you anniversary cards, too."

Mom's reserved Scottish upbringing kept her from lavishing praise out loud, yet every card, from the fanciest store-bought ones to the crudest childish drawings, was etched with my mom's hopes and dreams for us. More than that, these were the words she rarely expressed to us in life. She was proud of us. She loved us. She thought we were wonderful. We'd always known these things, but in her urgency to see us succeed and surpass her goals for us, more often she'd push and nag us.

I could see evidence of her own tears on the card that was signed by her first grandchild. I read of her joy as each of us married the men who would become the sons of her heart. I laughed as she shared her worries for us in a voice I could hear as clearly as if she were standing next to me. I was suddenly hungry to see my own cards. I quickly found one. Reading it, I began to sob. I reached for another . . . and another. Over and over, my mom told me I was beautiful and smart and funny. She wrote about how much it meant to her that I chose cards that were so beautiful and then put my own lovely words on them. She told me she wished she could express herself as well as I could.

In the months that followed, I wished I could have told her that the way she had expressed herself on all those cards would help her four daughters through some of the hardest days of their lives. And that she'd left behind a more lasting legacy than anything else she could have done.

The blue box is much lighter now that I've given the appropriate cards to each of my sisters, but there's a new layer forming. After each holiday, every card that I receive is put into the box with my own heartfelt message—and the vow that I'll say those words out loud as often as I can.

Even so, I will leave my own stack of cards behind so they can buoy up my dear ones when I'm gone, and keep my love for them alive . . . the way my mother's cards have for me.

Mary Ann Christie

Johnny and Jenny Wren

"Ooooooffff," I exhaled softly as I swung my legs over the edge of the bed. Could it be possible that every muscle in my body ached all at the same time? Gardener's muscles, that's what Mom called them. If she'd known how sore I was, I'd have been in for a scolding. "Lift with your legs, not with your back!" she'd told me more times than I could count.

But there'd be no lectures on lifting from Mom, I thought sadly. My heart ached with the familiar feeling I'd had since the morning a few weeks ago when my sister called with the news that Mom had died instantly and suddenly from a simple fall . . . a tiny misstep on the stairs in her own house.

In shock and grief, I'd rushed from my home, husband and child in Iowa, back to my childhood home in Pennsylvania, and spent the next weeks with my sisters and father. United in disbelief and sadness, we were busy with the rites of death. The busyness got us through our days and exhausted us to sleep at night; there was no time to indulge the grief, just getting through it was all we could do.

But now I was back in Iowa, and it seemed there was

nothing but time to feel the emptiness and ache of losing Mom. It was a Sunday morning. I would have been on the phone with her right then, cup of coffee in hand, discussing the week's events with her. Most of the talk would have been about our gardens. Gardening and the love of nature was something she and I had shared from the days of my toddlerhood, when I was granted a small section of the family garden to cultivate as I pleased. I learned all the rudiments of backyard agriculture at her knee, often *on* our knees, elbow-deep in fresh garden earth. The names of trees, plants, birds and animals all passed from mother to daughter in easy communion in the garden.

After I was married and had a family with my own home and gardens, each Sunday we'd talk to each other as we gazed out our windows, inventorying the birds at the garden feeders and the butterflies on the blooms.

But today there'd be no phone call. Only stiff muscles and the hollow feeling of being a motherless child. "Oh, Mom . . . ," I whispered.

Almost absentmindedly, I studied the landscape. The new green leaves on the oak and hickory trees fluttered in the spring breeze. With quiet surprise, I realized that the uppermost branches of a redbud tree had grown tall enough to be directly outside my second-story bedroom window.

It was a special tree to me. Mom and Dad had bought it for us when they visited the year after we'd built our house. Then a funny, unexpected little thought, almost like a whisper, popped into my head: "Why, that branch is so sturdy, I could hang a birdhouse from it."

I went out to the screened porch and pulled a little yellow birdhouse with a barn-red roof off the shelf. The next thing I knew, I was out in the yard behind the house, up on a ladder with my nightgown whipping in the wind. I hung the little birdhouse from a branch, facing southeast, like Mom had always taught. Then I ran back into the house and gazed out the bedroom window. Perfect! It was directly across from the window, tilting just so, providing me with a full view of the hole. "I wonder if I'll get any takers?" I mused, hopefully. The rest of the day I found myself making excuses to be in the bedroom, looking for any feathered visitors.

The next morning I was awakened by a warbling so loud it sounded as if it was on my pillow. I bolted up in bed and checked the birdhouse. Sitting on top was a little wren, singing its heart out and bouncing all around the redbud branches, as if to say, "Yahoo, I'll take it!" My heart soared in delight.

For the next week, my mornings always started at the crack of dawn with a loud serenade from my busy friend. My curiosity drove me to my bird books, and I learned that my bird buddy was a male who was looking for a mate. This particular male—Johnny Wren, as I called him—was the avian equivalent of a girl-crazy teenage boy with a bright yellow and barn-red hotrod. "Hey, Baby, check it out. Dig my house. Hey, Sweetie, what's your sign?" he seemed to relentlessly warble to any Jenny Wren within half a mile.

I began to root for him. "Go, Johnny, go!" I'd call out upon awakening to his love song every morning. My husband and daughter thought I was nuts but were thrilled to see me feeling some happiness again.

Within the week, I got to witness Johnny's first big date. A Jenny flew to the little house and began to examine it. Johnny perched on a branch above it and loudly extolled the virtues of his house, his manhood and his deep desire to wed her. Johnny's song now outshone the greatest Puccini aria as Jenny carefully investigated the interior of the house, the outside, the leafy branches around it. They fluttered about each other.

I knew Johnny's offer was accepted when Jenny flew to

a nearby woodpile, tore off a stem and returned to the house to stuff it in.

For the next several weeks I spent a lot of time at that window watching Johnny and Jenny Wren build their nest, lay their tiny eggs and raise a brood of wren nestlings. I watched the nestlings flutter away to start their own lives somewhere in our woods. I marveled at the miracle of it; I reveled in the magic of it. I celebrated the little cycle of life manifesting right outside my window in Mom's redbud tree.

It would be just like Mom to have sent Johnny and Jenny to me. The charm of their birdie lives simply lived was a wake-up call, a summons back to the larger cycles within my own life. And though I missed my wren friends over the winter, their magic lingered. As the months passed, I began to feel whole again.

The next spring I cleaned out my birdhouses to encourage my friends' return for another season. When I pulled out Johnny and Jenny's tidy nest, I held it for a moment and smiled, remembering the events of the previous summer.

I received a special surprise when I pulled out another nest from a birdhouse in a neighboring cedar. I noticed a shred of charred paper entwined in the sticks and straw. No doubt it was a bit of unburned trash the birds had plucked from the bin. Curious, I tugged at the scrap and straightened it out. It was a fragment of an old, shredded telephone bill. Suddenly, I gasped. There was Mom's phone number.

Of course, I saved that nest. Like Johnny and Jenny, it's an uncanny reminder that Mom and I are still connected. I consider it a gentle nudge from my first and best teacher, to tell me that, just like our gardens, life goes on.

Holly Manon Moore

Chocolate-Covered Cherries

[EDITORS' NOTE: *This Christmas letter was sent to friends and family along with a box of chocolate-covered cherries.*]

What a terrible way to spend Christmas! My oldest son, Cameron, had been diagnosed with acute myeloblastic leukemia the previous June. After a harrowing ride in a military helicopter to Walter Reed Hospital, three rounds of horrendous chemotherapy, an excruciating lung resection, and a disappointing bone marrow search, we were at Duke University Hospital. Cameron had undergone a cord blood transplant, a last-ditch effort to save his life, in early December. Now, here it was Christmas Eve.

Spending Christmas in the small room on Ward 9200 seemed strange—so different from our usual holiday setting at home. We had always spent weeks on our favorite holiday project: baking cookies. Now the cookies were sent from family and friends, since I tried to spend all my time with Cameron, helping to ease the long, tedious hours. He had been in isolation for weeks, because the chemotherapy and drugs they used to make his new bone marrow engraft left him with no immune system. When presents had arrived in the mail, we hadn't waited for Christmas, but had opened them immediately—anything to create a bright moment in that dull and painful time.

Always in the past, 6:00 P.M. on Christmas Eve was the "Magic Hour." This was the time when everyone in my family, in Iowa, Wisconsin, California and Washington, D.C., opened our presents. We all did this at exactly the same time, somehow bringing the family together, even though we lived so far apart. Cameron's father, step-mother, sister and brother also opened presents at their house at that time.

This year, the Magic Hour would find just Cameron and me in a small, almost-bare hospital room, since most decorations weren't allowed in the sterile environment.

We sat together, listening to the drone of the HEPA filter and the beeping of the six infusion pumps hooked to a catheter in his heart, as Cameron waited until 6:00 P.M. . . . exactly, to open the few presents I had saved aside for him. He insisted we follow this small tradition, to create some semblance of normalcy—all of which had been abruptly abandoned six months earlier. I watched him open the presents. His favorite was a Hug Me Elmo toy that said, "I love you," when you squeezed it.

All too quickly, Christmas was over. Or so I thought.

Cameron carefully reached over the side of his hospital bed and handed me a small green box. It was wrapped beautifully, obviously by a gift store, with perfect edges and a folded piece of ribbon held down with a gold embossed sticker.

Surprised, I said, "For me?"

"Mom, it wouldn't be Christmas unless you have something to unwrap, too," he replied.

For a moment, I was speechless. Finally I asked, "But, how did you get this? Did you ask a nurse to run down to the gift store?"

Cameron leaned back in his bed, and gave me his most devilish smile. "Nope. Yesterday, when you went home for a few hours to take a shower, I sneaked downstairs."

"CAMERON! You aren't supposed to leave the floor! You know you're susceptible to almost any germ. They let you leave the ward?"

"Nope!" His smile was even bigger now. "They weren't looking. I just walked out."

This was no small feat, because since the cord blood transplant, Cameron had grown weaker. He could barely walk, and certainly not unassisted. It took every ounce of strength just to cruise the small ward halls, pushing the heavy IV pole hung with medication and a pain pump. How could he possibly have made it nine floors to the gift store?

"Don't worry, Mom. I wore my mask, and I used the cane. Man, they really chewed me out when I got back. I couldn't sneak back in, since they'd been looking for me."

I couldn't look up. I held the box even tighter now and had already started to cry.

"Open it! It's not much, but it wouldn't be Christmas if you didn't have something from me to unwrap."

I opened the box of gift-store-wrapped chocolate-covered cherries. "They are your favorite, right?" he asked hopefully.

I finally looked at my poor eighteen-year-old baby. Cameron had begun all this suffering almost immediately after his high school graduation. Did he know how much he was teaching me about what being a family really meant? "Oh, absolutely my favorite!"

Cameron chuckled a little bit, "See, we still have our tra-ditions—even in here."

"Cameron, this is the best present I've ever received . . . ever," I told him, and I meant every word. "Let's start a new tradition. Every Christmas, let's only give each other a box of chocolate-covered cherries, and we'll reminisce about the year we spent Christmas at Duke University Hospital battling leukemia. We'll remember how horrible it all was and how glad we are that it is finally over."

We made that pact right then and there, as we shared the box of chocolate-covered cherries. What a wonderful way to spend Christmas!

Cameron died two months later, after two unsuccessful cord blood transplants. He was so brave—never giving in, never giving up. This will be my first Christmas without him and the first Christmas without something from him to unwrap.

This is my gift to you. A box of chocolate-covered cherries. And when you open it, I hope it will remind you what the holidays are really about . . . being with your friends and family . . . recreating traditions, maybe starting some new ones . . . but most of all—love.

What a beautiful way to spend Christmas.

Dawn Holt

I'll Make You a Rainbow

There is nothing that can truly prepare you to lose your own child. Looking back, I've often thought the doctors should have written a death certificate for me as well as my son, for when he died a part of me died, too.

Andy was almost twelve. For over three years he had been battling cancer. He'd gone through radiation and chemotherapy; he'd gone into remission and out again, not once but several times. I was amazed at his resilience; he just kept getting up each time his cancer knocked him flat. Perhaps it was his pluckiness and grit that shaped my own attitude about Andy's future, or maybe I was simply afraid to face the possibility of his death; whatever the cause I always thought that Andy would make it. He would be the kid who beat the odds.

For three summers, Andy had gone to a camp for kids with cancer. He loved it and seemed to relish the week he could forget about hospitals and sickness and just be a kid again. The day after he returned from his third camp adventure, we went to the clinic for a routine checkup. The news was bad. The doctor scheduled a bone marrow transplant for two days later in a hospital three hundred miles away from our home. The next day we threw our things in a suitcase and left.

One of the things I tossed into my suitcase was the present Andy had brought home from camp for me. A plastic suncatcher shaped like a rainbow with a suction cup to attach it to a window. Like most mothers, I considered any present from my child a treasure and wanted it with me.

We arrived at the hospital and began the grueling ordeal the doctors felt was my son's only chance. We spent seven weeks there. They turned out to be the last seven weeks of Andy's life.

We never talked about dying . . . except once. Andy was worn out and must have known he was losing ground. He tried to clue me in. Nauseous and weak after one of the many difficult procedures he endured on a regular basis, he turned to me and asked, "Does it hurt to die?"

I was shocked but answered truthfully, "I don't know. But I don't want to talk about death, because you are not going to die, Andy."

He took my hand and said, "Not yet, but I'm getting very tired."

I knew then what he was telling me, but I tried hard to ignore it and keep the awful thought from entering my mind.

I spent a lot of my day watching Andy sleep. Sometimes I went to the gift shop to buy cards and notepaper. I had very little money. The nurses knew our situation and turned a blind eye when I slept in Andy's room and ate the extra food we ordered off of Andy's tray. But I always managed to scrape a bit together for the paper and cards because Andy loved getting mail so much.

The bone marrow transplant was a terrible ordeal. Andy couldn't have any visitors because his immune system was so compromised. I could tell that he felt even more isolated than ever. Determined to do something to make it easier for him, I began approaching total strangers in the waiting rooms and asking them, "Would you write my son a card?" I'd explain his situation and offer them a card or some paper to write on. With surprised expressions on their faces, they did it. No one refused me. They took one look at me and saw a mother in pain.

It amazed me that these kind people, who were dealing with their own worries, made the time to write Andy. Some would just sign a card with a little get-well message. Others wrote real letters: "Hi, I'm from Idaho visiting my grandmother here in the hospital . . . " and they'd fill a page or two with their story, sometimes inviting Andy to visit wherever they were from when he was better. Once a woman flagged me down and said, "You asked me to write your son a couple of weeks ago. Can I write him again?" I mailed all these letters to Andy, and watched happily as he read them. Andy had a steady stream of mail right up until the day he died.

One day, I went to the gift store to buy more cards and saw a rainbow prism for sale. Remembering the rainbow suncatcher Andy'd given me, I felt I had to buy it for him. It was a lot of money to spend, but I handed over the cash and hurried back to Andy's room to show him.

He was lying in his bed, too weak to even raise his head. The blinds were almost shut, but a crack of sunlight poured in slanting across the bed. I put the prism in his hand and said, "Andy, make me a rainbow." But Andy couldn't. He tried to hold his arm up, but it was too much for him.

He turned his face to me and said, "Mom, as soon as I'm better, I'll make you a rainbow you'll never forget."

That was the one of the last things Andy said to me. Just a few hours later, he went to sleep and, during the night, slipped into a coma. I stayed with him in the ICU, massaging him, talking to him, reading him his mail, but he never stirred. The only sound was the constant drone and beepings of the life-support machines surrounding his bed. I was looking death straight in the face, but still I thought there'd be a last-minute save, a miracle that would bring my son back to me.

After five days, the doctors told me his brain had stopped functioning and that he'd never be "Andy" again. It was time to disconnect him from the machines that were keeping his body alive.

I asked if I could hold him, so just after dawn, they brought a rocking chair into the room and after I settled myself in the chair, they turned off the machines and lifted him from the bed to place him in my arms. As they raised him from the bed, his leg made an involuntary movement and he knocked a clear plastic pitcher from his bedside table onto the bed.

"Open the blinds," I cried. "I want this room to be full of sunlight!" The nurse hurried to the window to pull the cord.

As she did so, I noticed a suncatcher, in the shape of the rainbow attached to the window, left no doubt, by a previous occupant of this room. I caught my breath in wonder. And then as the sunlight filled the room, the rays hit the pitcher lying on its side on the bed and everyone stopped what they were doing, silent with awe.

The room was suddenly filled with flashes of color, dozens and dozens of rainbows, on the walls, the floors, the ceiling, on the blanket wrapped around Andy as he lay in my arms—the room was alive with rainbows.

No one could speak. I looked down at my son, and he had stopped breathing. Andy was gone, but even in the shock of that first wave of grief, I felt comforted. Andy had made the rainbow that he promised me—the one I would never forget.

Linda Bremner

A Christmas Memory

The snow fell softly, its delicate lace-patterned snowflakes lingering on my woolen poncho. I half-carried, half-dragged my cumbersome load—a large garbage sack loaded with gifts—across the whitening street. It was almost midnight on Christmas Eve, but I was in no hurry to get home. Tears blurred the kaleidoscope of multicolored lights that blinked cheerily from our neighbor's houses. More subdued candles dimly lit every window at our house in their halfhearted attempt to feign cheer. Suddenly I stopped and stared. A white-bearded, red-clad, overstuffed figure was tapping gently at our front door and muttering "Ho! Ho! Ho!"

What is he doing here? I thought bitterly.

Christmas wasn't coming to No. 5 Jodi Lane this year. I feared it might never come again. My mind raced back to that day in November, the day our joy seemed to disappear forever.

The fall weather was just turning crisp, and my husband Jack and I and our three children squeezed into the car to head out for the Junior Midgets Sunday afternoon football game. Our two older children, Tara, four, and

Sean, eighteen months, ran up and down the bleachers while I tended the baby, Christopher, who was three months old. He was snuggled up warmly in his carriage, napping on his stomach, oblivious to the noise and chill in the air.

"I haven't seen your newest addition yet," one of our friends, Tony, called, coming to my side. He smiled and peeked into the buggy. Always eager to show off the baby, I lifted him out, his face turned toward Tony. The smile faded from Tony's face, and horror filled his eyes. What was wrong? I turned Christopher to me. His beautiful, perfect little face was a contorted, grayish-blue. I screamed.

Another parent—a New York City policeman—leapt from the bleachers, grabbed Christopher from my arms and began applying CPR before the screams had died from my lips. An ambulance was on standby for the football game, and the policeman ran toward it with our lifeless baby cradled in his arms. Jack ran behind them. By the time they pulled away, I had collapsed, and a second ambulance was called to take me to the hospital.

When I arrived minutes later, the policeman who had carried Christopher away opened the door of my ambulance. His name was John, and his brown eyes were kind as he jumped up and sat by me in the ambulance. I didn't like what I saw in his eyes. He reached out one of his massive hands—hands that had tried to save my baby—and held mine.

"Let's pray for a moment before we go inside," he said gently.

"Is he alive?" I pleaded.

I didn't want to pray—not then, not for a long time afterwards. John led me into the hospital to Jack, and we stood together as we heard the medical explanation: SIDS (sudden infant death syndrome). Our son was another infant who had simply died in his sleep. No one knew why or how. There had been little anyone could do at the hospital. Christopher was dead when I lifted him from the carriage. He had died sometime during his warm, safe naptime.

We had set out that morning—a family with three happy, healthy children. Jack and I returned that evening huddled and bewildered in the backseat of John's car. Tara and Sean were at a friend's house. And Christopher, our baby, was dead.

John and his family lived about three blocks from us. A twenty-year veteran of the NYPD, John was experienced in dealing with death, but he was neither hardened nor immune to it. It was his patience and compassion that carried us through the worst hours of our lives.

The weeks that followed encompassed the two most joyous family holidays of the year—Thanksgiving and Christmas—but for us, they were a pain-filled blur. Jack and I were so overwhelmed with grief, we cut ourselves off from everyone and each other.

By the beginning of December, if I could have stopped Christmas from coming for the entire world, I would have done it. *Christmas has no right coming this year,* I thought angrily.

But now, close to midnight on Christmas Eve, Santa Claus was intruding at my front door. If ever I had entertained a belief in the existence of Santa Claus, this was certainly the moment of stark reality—the time I knew he didn't, never did and never would exist.

Angry and exhausted, I set down the load of packages I'd bought for the children weeks ago. I had donated Christopher's presents to Birth Right shortly after his death. Tara's and Sean's gifts had been hidden safely from their spying eyes at a neighbor's house until this evening. I felt a pang of guilt. Jack and I probably hadn't done a very good job of preparing for Christmas this year; we had numbly gone through the motions of selecting and decorating a tree with Tara and Sean.

By the time I reached the front steps, Jack had opened the door and was looking blankly at the bulky figure. His eyes landed on me, behind the Santa; he probably thought I had dragged the guy home in a feeble attempt to revive some Christmas spirit. I shrugged my shoulders, indicating I was just as bewildered as he, and entered the house behind the red-suited man.

Santa ignored us. He merrily bounced up the stairs and made a beeline to the children's bedrooms. He woke Tara first, gently calling her by name. She sat straight up and smiled. Of course Santa was standing by her bed! What else could you expect on Christmas Eve, her four-year-old mind reasoned, and she immediately launched into a recital of her wish list. "A Barbie doll with lots of clothes, a tea set, Candyland and a doll that really wets," she finished happily. Santa hugged her and made her promise she would go right back to sleep. "Don't forget, I've been a very good girl," she called after him.

Santa walked into Sean's room. Sean wasn't so enthusiastic about waking up (he never was), and he was a bit skeptical, but he remembered getting a reindeer lollipop at the mall from some guy who looked like this and decided to let him stay. Santa lifted him out of his crib. Sean smiled sleepily and gave Santa a hug.

I looked at the big strong hands that gently held my son and, lifting my eyes to Santa's face, saw kindly brown eyes gazing at me over the folds of his fluffy white beard. I remembered those strong hands and the warmth of those eyes.

"Oh, John!" I cried and burst into tears. Santa reached out to Jack and me and held us close. "Thought you might all need a little Christmas tonight," he said softly.

Soon Santa left, and we watched him walk out into the snow-covered street toward the warmth of his own home and family. Jack and I wordlessly placed our packages under the tree and stepped back to see their bright paper glow under the Christmas tree lights. Santa had come to No. 5 Jodi Lane. And so had Christmas.

Lenore Gavigan

11

A GRAND-MOTHER'S LOVE

*P*erfect love sometimes does not come until the first grandchild.

Welsh Proverb

THE FAMILY CIRCUS® By Bil Keane

"Grandmas are good at hugging because they've had years and years of practice."

Grandma's Soup Night

The best thing to spend on children is your time.

Joseph Addison

It had been a busier than usual week, and trying to cope with a stiff neck had made it worse. By Thursday afternoon I had used up my supply of energy and patience. All I wanted to do was to get home, put on a comfortable robe, fix a bowl of good hot soup and collapse with my feet up.

So when I pulled into the driveway and saw my daughter-in-law Wanda's car, I groaned in despair. I had forgotten it was Bryan's night.

Since his parents' separation, I had tried to have my six-year-old grandson spend a few hours with me at least once a week. I always tried to make it a special time for him. We cooked his favorite meal—chicken and cranberry sauce—or went to his favorite hamburger place. Then either a movie or a walk through the park, and home for some fun together. We'd get down on the floor and have car races. Sometimes we'd make candy, or maybe read some silly or scary book. Bryan delighted in all these activities, and so did I. Usually.

Tonight there was no way I could handle it. I was going to have to postpone our evening together until next week. I hugged them both and then explained how badly I was feeling.

"Bryan, honey, I'm sorry," I said. "Tonight your Grandma Joan isn't up to any fun and games. Just a nice hot bowl of soup, a lazy hour of TV and then early to bed. We'll have our night together some other time."

Bryan's smile faded, and I saw the disappointment in his eyes. "Dear Lord, forgive me," I prayed, "but I'm really not up to it tonight. I need this night to relax and renew myself."

Bryan was looking up at me solemnly. "I like soup, Grandma."

My grandmother's heart knew what he was really saying. In his own way, he was saying, "Please don't send me away. Please let me stay."

I heard Wanda say, "No, Bryan. Grandma Joan's too tired tonight. Maybe next week."

But in Bryan's eyes, I saw the shadow, the uncertainty. Something else was changing. Maybe Grandma Joan wouldn't want to have him come anymore. Not tonight, not next week, not ever.

I hesitated and then tried again. "Just soup and TV, Bryan. No car games on the floor for me tonight, no baking cookies, no books. I probably won't be awake very long."

"I like soup," he repeated.

With a sigh of resignation, I gave in and placed my hand on his shoulder. "Then you are cordially invited to dine at my castle. The meal will be small, but the company will be delightful. Escort the Queen Mother in, please, Sir Bryan."

It was worth it to see his eyes light up and hear him giggle as he made a mock bow and replied, "Okay, your Royal Highness."

While I put the soup on the stove and changed into my robe, Bryan set up trays and turned on the television set.

I must have dozed off after the first few sips of soup. When I woke up, there was an afghan over my legs, the bowls and trays were gone. Bryan was sprawled on the floor, dividing his attention between a coloring book and a television show. I looked at my watch. Nine o'clock. Wanda would be coming to get Bryan soon. Poor boy, what a dull time he must have had.

Bryan looked up with a smile. Then, to my surprise, he ran over and gave me a big hug. "I love you, Grandma," he said, his arms still around my neck. "Haven't we had a nice time together?"

His big smile and happy eyes told me that this time he meant exactly what he was saying. And, to my surprise, I knew he was right. We really had had a nice time together.

That was the key word—*together.* We had done nothing exciting or special. I had slept in the chair. Bryan had colored and watched TV. But we were together.

That night I realized something important. Bryan's visits don't have to be a marathon of activity. The important thing is that he knows I love him and want him. He knows he has a place in my life, which is reserved particularly for him. A time that is just for us to be together.

Bryan still comes once a week. We still bake chicken or eat out, make cookies or go for a walk in the park. But every now and then we enjoy our favorite together time, our special feast of love—soup night.

Joan Cinelli

Becoming a Grandma

To understand your parents' love you must raise children.

After three days of labor, my daughter Déjà had her first child, a beautiful seven-pound four-ounce girl. I was amazed to observe that the instant she saw her new baby, the pain of childbirth was immediately replaced by the bliss of motherhood.

In those first few heart-stopping minutes of becoming a grandmother, one particular moment stands out for me. A moment set apart from everything else that was happening by the sudden depth of our connection—daughter, mother and grandmother.

My beautiful daughter turned to me, her eyes shining with a light I had never seen there before. "Mom," she said, "now I know how much you love me."

Robin Lim

The Secret Handshake

Dear John,

I must confess that your son—my new grandson—and I have a little secret. We made a pact that very first day you brought him home from the hospital and placed him in my arms. When no one was looking, I unfolded the loose cloth of his soft cotton sleeve to find his warm little fist, and I freed his fingers so they could wrap around one of mine. His grip was sure and steady and strong, as I knew it would be, and for an instant, as he clutched me, thoughts of what he meant to me were almost overwhelming.

I dreamed of all he has yet to do and be, and I remembered how you, my own brand-new baby not so many years ago, had also held on tightly. You, too, latched onto my finger and squeezed, not in fear, but in determination, as if to say, "This is my strength, my courage for now. I'm going to hold on tight, but only until I'm ready to handle the world on my own."

Then, it seems that I merely blinked and you

were letting go, long before I thought you would. A bright-colored rattle with an interesting noise caught your attention, and you needed to explore this new object with both of your smooth, round hands. I blinked again and you were stacking blocks to build a house that made you sit back with chest puffed out and stare in wide-eyed pride at a job well done.

Those precious fingers grew and moved on to hold a crayon, drawing pictures of sunny skies and stick figures as a pink triangle tip of a tongue darted out of the corner of your mouth in concentration. They molded clay animals, learned to tie shoes and held a knife to butter your own bread. I watched as they gripped your lunch box handle, a little too tightly in the Septembers of your childhood, more relaxed and swinging it by your side in May.

Those once-plump hands lost their rounded softness, and the fingers had grown long and slender by the time they gripped tools, dribbled a basketball and rested far too casually on the steering wheel of the first car you drove. Before I knew it, they had become the hands of a man, though some of their gentleness has remained, and I'm pretty sure my fond memories are not just making it so in my mind.

Then, the day came when I watched the hand that first gripped mine hold the hand of another woman. It felt strange, but somehow not wrong as you cupped your hand around her waist and danced with her.

I knew those many years ago, that fleeting instant when you first held on tight to my finger, we had made an agreement, sealed with a secret handshake, acknowledging that both of us would let go when the time was right. At that same instant, I knew that while we'd let go with our hands, we'd always remain connected in a beautiful, special way.

Now, as I think of my new grandson's perfect little fist, with his fingers wrapped around mine, I know I could blink and he'll be sitting up, wanting to hold his own spoon, prefer petting a dog or throwing a ball to holding onto Grandma's hand or even his mommy's or daddy's. We could blink again, and he'll be working math problems, casually cradling the phone on a broad shoulder as he talks to a girlfriend.

If I'm lucky, I'll see him grow into a man, and as he slips a ring on the hand of his bride, I'll be amazed at how large his hands have become.

I could think about these things and more, as I lament your passing youth and my own. For now though, I'd rather relish completely and selfishly the thrill I got as my precious new grandson gripped my finger and stared intently into my eyes. I know without a doubt that he was telling me he'd trust us to hold on, to teach him what he needs to know of life, to be there as long as he needs us. Then, when it's time, we'll all let go with our hands, but continue to hold on tight with our hearts.

Love always,
Mom

Lynn Stearns

Second Chance

When they were small and I was young,
I often had no time for fun.

There was cleaning to do and bills to pay.
I rushed upon my busy way.

And when I tucked them in to sleep,
I'd obligations still to keep.

I kissed them, and I turned away
My promises broken another day.

We had good times. I loved them dear,
But interruptions grew each year.

Then suddenly, they'd grown and gone.
I felt like life's discarded pawn.

But then, a miracle. It's true.
This time I recognized my cue,

And let each precious moment be
Embraced and savored happily.

My children's children now I see,
Gathered sweetly at my knee.

I send an upward, grateful glance,
That God gave me a second chance.

L. D. Hindman

THE FAMILY CIRCUS ®   **By Bil Keane**

"I need a new football. I don't know if I should send up a prayer, write a letter to Santa Claus or call Grandma."

The Christmas I Was Rich

There was a tree that Christmas. Not as big and full as some trees, but it hung with all the treasured ornaments and glowed with lights. There were presents, too. Gaily wrapped in red or green tissue paper, with colorful seals and bits of ribbon. But not as many as presents as usual. I had already noticed that my pile of gifts was very small.

We weren't poor. But times were hard, jobs scarce, money tight. My mother and I shared a house with my grandmother and my aunt and uncle. That Depression year, they all stretched meals, carried sandwiches to work and walked everywhere to save bus fares.

Years before the World War II slogan became famous, we, like many families, were living it: "Use it up, wear it out; make it do, or do without." There were few choices.

So I understood why my pile of presents was so small. I understood, but I still felt a guilty twinge of disappointment.

I knew there couldn't be any breathtaking surprises in those few gaily wrapped boxes. I knew one would be a book. Mom always managed a new book for me. But no new dress, or sweater or warm quilted robe. None of the hoped-for indulgences of Christmas.

But there was one box with my name on it. From my grandmother. I saved that box for last. Maybe it would be a new sweater, or even a dress—a blue dress. Grandmother and I both loved pretty dresses, and every shade of blue.

Dutifully ooh-ing and aah-ing over the fragrant bar of honeysuckle soap, the red mittens, the expected book (a new Nancy Drew!), I quickly reached that last package. I began to feel a spurt of Christmas excitement. It was a fairly big box. Ashamed of myself for being so greedy, for even hoping for a dress or sweater (but hoping anyway), I opened the box.

Socks!

Nothing but socks!

Anklets, knee-highs, even a pair of those awful long white cotton stockings that always sagged and wrinkled around my knees.

Hoping no one had noticed my disappointment, I picked up one of the four pairs and smiled my thanks to my grandmother. She was smiling, too. Not her polite, distracted, "Yes, dear," smile, but her sparkling, happy, "This is important woman-to-woman stuff, so pay attention!" smile.

Had I missed something? I looked back down at the box. Still socks—nothing but socks. But now I could see there was another pair under the pair I had picked up. Two layers of socks. And another. Three layers of socks!

Really smiling now, I began taking them out of the box. Pink socks, white socks, green socks, socks in every imaginable shade of blue. Everyone was watching now, laughing with me as I tossed socks in the air and counted. Twelve pairs of socks!

I got up and squeezed Grandmother so tight it hurt us both.

"Merry Christmas, Joan-girl," she said. "Every day now

you'll have choices to make—an abundance of choices. You're rich, my dear."

And so I was. That Christmas and all year. Every morning, as I chose which pair of socks to wear from my elegant hosiery wardrobe, I felt rich. And I still do.

Later, my mother told me that Grandmother had been hiding those socks away for almost a year—saving nickels and dimes, buying a pair at a time; once, seeing a lovely blue pair with hand embroidery on the cuff, she had actually asked the understanding salesclerk to take a deposit and hold it for her for three weeks.

A year of love had been wrapped in that box.

That was a Christmas I'll never forget.

My grandmother's gift, her extravagance of socks, showed me how wonderful and important little things can be.

And how enormously wealthy love makes us all.

Joan Cinelli

The Surrogate Grandmother

The giving of love is an education in itself.

Eleanor Roosevelt

All the way to the nursing home, I could hear Pam complaining.

"I don't like this idea. I hate being around old people, and I think nursing homes are gross."

I had suggested to my teen Girl-Scout troop that each girl adopt an elderly lady in the nursing home as a grandmother. I thought it would be good for the girls to learn about the elderly and the hardships they have with ill health and loneliness. It would teach them, I hoped, to have compassion for others. Most of the girls thought it was a good idea, except for Pam.

If anyone needs to learn about compassion, it's Pam, I thought. She was an only child and very spoiled. She seemed to care about nothing but her looks, clothes and boys.

"Phew! It stinks in here."

"Shhh," I told Pam. "It's not the most pleasant smell,

I know. Just be grateful you're not in here all the time, like they are."

I turned away to talk to the administrator. After a few minutes, I went to the main sitting room to check on the girls. They had all found an elderly woman and seemed to be getting along fine. All except Pam. She was nowhere to be seen.

I started down the long hallway in time to see Pam enter a room. I stopped beside the door.

"Hello." The weak shaky voice had come from a small hump lying in a narrow bed. "I'm Hannah."

"Hi. I'm Pamela."

"My, you're a pretty girl, Pamela. I've never had anyone as pretty as you to visit me before."

"Really?"

I could tell Pam was very pleased over this comment.

"Really." The bright, little eyes looked Pam over. "You're not one of those feisty girls, are you?"

"Feisty?" Pam couldn't keep from smiling at the way Hannah had said the word. Like it was something bad.

"Yes. Feisty. In my day, bad girls were called feisty."

"They were?" Pam couldn't hide her surprise. "When was that, Hannah? Would you mind if I ask how old you are?"

Grinning wide and showing her toothless gums, Hannah proudly said, "I'm 104."

"A hundred and four?" Pam's mouth gaped opened. "You're really 104?"

Hannah chuckled. "I bet you didn't think anyone could live that long, right? Well, you drag that chair over here and sit a spell. It's been a long time since I've had anyone to visit with."

"Don't you have any family?" Pam asked.

"Oh no. They're all dead and gone. I'm the last member of my family left."

I walked in and introduced myself to Hannah and reminded Pam why we were there.

Pam looked at me and whispered. "She's 104!"

I explained to Hannah about the girls wanting to adopt an elderly lady as their grandmother.

A little reluctantly, Pam asked Hannah if she could adopt her.

Hannah smiled her big, toothless grin. "I would be right proud to be your grandma."

I took the girls to visit their surrogate grandmothers every week. I don't know who was enjoying it more, the girls or the grandmothers. At first, Pam was quiet, but over the weeks, I could see a change in her.

"She's amazing!" Pam told the other girls. "Do you know, she can remember when there was trouble with Indians! Some of the things we study about in American history—she witnessed."

"You've come to really love her in these last few months, haven't you?" Pam's best friend asked.

"You know, I really have. She's the most interesting person I know. And the stories she tells! She's so interested in everything that's going on. She's crippled with arthritis and completely bedridden, but she never complains."

I could see the affection between Pam and Hannah grow with each visit. Pam would brush Hannah's long white hair while listening to stories about the way Hannah and other young ladies in her day dressed and wore their hair. In turn, Pam told Hannah all her thoughts and fears, and Hannah would share her wisdom, born of long experience, with Pam. They laughed together often.

Pam brought little gifts that made Hannah's eyes light up. Hannah's favorite was the milk-chocolate drops that Pam sneaked in. Smiling, Hannah would let them melt in her mouth.

On our way to visit one day, I noticed Pam was carrying a big bouquet of lilacs.

"Those are beautiful, Pam."

"I'm taking them to Hannah. They're her favorite flower."

When we arrived, Pam rushed into Hannah's room. "Hannah?"

I heard her call out Hannah's name and went into the room. The bed was made up with white, starched sheets as though no one had ever been in it.

"Can I help you?" One of the attendants walked into the room.

"Yes, we're looking for Hannah," I told her.

"Oh dear, didn't anyone tell you? Hannah passed away last night."

"Passed away?" Pam whispered.

"Yes, her heart stopped. She went very peacefully."

"Pam, I'm sorry." I put my arm around her.

Throwing the lilacs on the floor, Pam turned to me. "It's all your fault!" she yelled. "I didn't want to adopt an old person. Then, I met Hannah. I loved her, and now she's gone. It's not fair."

I put my arms around her and let her cry. She had never lost anyone before.

"Hannah wanted you to have this." The attendant held an old, worn Bible out to Pam. With it was a note, addressed to: My Granddaughter, Pamela. The note simply said, "Love never dies."

I attended Hannah's funeral with Pam. She never said a word through the whole service. She just held Hannah's Bible.

I wasn't surprised that Pam started skipping our scout meetings on the days we visited the nursing home. I didn't know what to say to her. *Maybe it hadn't been such a good idea after all,* I thought.

A few months later, at one of our regular meetings, Pam asked, "Can I go back to the nursing home with the rest of you next week?"

"Of course you can, but are you sure you want to?"

Pam smiled and said, "Yes. No one can ever take Hannah's place, but I know there are other grandmothers, just as wonderful, waiting to be adopted."

"Yes, I bet there are. What a good idea, Pam."

She had learned and in doing so, she had reminded me: Love is always a good idea.

Pat Curtis

12

THANK YOU, MOM

The people who make a difference are not the ones with the credentials, but the ones with the concern.

Max Lucado
And the Angels Were Silent

Lessons on Napkins

In a child's lunch basket, a mother's thoughts.

Japanese Proverb

In 1974, my mother was a junior at an all-girls Catholic college in New York. She was an excellent student and wanted to be a special education teacher. But, her dreams of becoming a teacher were interrupted by an unexpected child: her own. My mother became pregnant with me during her junior year of college and left school to marry my father. Yet even though my mother left the field of education formally, she did not leave it entirely.

When I was born my mother immediately made learning an integral and fun part of my life. Everything we did was a positive learning interaction, whether we were baking cookies or spending the day at the library. I never watched television, not because I was not allowed to, but because it was more fun writing stories with my mom. There was never a lot of money in our home, but with all of the books, laughter and hugs, it was a scarcity I never felt.

When I finally entered a school classroom at age five, I was excited, but terrified. That first day of kindergarten I quietly sat at my desk during snack time and opened my Miss Piggy lunch box. Inside the lunch box I found a note from my mother written on a napkin. The note said that she loved me, that she was proud of me and that I was the best kindergartner in the world! Because of that napkin note I made it through my first day of kindergarten . . . and many more school days to follow.

There have been many napkin notes since the first one. There were napkin notes in elementary school when I was struggling with math, telling me to "Hang in there, kiddo! You can do it! Don't forget what a great writer you are!" There were napkin notes in junior high school when I was the "new girl" with frizzy hair and pimples, telling me to "Be friendly. Don't be scared. Anyone would be lucky to have you as her friend!" In high school, when my basketball team was the first team in our school's history to play in a state championship, there were napkin notes telling me, "There is no 'I' in team. You have gotten this far because you know how to share." And, there were even napkin notes sent to me in college and graduate school, far away from my mother's physical touch. Despite the tumultuous changes of college—changing majors, changing boyfriends, changing the way I looked at the world—my one constant was my mother's encouragement, support and teachings, echoed in years of love, commitment and napkin notes.

My nineteen-year-old sister is now a college sophomore. Somewhere in her dorm room, amid her varsity basketball uniform and her nursing books, she has a box of well-read napkin notes hidden, but accessible. At home, my sixteen-year-old sister and nine-year-old brother also have their own private stashes of napkin notes. When they read them I know they feel the same warm surge of confidence that I felt all through my school years.

For Christmas this year, my mother received a book

bag, a daily planner, notebooks and a full-tuition college scholarship. These gifts reflected an impending change in her life. After a twenty-five-year hiatus, my forty-four-year-old mother was finally going back to school to earn her degree in teaching. And although I was immensely proud of my mother for following her dreams, I wanted her to know that she didn't need a degree to make her a stellar teacher.

So I also gave her a Christmas gift for school: a lunch bag filled with her favorite foods. She laughed as she opened the lunch bag and took out cans of tuna fish and V-8. Then she pulled out a napkin with writing on it.

As she opened up her "You can do it!" napkin note from me, tears began running down her face. When her eyes met mine, I saw she understood my unspoken message: My mother is—and has always been—a teacher.

Caurie Anne Miner

A Worthy Investment

The best way to keep children home is to make the home atmosphere pleasant—and let the air out of the tires.

Dorothy Parker

When we were growing up, we always suspected our mother was a little bit crazy. One day in particular stands out in my mind. It was a Saturday afternoon in the fall, and Mom had been running errands all day. We five kids were raking leaves in the front yard when Mom pulled into the driveway. She was driving our beat-up old pickup truck. (It still amazes me that she wasn't embarrassed to be seen in that thing.)

"Hey kids, come see what I got!" Mom yelled excitedly, and we rushed over to investigate. We never knew what Mom would be up to. She climbed up into the back of the truck, flung her arms open wide, and cried, "Ta-daa! Can you believe it was free?" She wore an enormous smile of anticipation.

Climbing into the pickup to join her, we saw the ugliest couch in the world. It had once been blue and red plaid, but now it was faded, stained and the stuffing was coming out in spots.

"*Mother,* please tell me you're not putting this in the living room!" I groaned, dreading the embarrassment of explaining this monstrosity to my friends. Teenage boys were supposed to pull stunts like this, not mothers! *Sometimes,* I thought, *Mom was just nuts.*

"Of course not!" Mom laughed. "I'm going to put it in the garage. You see, I had this idea that we could clean out the garage a little bit and make it into a kids' hangout room. Mr. Larson down the street said we could have his old Ping-Pong table for only ten dollars if we wanted it, and we'll set that up in there, too. Then, when friends come over you can hang out in the garage, stay up late and not bother anybody! So what do you think?"

I looked at my brothers and sisters, who were obviously excited by the idea. "Hooray!" Chris yelled. "It can be a guys-only hangout. No girls allowed. Right, John?" John was quick to agree, but Mom interrupted as my sisters and I began to protest.

"We'll all share it. You know that's how we do things around here! But before we do anything else, we've got to get that garage cleaned out. Let's go!" Rakes and leaf piles were deserted as we followed Mom to the garage. I had to admit, as crazy as Mom was to bring home a nasty couch, the idea of a hangout room was starting to grow on me. There was already a basketball hoop and a dartboard outside the garage. This could actually become a pretty cool place to hang out. I wasn't so sure my girlfriends were into Ping-Pong, but at least we could sit on the couch (once I found a *clean* blanket to cover those spots) and talk.

Our garage quickly became a neighborhood favorite where kids in the neighborhood could hang out and relax. Mom couldn't have been happier. She loved having lots of young people around the house. They all loved her, too, and treated her like one of the gang. Sometimes I would come home at night with friends and end up going to bed while Mom and my friends were still sitting up chatting! Everyone considered her their friend, and I was secretly very proud of having a "cool" mom.

Mom made our house a place that was always open to our friends, no matter who they were or what their background and reputation were. Our parents were always very strict about our going out at night to parties and on dates, but Mom was always quick to remind us that she was glad to have all our friends come to our house. We could always bring the party home!

Her real concern was that we were safe. She was much happier knowing that the party was going on downstairs instead of somewhere else! I think that Mom and Dad probably passed many sleepless hours, while Ping-Pong games and basketball tournaments went on outside their bedroom window at all hours of the night. But we never once heard them complain. To them, it was a worthwhile sacrifice.

Mom wasn't the kind of mother who always had cookies and milk waiting for us and our friends. Instead she had refrigerated cookie dough, brownie mixes and microwave popcorn available twenty-four hours a day. Even now, when my husband and I come to visit my parents, we can count on seeing my brothers and sisters and friends there in the kitchen. Sometimes, even when my siblings aren't there, their friends are! Mom has so endeared herself to them by her open heart and open house policy, they know they can count on her to listen when no one else will.

We still have that old couch in the garage. Although it's pretty much destroyed, no one wants to part with it. For us, it's a very special monument to Mom's investment in our lives and our relationships.

Allison Yates Gaskins

Unstoppable

My mother, Beulah Hill Wetchen, was born in rural Alabama in 1908, a time when most women could not even think about having a career. As a small child, she would rise during the early hours of dawn and work long days in the cotton fields, enduring the unrelenting Alabama heat. She told me that it was at these times that she vowed to herself to become educated and pursue a career in nursing. In that era, it would take tremendous determination and ambition to fulfill her dream and goal of becoming a registered nurse.

The eldest of eleven children, Beulah was the one that her parents relied upon to help with the rest of the family. Many days she would stay home from school to help watch after the younger children while her mother and father worked in the fields. This made the decision to leave home and attend nurses' training in Tuscaloosa even more difficult because she knew her mother and father would desperately miss her assistance. In the end, however, it was this very decision which came to be more valuable to the family than any of them could have foreseen.

After my mother finished her nursing education, she stayed in Tuscaloosa, doing private-duty nursing and living in her own apartment. She was especially skilled in bedside nursing care, which at that time was at the heart of nursing.

One evening, she received a frantic call from her father. Howel, her seventeen-year-old brother, was gravely ill. He had been having abdominal pains for two days and was becoming progressively worse with fever and chills. The doctor, who had just left the house after administering an injection to Howel for pain, had told my grandparents, "If the boy lives until morning, he will probably be all right." Beulah's mother was not about to accept this extremely chilling statement and do nothing until morning. She told her husband, "We have to reach Beulah. She will know what to do."

Having no car and no phone, Beulah's father walked to the telephone office in the nearby town of Moundville to make the call. When he reached Beulah, she told him that she would take the midnight train bound for New Orleans. She immediately left for the Tuscaloosa train depot. She knew that the train was not scheduled to stop in Moundville, but she decided she would face that obstacle when she arrived at the depot.

Sure enough, when she arrived there and told the ticket agent where she needed to go, she was told the train would not be stopping in Moundville. Undeterred, my mother boarded the train and told the conductor, "You *will* stop this train in Moundville. My brother is very ill and may be dying. I must get to him right away, and I *will* be getting off this train where I need to!"

Apparently, the look in her eyes and the tone of her voice had the necessary impact on the conductor because the train stopped briefly—ever so briefly—in Moundville. My mother told me that she hadn't even completely taken her foot from the bottom step of that train when it started to move.

When my mother arrived at the house, her brother Howel was lying on a low cot in the living room. She knelt down by his side, and smelling a very distinct odor on his breath—and noting his pale, clammy skin—was certain he had suffered a ruptured appendix. She told her parents that they needed to get him to the hospital right away.

The same neighbor who had driven my grandfather to the train depot took them to the hospital in Tuscaloosa. Upon arrival at the hospital, my mother told the night nursing supervisor what she thought Howel's problem was and a surgeon was called. Within two hours after the phone call to my mother, Howel was in surgery. Beulah was allowed to stay in the operating room during the surgery. Opening the abdomen, the surgeon turned to her and said, "Miss Hill, your diagnosis is right. Your brother's appendix has ruptured. It's like muddy water in here, but we will do what we can to save him."

One week after the surgery, my uncle was recovering and on his way to good health again.

Last year my mother celebrated her ninetieth birthday and, in her true style, the party was everything she wanted it to be with music and dancing and friends and family around her. As I watched her mingle with the guests, I pictured how she must have looked on that night long ago when she rose to her full five-foot two-inch height, looked that train conductor in the eye and said, "You *will* stop this train because I *am* going to get off!"

My Uncle Howel lived to serve his country during two world wars, marry, raise a fine family and become a loved and respected member of his community. All thanks to my mother, a woman with sufficient spirit to set out on a difficult path, ample courage to follow her dreams and enough determination to even stop a train.

Dixie Jane Sokolik

The Power of My Mother's Love

Motherhood is being available to your children whenever they need you, no matter what their age or their need.

Major Doris Pengilly

I discovered the power of my mother's love the spring I was twenty-six years old. I was hard at work in graduate school, busily moving toward my doctoral degree in psychology. It was early spring, the grass still brown and crunchy beneath my feet, as I walked from my car to the hospital entrance. I had been sick for a month with infections so resilient that not even the most powerful antibiotics were able to eradicate them. I felt incredibly weak, but had so much to do, I was eager to be done with this appointment.

As I walked wearily through the sliding glass doors into the admissions area, I anticipated a diagnosis of anemia or some other vitamin deficiency, a lecture about improper eating habits, finishing with a new regimen of vitamin horse-pills and a strict diet. I could hear my mother's voice, "I told you—you should be eating more protein.

You're just not taking care of yourself. You're studying too hard." *Why is this happening now?* I thought resentfully. *It is so inconvenient.*

After what seemed like hours of waiting, a doctor appeared from behind the sherbet-striped curtains and entered the cubicle where I lay stretched out on the gurney. Startled to find me alone, he inquired where my family was. I told him that my husband had to work that morning and that my mother and father were living in a different state. The concern on his face deepened.

"I have reason to believe that you have leukemia," he said. The statement hung in the air and then fell like a ton of bricks, shattering my world as I knew it and rocking me at my very foundation. My first question after that initial moment of shock was, "Am I going to die?"

The doctor explained his diagnosis needed to be confirmed immediately with additional testing. After that chemotherapy treatments would start immediately. Bottom line, I would be admitted immediately to the hospital and would not be released for at least a month. My condition was life-threatening. He told me that if I had waited a day or two longer my condition could have been fatal. My body was shutting down because of the rampant takeover of the quickly proliferating white blood cells. I could still die—suddenly—at any time.

After a painful test that confirmed the diagnosis of acute leukemia, my family began to arrive. I remember vividly the expression of shock and anguish on my mother's face. She looked as if the world had dealt her a deathly blow, as if her world had been shattered as well. It was this sense of shared trauma that would see us through the ordeal of the following five months.

Time passed in a blur of treatments. There were three extended hospital stays, rounds of chemotherapy, endless waiting for blood counts to return to normal from the devastating effects of chemo and even longer days and nights spent fending off the fever of infection. During this time, my mom was my rock, ever present and ever supportive. Every day, twelve to sixteen hours a day, she was there with me at the hospital.

One of the most trying parts of the hospital routine was the mask she was required to wear anytime she was in my room to protect me from the potential deadly germs of the outside world. Yet she wore her mask every day without hesitation or complaint, enduring with me the boring and cramped confines of the Isolation ward.

Later, I came to see that time of shared isolation as a time of immeasurable bonding, not unlike my time in her womb. I was dependent on her for life support, trusting that she would nourish and protect me. I came to appreciate the enormity of the responsibility she had taken for me years ago at my conception. And now, without a moment's hesitation, she had taken that responsibility again. The beauty and power of our bond and her commitment to care for me were profound healing forces in my recovery.

During those months, my mother and I had many rituals that came to sustain us. Each morning, I would awaken early and sit by the window waiting for my mother's familiar red car to tool down the street and into the visitor's parking lot. When I spotted her car, I immediately felt that I could make it through another day—as if she were my guardian angel, guiding and protecting me through the most difficult battle of my life. As she walked from the parking lot to the hospital I would wave at her. Each morning she looked up and cheerfully waved back. She was happy to see me as well.

During that time, I began to understand that a mother does what she needs to do to nurture and protect her child, even if that means enduring horrible conditions herself. Those long days at the hospital, I later learned, were very stressful for my mom. There were days when she broke out in itchy, painful hives and went downstairs to the emergency room for treatment. She hid it so well, I never knew she was in discomfort. Most of the time, she sat by my bed and we talked, played cards and watched "Oprah" together. Other times, she read quietly and watched me sleep.

My mother had no other purpose in those days except to tell me she loved me with her presence. I especially felt her love the times she reached out and rested her hand on top of mine. Such a small gesture, but one that immediately brought me calm and peace—a sense that the world was all right and that I was okay.

I also cherished our evening ritual. Many nights I experienced panic and anxiety when I knew it was time for Mom to leave. My mother would kiss me goodnight and assure me I would see her tomorrow. Again, I would perch in the windowsill and wait until I saw her walking into the night, toward her car. She would turn as she neared the end of the sidewalk and look up into the darkened windows of the hospital and find me, waving to her. She would give one last wave before getting into the car. Then I'd watch the taillights of her car fade into the dark, knowing that in the morning, we would start our rituals all over again. This is how we survived those challenging months—together.

Eventually, I recovered from my leukemia and have been in remission for seven years now. Battling for my life was painful in every way, yet sharing that ordeal with my mother produced some of the most precious moments in our relationship. I experienced firsthand the overwhelming power of a mother's love to bring peace and healing in even the most difficult of life's circumstances.

Shana Helmholdt

A House for Momma

There was never a great man who had not a great mother.

Lyndall in Olive Schreiner's
The Story of an African Farm

My mother grew up in the poor, upland South where life was harsh, where men coaxed crops to grow in clay and women worked themselves to death. Poor was all she had ever witnessed, tasted, been.

The first memory I have is of a tall blond woman dragging a hundred-pound canvas sack through a field that seems to reach into the back forty of forever. I remember the sound the sack makes as it slides between the chest-high stalks that are so deeply, darkly green they look almost black, and the smell of kicked-up dust and sweat. The tall woman is wearing a man's britches and old straw hat, and now and then she looks back over her shoulder to smile at the three-year-old boy whose hair is almost as purely white as the cotton bolls she picks, who rides the back of the six-foot-long sack like a magic carpet. It is my first memory, and the best. The memory that continues to ride and ride in my mind because it so perfectly sums up the way she carried us, my two brothers and me, with such dignity.

She picked cotton for a few dollars a day. And when that work was gone, she stripped long rows of sugar cane, picked tomatoes and picked up pecans—backbreaking stoop labor. Manual labor slowly turned her from a beautiful young woman into one who was old before her time.

At night, Momma ironed in the bedroom I shared with my brothers in my grandma's tiny house. I used to go to sleep with the clothes of strangers heaped around my bed. She made only a few pennies a shirt, but she worked hours and hours, dripping sweat.

She signed us up for welfare and free lunches. She stood in line for government cheese. She hated it, but she did it.

She stood in line at the Goodwill, waiting to buy dresses draped across her sunburned arms. I remember we scavenged the city dump, burrowing into mountains of trash for treasure Momma could sell: copper wires, aluminum, Coke and Royal Crown bottles, worth a penny.

It seemed all Momma did was work, going out only to buy groceries. It was a long time before I realized she stayed home because she was afraid we might be ashamed of her.

I do not ever remember being ashamed of her when I was a little boy. But later, when I was discovering girls and making friends, I admit I was content to let her remain in her own exile.

I remember the summer before I started high school, I was going steady with a fourteen-year-old cheerleader who was the daughter of a respected family in the small community where I went to school, but which was not the one where I lived. I had told her nothing about my background. I thought I was safe.

One day there was a knock on my door. It was her,

flanked by girlfriends. They came by to invite me to a picnic. I will never forget the look on their faces as they took in the tiny living room with its ripped couch, worn-out rug and bare bulb hanging from the ceiling. And I saw the way they looked at my momma, in her flip-flops and old pants cut off at the knees.

I was ashamed of who I was. Worse, I was ashamed of my momma.

By the time I was twenty-seven, I had not lived at home for a long time, and any embarrassment I ever felt was long gone. I tried to help Momma with little things, such as groceries and doctor bills to make up for any wrong I had ever done her. But the thing I wanted most to do was beyond my reach.

All her life, Momma had lived in other people's houses: "Momma," I said, "one of these days, I'm gonna buy you a house." She just nodded. She thought I was dreaming.

She never even said she wanted a house. She never even hinted. But if you could have seen her face when we rode down the rural roads of our county, heard her talk about how this is an A-frame and that is a Victorian, about how this one will need painting and that one just got new aluminum siding, you would have known.

I could have bought her a house on credit, but I was afraid something would happen, taking away my ability to pay for it. The only thing worse than doing without is to be given something and then have it snatched away. I could not take that chance and decided I would have to buy a house outright.

The problem was I had picked just about the lowest-paying profession in America, journalism. In high school, the only thing I was any good at was telling stories, and there was no profit in that.

I joined the school newspaper because the press badge gave me freedom to roam the halls and goof off. I had no way of knowing that it would be my salvation.

After high school, I enrolled at Jacksonville State University for one class in feature writing. I wandered over to the school newspaper and volunteered to write. I covered sports and got the facts right, mostly.

A few weeks later, the editor of the local paper, the *Jacksonville News,* called and asked if I wanted a job writing for fifty dollars a week.

My momma cut out my first story and put it in a scrapbook, as she would every story I wrote that she could find. I wrote sports at first and dropped out of college because I had what I wanted from it: a coat-and-tie job. Soon I lent my meager talents to progressively larger papers, and eventually I became a sort of roving national reporter. In 1994, I went to work for the *New York Times,* the temple of the profession. That job has carried me to the other side of the world and into the same columned mansions where my momma used to clean bathrooms.

And then, when I was thirty-six, I won a Pulitzer Prize.

Momma had never heard of the Pulitzer. When I told her we would have to travel to New York to accept it, she said no. I think she was afraid that all those fancy people would spot the impostor in their midst, that they would ask her to clear the table. I gave up after a while.

But after the news broke, her phone rang steadily for days. Kinfolk we had not heard from in years, teachers, perfect strangers called to say how proud they were that I had won something so grand. People spoke to her on the street, people who had never talked to her before.

I called her one last time to beg her to go. "I been thinking about it," she said, "and I reckon I can do it." I almost dropped the phone. She had decided that if this thing was so important to everyone, then it must be ever so important to me.

My mother was not afraid of much. But the day of the

Pulitzer lunch, she was scared. When we got to the reception, the place was full, so we stood just inside the door. I touched her shoulder, and it was shaking.

Then, one by one, the editors of the *New York Times* came by to pay my mother homage, to tell her what a fine son she had raised. We sat at a table with Arthur Sulzberger Jr., the publisher of the *Times,* who treated her like a queen.

I had often seen my mother cry from pain and grief and misery when I was a child. I had never seen her cry from happiness until they called out my name and I walked up to get that prize, then handed it to her.

That same year, I kept my promise to my mother. I took every dollar I had and bought her a house, a good house, the first thing of any real value she has ever owned. We must have looked at a hundred before this one caught her eye and her heart.

"It's a dream, ain't it? It's just a dream," she said.

My momma believes that she failed, that her three sons did not get enough of the fine things in life. She blames herself for that.

But through the leg up she gave me and a series of happy accidents, I wound up at the temple of this profession, working under legends at the *New York Times* and winning the highest honor my profession bestows. I am as proud of that as I am of being the son of a woman who picked cotton and took in ironing. I have always believed that one could not have been without the other.

I hope she blames herself for that, too.

Rick Bragg
Condensed from It's All Over But the Shoutin'

More Chicken Soup?

Many of the stories and poems you have read in this book were submitted by readers like you who had read earlier *Chicken Soup for the Soul* books. We are planning to publish five or six *Chicken Soup for the Soul* books every year. We invite you to contribute a story to one of these future volumes.

Stories may be up to 1,200 words and must uplift or inspire. You may submit an original piece, something you have read or your favorite quotation on your refrigerator door.

To obtain a copy of our submission guidelines and a listing of upcoming *Chicken Soup* books, please write, fax or check one of our Web sites.

Please send your submissions to:

Chicken Soup for the (Specify Which Edition) Soul
P.O. Box 30880, Santa Barbara, CA 93130
Phone: 805-563-2935
Fax: 805-563-2945
Web site: *www.chickensoup.com*

You can also visit the *Chicken Soup for the Soul* Web site on America Online at keyword: chickensoup.

Just send a copy of your stories and other pieces to the above address.

We will be sure that both you and the author are credited for your submission.

For information about speaking engagements, other books, audiotapes, workshops and training programs, please contact any of our authors directly.

Supporting Mothers and Children Around the World

In the spirit of supporting mothers and children of the world, the publisher and coauthors of *Chicken Soup for the Mother's Soul 2* will donate a portion of the proceeds from this book to the following non-profit organizations. Please contact them directly for more information. We invite you to join us in supporting these organizations:

The March of Dimes is dedicated to improving the health of babies by:

- Funding lifesaving research on birth defects and low birthweight.
- Providing expectant parents with the latest scientific information.
- Fighting for health care for all our kids.
- Helping women get quality prenatal care.

For free help or information about pregnancy or birth defects, contact:

March of Dimes™
1275 Mamaroneck Ave.
White Plains, NY 10605
Phone: 888-MODIMES (888-663-4637)
Web site: *www.modimes.org*

Children's Relief Network is dedicated to saving and rehabilitating the lives of abandoned and orphaned street children in Bucharest, Romania. In 1994, Angie Thomson founded the organization after a trip to Bucharest where she found young children left on the streets to survive on their own. Since then, Children's Relief Network has developed The Villa of Hope for Boys, The House of Hope for

Girls, The Hope Rescue Center, The Refuge of Hope for Girls, The Hope Orphanage Outreach, and the Village of Hope. Contact:

Children's Relief Network, Intl.
P.O. Box 67059
Scotts Valley, CA 95067
Phone: 800-326-6500
Web site: *www.romanianchildren.org.*

The House of Umoja was established in 1968 as a home for troubled urban youth. The unique methods employed by the founders, Dave and Falaka Fattah, have been successful in turning around the lives of thousands of young men. Authorities credit the House of Umoja for playing a major role in eliminating the gang warfare that plagued Philadelphia in the 1970s. Today, the House of Umoja is one of the most acclaimed and successful youth service programs in the country and was selected as a crime prevention model by the Department of Health and Human Services and the Police Foundation. A successful replication of the House of Umoja is in operation in Portland, Oregon. Contact:

The House of Umoja
1410 N. Frazier St.
Philadelphia, PA 19131
Phone: 215-473-5893

The Alliance for Bio-Integrity is dedicated to promoting technologies that foster human and environmental health and addressing the problems of those that do not. The Alliance is dedicated to preserve the safety of our food supply, the health of the environment and the harmony of our relationship with nature. Contact:

The Alliance for Bio-Integrity
Phone: 641-472-5554
Web site: *www.biointegrity.org*

Humanity in Unity is dedicated to supporting humanitarian and educational projects which address issues of poverty, disease, and inequality. The organization's activities currently include sponsoring inner city programs, funding AIDS facilities, and ministering to women who have suffered abuse or are undergoing rehabilitation. Humanity in Unity is dedicated to improving conditions for women and children, and unifying our world family through bridging economic, social and cultural differences. Contact:

Humanity in Unity
500 Hartford Dr.
Boulder, CO 80305
Phone: 303-554-0880

Homes for Change is a volunteer organization dedicated to building basic, inexpensive, yet durable housing for the poorest families worldwide. Frequent recipients of these homes are women with children, often victims of abuse and neglect, all of whom must work for meager wages simply to survive. Homes for Change provides a foundation for these families to live independently, to grow materially and socially and to become contributing members of their communities. Contact:

Homes for Change
13029 Triadelphia Mill Road
Clarksville, MD 21029
Phone: 301-854-0087

Who Is Jack Canfield?

Jack Canfield is one of America's leading experts in the development of human potential and personal effectiveness. He is both a dynamic, entertaining speaker and a highly sought-after trainer. Jack has a wonderful ability to inform and inspire audiences toward increased levels of self-esteem and peak performance.

He is the author and narrator of several bestselling audio and videocassette programs, including *Self-Esteem and Peak Performance, How to Build High Self-Esteem, Self-Esteem in the Classroom* and *Chicken Soup for the Soul—Live.* He is regularly seen on television shows such as *Good Morning America, 20/20* and *NBC Nightly News.* Jack has co-authored numerous books, including the *Chicken Soup for the Soul* series, *Dare to Win* and *The Aladdin Factor* (all with Mark Victor Hansen), *100 Ways to Build Self-Concept in the Classroom* (with Harold C. Wells), *Heart at Work* (with Jacqueline Miller) and *The Power of Focus* (with Les Hewitt and Mark Victor Hansen).

Jack is a regularly featured speaker for professional associations, school districts, government agencies, churches, hospitals, sales organizations and corporations. His clients have included the American Dental Association, the American Management Association, AT&T, Campbell's Soup, Clairol, Domino's Pizza, GE, ITT, Hartford Insurance, Johnson & Johnson, the Million Dollar Roundtable, NCR, New England Telephone, Re/Max, Scott Paper, TRW and Virgin Records. Jack is also on the faculty of Income Builders International, a school for entrepreneurs.

Jack conducts an annual eight-day Training of Trainers program in the areas of self-esteem and peak performance. It attracts educators, counselors, parenting trainers, corporate trainers, professional speakers, ministers and others interested in developing their speaking and seminar-leading skills.

For further information about Jack's books, tapes and training programs, or to schedule him for a presentation, please contact:

Self-Esteem Seminars
P.O. Box 30880
Santa Barbara, CA 93130
Phone: 805-563-2935 • Fax: 805-563-2945
Web site: *www.chickensoup.com*

Who Is Mark Victor Hansen?

Mark Victor Hansen is a professional speaker who in the last twenty years has made over 4,000 presentations to more than 2 million people in thirty-two countries. His presentations cover sales excellence and strategies; personal empowerment and development; and how to triple your income and double your time off.

Mark has spent a lifetime dedicated to his mission of making a profound and positive difference in people's lives. Throughout his career, he has inspired hundreds of thousands of people to create a more powerful and purposeful future for themselves while stimulating the sale of billions of dollars worth of goods and services.

Mark is a prolific writer and has authored *Future Diary, How to Achieve Total Prosperity* and *The Miracle of Tithing.* He is coauthor of the *Chicken Soup for the Soul* series, *Dare to Win* and *The Aladdin Factor* (all with Jack Canfield), and *The Master Motivator* (with Joe Batten).

Mark has also produced a complete library of personal-empowerment audio and videocassette programs that have enabled his listeners to recognize and use their innate abilities in their business and personal lives. His message has made him a popular television and radio personality, with appearances on ABC, NBC, CBS, HBO, PBS and CNN. He has also appeared on the cover of numerous magazines, including *Success, Entrepreneur* and *Changes.*

Mark is a big man with a heart and spirit to match—an inspiration to all who seek to better themselves.

For further information about Mark, write:

MVH & Associates
P.O. Box 7665
Newport Beach, CA 92658
Phone: 949-759-9304 or 800-433-2314
Fax: 949-722-6912
Web site: *www.chickensoup.com*

Who Is Marci Shimoff?

Marci Shimoff is coauthor of the *New York Times* bestsellers *Chicken Soup for the Woman's Soul, Chicken Soup for the Mother's Soul, A Second Chicken Soup for the Woman's Soul, Chicken Soup for the Single's Soul.* She is a top-rated professional speaker who, for the last eighteen years, has inspired thousands of people with her message of personal and professional growth. Since 1994 she has specialized in delivering *Chicken Soup for the Soul* keynote speeches to audiences around the world.

Marci is cofounder and president of The Esteem Group, a company specializing in self-esteem and inspirational programs for women. She has been a featured speaker for numerous professional organizations, universities, women's associations, health-care organizations and Fortune 500 companies. Her clients have included AT&T, American Airlines, Sears, Junior League, the Pampered Chef, Jazzercise and Bristol-Myers Squibb. Her audiences appreciate her lively humor, her dynamic delivery and her ability to open hearts and uplift spirits.

Marci combines her energetic and engaging style with a strong knowledge base. She earned her MBA from UCLA; she also studied for one year in the United States and Europe to earn an advanced certificate as a stress-management consultant. Since 1989, Marci has studied self-esteem with Jack Canfield, and has assisted in his annual Training of Trainers program for professionals.

In 1983, Marci coauthored a highly acclaimed study of the fifty top businesswomen in America. Since that time, she has specialized in addressing women's audiences, focusing on helping women discover the extraordinary within themselves.

Of all the projects Marci has worked on in her career, none have been as fulfilling as creating *Chicken Soup for the Soul* books. Currently at work on future editions of *Chicken Soup for the Soul,* she feels blessed to have the opportunity to bring inspiration to millions of people throughout the world.

To schedule Marci for a *Chicken Soup for the Soul* keynote address or seminar, you can reach her at:

The Esteem Group
369-B Third St. Ste. 111
San Rafael, CA 94901
Phone: 877-472-9394 • Fax: 877-472-5065

Who Is Carol Kline?

Carol Kline is a speaker, self-esteem facilitator and certified instructor of the parenting skills program, *Redirecting Children's Behavior* (RCB). The first RCB instructor in Iowa, Carol has offered workshops, weekly classes for parents and in-service programs for child-care providers since 1993. In addition, she has served as a counselor at a self-esteem camp for teens and kids. Since 1975, Carol has also taught stress-management programs to the general public.

In 1990, she began studying the area of self-esteem with Jack Canfield and has assisted as a facilitator in his annual Train the Trainers program. Her dynamic and engaging style has won her enthusiastic receptions from the various audiences she addresses.

Carol is also active in many volunteer programs in her community including animal rescue work, fund-raising for local youth groups and humane education for children.

In addition to her parenting, self-esteem and volunteer work, Carol has been a freelance writer for fourteen years. Carol, who has a B.A. in literature, has written for newspapers, newsletters and other publications. She has presented seminars for writers on effective story writing and has spoken at writing conferences around the country. She is the coauthor of the *New York Times* best-selling *Chicken Soup for the Pet Lover's Soul* and *Chicken Soup for the Cat and Dog Lover's Soul*. She has also contributed stories and her editing talents to many other *Chicken Soup for the Soul* books.

Carol has the good fortune to be married to Larry Kline, and is proud stepmother to Lorin and McKenna. To contact Carol:

P.O. Box 1262
Fairfield, IA 52556
Phone: 641-469-3889 • Fax: 641-472-3720
E-mail: *motherschickensoup@yahoo.com*

Contributors

Pamela Albee is a dental ceramist who also offers holistic healing and energy medicine to private clients. She has always loved children. After adopting her daughter she founded and facilitated an adoption support group and developed infant care and parenting classes for adoptive parents in Spokane, Washington.

Beverly Beckham is an award-winning columnist for *The Boston Herald.* She is the author of *A Gift of Time,* a collection of personal essays and *Back Then–A Memoir of Childhood.* Her stories have also appeared in *A Second Chicken Soup for the Woman's Soul* and *A 6th Bowl of Chicken Soup for the Soul.* An at-home mother who embarked upon a writing career at age thirty, she routinely ponders the universal experiences that connect family and friends. She can be reached at 298 Chapman Street, Canton, MA 92021 or by e-mail at *BevBeckham@aol.com.*

Mildred Bonzo is a ninety-two-year-old widow who lives alone in a 180-year-old log house that has been in her husband's family for four generations. A few years ago she wrote a book of family memories for her grandchildren and great-grandchildren which includes her story, "A Sweet Lesson." She is the oldest member of the Sunshine Church of Christ where she has served for over eighty years.

Trudy Bowler lives in Gregory, Michigan, with her husband Carl, the love of her life, and her children James and Pamela. She began writing when she returned to college at the age of thirty. Her children and husband are her main inspiration for the stories she writes. Trudy believes that providing a happy home for her family is her greatest joy and success in life.

Linda Bremner is a mother and grandmother, although her business card reads "Founder and Executive Director" of Love Letters, Inc. At fifty-two, she has been involved with the art community, especially paper crafts, for over thirty years. She has had several articles published and is also a lecturer and motivational speaker. To make a tax-deductible contribution to Love Letters, Inc. or to find out about volunteering, contact Linda at P.O. Box 416875, Chicago, IL 60641.

Thomas Brown, hairstylist and developer of various hair care products, is currently working on his own book. He is originally from Geneseo, New York, and now resides in Fairfield, Iowa. He is deeply grateful to his aunt and uncle, Jan and Vernon Horras, for the loving care they gave his mother. You can reach Thomas by writing to him at 108 W. Broadway, Fairfield, IA 52556.

Carol Bryant, one of the original baby boomers, is a freelance writer whose topics include the concerns of the elderly and the people who care for them.

She lives in Delaware with an extensive Tupperware collection. You can reach her on e-mail at *carol33@gateway.net.*

Patricia Bunin is a writer and breast cancer survivor from Altadena, California. She writes regularly for the *Pasadena Star News* and is working on an inspirational book about her experience with cancer. She is available for freelance writing assignments or speaking engagements. You can reach her at 626-797-8255 or e-mail her at *patriciabunin@ix.netcom.com.*

George Burns, born Nathan Birnbaum on Manhattan's Lower East Side, began performing in 1903, at age seven. Not only did he survive all the shifts in popular entertainment over the course of the century—vaudeville, radio, movies, television, publishing—he prevailed in every one. He had a hit TV series, *The George Burns and Gracie Allen Show,* from 1950 to 1958, won an Oscar for his 1975 performance in the movie, *The Sunshine Boys,* and of the ten books bearing his byline, four were bestsellers. Burns died just weeks after his hundredth birthday in 1996.

Martha Campbell is a graduate of Washington University St. Louis School of Fine Arts, and a former writer/designer for Hallmark Cards. She has been a freelance cartoonist and book illustrator since 1973. She can be reached at P.O. Box 2538, Harrison, AR 72602, 870-741-5323, or *marthaf@alltel.net.*

Bill Canty's cartoons have appeared in many national magazines, including the *Saturday Evening Post, Good Housekeeping, Better Homes and Gardens, Woman's World, National Review* and *Medical Economics.* His syndicated feature "All About Town" runs in thirty-five newspapers. Bill can be reached at P.O. Box 1053, S. Wellfleet, MA 02663; phone and fax: 508-349-7549; e-mail: *wcanty@mediaone.net* or his Web site: *www.reuben.org.Canty.*

Dave Carpenter has been a full-time cartoonist since 1981. Dave's cartoons have appeared in such publications as *Reader's Digest, Harvard Business Review, Barron's, The Wall Street Journal, Better Homes and Gardens, USA Weekend,* as well as numerous other publications and *Chicken Soup for the Soul* books. Dave can be reached at P.O. Box 520, Emmetsburg, IA 50536.

Mary Chavoustie is a photojournalist with a passion for travel writing, small towns and family. Her contributions have been included in AAA's Texas and New Mexico *Journey* magazines, *Grit, Houston* and *New Mexico House and Home* and most recently, her call for lupus awareness in the anthology, *Women Forged in Fire.*

Mary Ann Christie is the Webmistress of successful sites devoted to love (*hugkiss.com*), marriage (*bridalzine.com*) and fun (*funlinked.com*), and her humorous outlook has earned her a place as a NetWit, a highly regarded group of humor writers. She can be reached at *maryann@hugkiss.com.*

Joan Cinelli is a South Carolina writer whose work has appeared in *Good Housekeeping, Guideposts, Christian Century, Catholic Digest* and in an anthology, *Get Well Wishes.* Joan edits and publishes *Timelapse,* a poetry journal.

Her three sons and three grandchildren are the inspiration for much of her writing.

Cynthia Coe is a Phi Beta Kappa Graduate of the University of Tennessee, Knoxville and a former lawyer. She is currently pursuing a Masters of Arts in Christian Education degree at Virginia Theological Seminary and is on staff at Episcopal Church of the Ascension in Knoxville, Tennessee.

Conari Press, established in 1987, publishes books on spirituality and women's history to sexuality and personal growth. Their main goal is to publish quality books that will make a difference in people's lives—both how people feel about themselves and how they relate to one another. To contact Conari Press: 2550 Ninth Street, Suite 101, Berkeley, CA 94710, 800-685-9595. E-mail: *conari@conari.com*. Web site: *www.conari.com*.

Christie Craig is a writer, photographer and teacher. With over five hundred national credits and one published novel, her work has appeared in a variety of publications, including *Reader's Digest, Woman's World, Redbook, The Lookout, Signs of the Times, Cats* and *PetLife*. Known for her inspiration and encouragement, she teaches writing classes in Houston, Texas. For information, contact her at *ccraig@comwerx.net*.

Pat Curtis is a mother and grandmother who, along with her husband Max and their two Yorkies, Dollie and Skeeter, live in Joplin, Missouri. She enjoys writing inspirational stories of real-life events along with writing stories and novels for children.

Holly W. Danneman was born and raised in Texas. She graduated from Brigham Young University in 1974 with a degree in business. She married while living in San Francisco and has also lived in New York, Frankfurt and London. Holly is currently writing a travel guide called American Mini-tours of London and a novel about her childhood called In Defense of Men.

Lisa Duffy-Korpics is a freelance writer and high school social studies teacher in Montgomery, New York. Her work has appeared in magazines and regional newspapers, as well as in *Chicken Soup for the Cat and Dog Lover's Soul*. Lisa lives in Dutchess County, New York, with her husband Jason, her six-year-old son Charles and three-year-old daughter Emily. Her mother, Kathleen, is currently on her twenty-eighth year of dialysis. Lisa can be reached at *Memleigh@msn.com*.

Patty Duncan recently graduated from college a second time, at age fifty, with a degree in elementary education. She's a substitute teacher and likes working with middle schoolers best. She enjoys chatting with her mother, who is now eighty years old, on the phone every evening.

Benita Epstein's cartoons appear in hundreds of publications such as *The New Yorker, Reader's Digest* and *Better Homes and Gardens*. She has three cartoon collections: Suture Self, Interlibrary Loan Sharks and Seedy Roms and Science of

Little Round Things. (McFarland & Co. 800-253-2187) E-mail: *BenitaE2aol.com;* Web site: *www.reuben.org/benitaepstein/.*

Debbie Farmer is a nationally syndicated humor columnist. Her column "Family Daze" is distributed by Paradigm TSA Syndicate (*www.paradigm-tsa.com*). Her column has been internationally published in parenting magazines in the U.S., Canada and Australia. Her essays have also appeared nationally in *Disney's Family Fun Magazine, Christian Parenting Today* and Sunset Publications *Specialty Magazines.* Visit her Web site at: *www.family-daze.com.*

Falaka Fattah is the founder and Chief Executive Officer of the House of Umoja in Philadelphia, a home established almost thirty years ago for troubled urban youth. When asked once how she managed to convert the boys under her care into such well-behaved young men, she responded, "I treat them with respect, I demand that they respect me and I love them with an unconditional love." To make a tax-deductible donation, please send checks to: House of Umoja, Inc., 1410 N. Frazier St., Philadelphia, PA 19131. Or contact Mrs. Fattah at (215) 473-5893, Fax: (215) 879-5340, e-mail: *falakafattah@aol.com.*

Alice Ferguson was born and raised in Derry, New Hampshire, and currently resides in Reno, Nevada. Alice holds a masters degree in Liberal Arts and teaches English Composition at the University of Nevada/Reno. When not teaching, Alice divides her time between travel in her RV and spending time with her two children.

Carol Frink resides in New York State with her husband and two children. She has been a full-time "stay-at-home" Mom since 1994 and does computer work part time from home. Writing has always been a hobby. She considers her family to be her greatest asset and even being considered for publication by *Chicken Soup for the Soul* one of her greatest honors.

Allison Yates Gaskins is the coauthor of *Thanks, Mom, for Everything, Thanks, Dad, for Everything* and *Tightening the Knot.* She, her husband Will and their children live at Summer's Best Two Weeks Camp in Boswell, Pennsylvania. She is currently a full-time mom and occasional freelance writer.

Lenore Gavigan has been a teacher for thirty-two years. She currently teaches English, as well as English as a Second Language for the North Rockland School District in New York State. As an adjunct instructor for the Regional Training Center, she conducts courses for teachers on how to convey the art of writing to their students. She and her husband of thirty-two years, Jack, have three children, Tara (married to Sinclair), Sean and Mary Beth, and two grandchildren, Meghan and Justin, who bring great joy to their lives.

Dorothy Raymond Gilchrest is the mother of two and a true Mainer. She is presently a self-employed radiographer in occupational medicine. She is a dynamic lecturer on motivational topics for the working woman. Her inspirational writing has produced published journal articles as well as nostalgic lifetime stories and poetry offering spiritual balance between work and family. If you would like your family story portrayed in print, she may be reached through e-mail: *gilcrest@exploremaine.com*.

Debbie (Fletcher) Gilmore—a full-time mother—lives in Germany with her husband, Gene, and her son, Brandon. She began writing after her first son, Matthew, died, and her essay, in his memory, was published in the book *Heart of a Mother*. You can reach her at *dgilmore@cms3.com*.

Randy Glasbergen is one of America's most widely and frequently published cartoonists. More than 25,000 of his cartoons have been published by *Funny Times, Glamour,* Hallmark Cards, AOL, *Good Housekeeping* and many others. His daily comic panel, "The Better Half," is syndicated worldwide by King Features Syndicate. Randy is the author of many cartoon books, including *Oh Baby!*, a collection of cartoons for new parents. You can find more of Randy's cartoons online at: *www.glasbergen.com*.

Marcy Goodfleisch is the divorced mother of two "terrific" adult sons, Kevin and Eric. A writer and public relations professional, she has had more than five hundred articles and stories published in national and regional (Central Texas) magazines and newspapers. Marcy manages a team of writers and PR professionals for Academic Computing at the University of Texas. She is active in her church and community, and loves music, art, travel, camping and literature. She is a member of MENSA, has a B.S. in Liberal Studies and is completing her masters degree in liberal arts. She may be reached at 512-288-8894, or P.O. Box 13322, Austin, TX 78711-3322.

Stuart Hample and **Eric Marshall** are co-editors of the million-copy bestseller, *Children's Letters to God*, as well as *Grandma, Grandpa and Me*. Mr. Hample is also the editor of *Me and My Dad* and *My Mom's the Best Mom*. Their books, along with many other children's, humor, gift and other titles, are published by Workman Publishing (*www.workman.com*).

Bonnie Compton Hanson, editor, artist and author, is also represented in *Chicken Soup for the Pet Lover's Soul*. Her lively family includes husband Don, children, grandchildren, birds, cats and possums. You may reach Bonnie at 3330 S. Lowell St., Santa Ana, CA 92707; phone: 714-751-7824; e-mail: *bonnieh1@worldnet.att.net*.

Karie Hansen is a single mother and a full-time student studying Elementary Education in Iowa. Her inspiration for writing is her daughter Loreena.

Johnny Hawkins's cartoons have been published by more than 250 publications over the last fifteen years. His work has been in *The Saturday Evening Post, Woman's World, First, Barron's, Air and Space* and many others. More of his work can be seen at Hawktoon.com. Contact him at: P.O. Box 1888, Sherwood, MI 49089; phone: 517-741-3668; e-mail: *cartoonist@anthill.com*.

Shana Helmholdt is a licensed clinical psychologist in private practice in the Chicagoland area. She is passionate about writing and about her life's work—helping others to see the opportunities for growth and healing in crisis and in life's transitions. She can be reached at 312-490-4150.

L. D. Hindman is a grandmother whose avocation is writing poetry. She recently completed a small volume of verse, *Among Stones*, written to bring comfort to those who have experienced the loss of a loved one. She lives in Colorado with her husband of thirty-eight years, where she enjoys all activities that involve her family.

Dawn Holt is currently a school counselor at Westover High School in Fayetteville, North Carolina, fulfilling her son Cameron's last wishes that he not be forgotten, and that she come back to his high school to make a difference in the lives of the students. After giving the chocolate-covered cherries story to family and friends in December of 1998, they encouraged her to submit the story to *Chicken Soup for the Soul*. She still makes the box of candy her annual gift to them.

Ann Hood is the author of the nonfiction book, *Do Not Go Gentle: My Search for Miracles in a Cynical Time* (Picador), and seven novels: *Somewhere Off the Coast of Maine, Waiting to Vanish, Three-Legged Horse, Something Blue, Places to Stay the Night, The Properties of Water* and *Ruby*. She has published short stories, essays and book reviews in many magazines and newspapers including *Parenting, Redbook, Self, The New York Times, The Washington Post* and *The Los Angeles Times*. She lives in Providence, Rhode Island, with her husband, son and daughter.

Amberley Howe is currently a junior in college majoring in English and Behavioral Science with goals to write inspirational material for families. She wrote her story, "Mother's Christmas Stocking," during her freshman year for her Composition 101 final examination. She had three hours to write something she remembered about her childhood holidays. Her instructor, Mrs. Pyke, who usually destroyed graded finals, returned this one to Amberley with orders to find a place to publish it. Amberley can be reached at 2810 E. Westfall Rd., Mariposa, CA 95338.

Susan Hubbs is a freelance writer who lives in Orlando, Florida, with her husband, Rick, and two children, Christopher and Elizabeth. She is published in a variety of magazines and is the author of two nonfiction books, *Pamper Your Partner* and *Dig Up Your Roots and Find Your Branches*.

Earle Irwin, mother of Richard Irwin-Miller, is a psychiatric clinical nurse specialist who writes avocationally. She is a member of a women's writing group and a prolific journal keeper. She resides in Blacksburg, Virginia.

Richard Irwin-Miller is now seventeen. He is a junior in high school and a member of the National Thespian Society. He hopes to major in drama in college and pursue a career in theater.

Linda Jones considers the two most important things in life to be her relationship with the Lord and with her daughter. They became Christians—she as a young single mom and Kelly as a young girl—and "grew up" together in the Lord. She has worked for JCPenney for twenty-four years and loves to teach women's Bible studies.

Bil Keane started "The Family Circus," based on his own family (his wife Thel and their five children) in 1960. It now appears in more than 1,500 newspapers and is read daily by 188 million people. The award-winning feature is the most widely syndicated panel cartoon in America.

Marie Kennedy is a wife, mother, motivational speaker and freelance writer. She is published in numerous online magazines, and has been a guest speaker at schools, hospitals and conventions. She is a new member of NLAPW (National League of American Pen Women) and author of *My Perfect Son has Cerebral Palsy*. The book is available nationwide; call your local book store for details or visit *www.mariekennedy.com*. Contact Marie from her Web site or e-mail *MarieKennedy@aol.com*.

Janet Konttinen is a syndicated columnist with Universal Press Syndicate, and the mother of a six-year-old son and triplet daughters, age five. In her writing she shares her family's chaos. She also appears in *Baby Talk Magazine* where she answers readers' questions about kids, parenting and life's ins and outs.

Kathryn Kvols is the mother/stepmother of five. She is a dynamic speaker and is best known for her life-changing course and book *Redirecting Children's Behavior (RCB)*. Kathryn is president of the International Network for Children and Families. She resides with her husband, Brian, and her children, Tyler and Brianna. For more information about RCB, call Kathryn at 352-375-7698 or visit her Web site at *www.incaf.com*.

Cynthia Laughlin is the proud mother of Skyler, an active eight-year-old son who is autistic. She is currently working on a book about Skyler's life and takes every opportunity to share with others the joys and heartaches of life with an autistic child.

Pat Laye, author of seven novels, numerous short stories and a frequent contributor to other *Chicken Soup* books, teaches at writers' conferences and colleges throughout the South. She resides in Cuthbert, Georgia, where she is currently working on a mystery. She travels worldwide exploring new settings for her novels.

Robin Lim is the mother of seven, grandmother of "Zhou" and midwife of many. She lives with her large family in the mountains of the Philippines, and can sometimes be found in Iowa. Her book, *After the Baby's Birth: A*

Woman's Way to Wellness, is a wonderful guidebook for new mothers. Lim is director of Healthy Mother–Healthy Baby, an international not-for-profit foundation which supports gentle, culturally sensitive childbirth and breastfeeding. Donations may be sent to HEALTHY MOTHER—HEALTHY BABY, 4286 Redwood Hwy., #330, San Rafael, CA 94930.

Marnie O. Mamminga is a freelance writer and teacher in Batavia, Illinois. She has been married to her high school sweetheart for thirty years and has three wonderful sons. All four guys have graciously, though perhaps unknowingly, provided much material for her writing. For this, she is sincerely grateful.

Mary Marcdante is an inspiring and dynamic professional speaker and author whose mission is to help people deepen and expand their appreciation of themselves, their relationships, their work and life. She speaks on communication, stress management, self-awareness and personal change at business and association meetings and conventions. She is the author of *My Mother, My Friend: The Ten Most Important Things to Talk About with Your Mother* (Simon & Schuster/Fireside) and *Inspiring Words for Inspiring People* (self-published). She can be reached at *mary@marymarcdante.com* or P.O. Box 2529, Del Mar, CA 92014.

Scott Masear lives in Portland, Oregon, and has been cartooning professionally for fifteen years. Some of the magazines that he sells to regularly are *Harvard Business Review, Medical Economics, Air and Space, Phi Delta Kappa, National Law Journal* and *Travel Weekly.*

Michael McClelland has established a reputation as one of the leading viola teachers and performers in the United States. He received his bachelor's degree in music from the Peabody Conservatory of Music, and is now a violist with the Florida Philharmonic.

W. W. Meade started writing at the age of fourteen. When he was twenty-two, his first story was published in *Colliers* magazine. He wrote short fiction stories for the *Saturday Evening Post, Gentleman's Quarterly* and several others. He then turned to writing nonfiction for magazines such as *Cosmopolitan, Redbook* and *Reader's Digest.* Later he became the managing editor of *Cosmopolitan* and then the managing editor of the Reader's Digest Book Club. His last position in publishing was president and editor in chief of Avon Books. Today, Walter is retired and writing short stories for *Reader's Digest* as well as many other magazines and periodicals. He can be reached at 4561 N.W. 67 Terr., Fort Lauderhill, FL 33319.

Caurie Anne Miner is the daughter of Dawn and Gregory Miner and sister of Stephanie, K. T. and Christopher. Caurie—a freelance writer—was raised on the family's tree farm in upstate New York. She earned her bachelor and masters degrees from the University of Rochester and is a former Fulbright Grant recipient. Caurie's mom recently graduated from Green Mountain College with her "official" teaching credentials. You can reach them both at 217 Scotch Hill Road, Cambridge, NY 12816 or *caurieanne@hotmail.com.*

Holly Manon Moore is grateful to be a full-time mom and wife-at-home to daughter, Mira, and husband, Bob, in Fairfield, Iowa. She has a B.F.A. in art and an M.A. in educational administration, which happily qualifies her for her activities as artist, writer, organic gardener and adult volunteer for the Girl Scouts of the USA. She has also been a teacher of the Transcendental Meditation Program for over twenty-five years.

Marilyn Neibergall holds a Bachelor of Science Degree in Nursing from Arizona State University and is an R.N.—community health nurse—at Maricopa County Department of Public Health in Phoenix, Arizona. She is also a freelance writer with several articles in *Woman's World* magazine. She can be reached at 1030 W. Emelita Avenue, Mesa, AZ 85210 or call 480-969-1794.

Doris Hays Northstorm is a nationally published writer, inspirational speaker and creative writing teacher. She has four children, six grandchildren, and finds her motivation for writing in her family and living in the Pacific Northwest. Her hobbies include biking, hiking and skiing with her children and gardening, tennis, and dancing with her husband, Ron. Contact her at 1308 N. Cascade Ave., Tacoma, WA 98406, or e-mail at *3434@earthlink.net.*

Christina Chanes Nystrom is a southern California-based free-lance writer and photographer. Christina has published more than nine hundred newsprint, Web and magazine articles. She is married and has a daughter. Her cover and feature publication credits include *Tradeshow Week, Casinogaming.com, PEO Record, San Gabriel Valley Tribune, Whittier Daily News, Highlander Weekly News, American City and County Magazine, MAMM Magazine, El Restaurante Magazine, Design Build Business* and the *Design Journal.*

Shirley Pease, a writer and speaker for ten years, has written for both secular and Christian magazines. She has coauthored one book and is working on two more. This is her second story in the *Chicken Soup* series. Recently she began a writer's group for senior citizens in Wenatchee, Washington. E-mail Shirley at: *mocrane@aol.com.*

Diane C. Perrone is a freelance writer and has been a marketing/ PR consultant since 1966. She is the mother of five and is reframing life through the eyes of her seven (so far) grandchildren and the lens of faith. She speaks to "seasoned" citizens and the companies that market to them, and also teaches skin care for Mary Kay Cosmetics.

Carol McAdoo Rehme is a freelance writer, professional storyteller and public speaker. With her four children providing ample fodder for stories, she is a regular contributor to other *Chicken Soup for the Soul* books,

Whispers from Heaven and various publications. Contact Carol at 2503 Logan Dr., Loveland, CO 80538; phone (970) 669-5791 or e-mail her at *crehme@verinet.com.*

Staci Ann Richmond is a former reporter, award-winning columnist and freelance writer who left the wild world of print journalism to pursue a degree in secondary English education. However, her most prized accomplishment has been the establishment of an in-home brokerage firm she operates with her husband of ten years, Bart. The two deal primarily with futures—those of their four children, Addi Rose, Jasper, Sage and Zane. She can be reached at 101 E. Fillmore Ave., Fairfield, IA 52556.

Patricia Rinaldi has built a career on what she does best: making things safer to protect children, creating order from chaos and demonstrating leadership in times of trouble. A high school drop-out, Patricia is currently working on her master's thesis at the University of Michigan. In addition, she is the Director of Michigan Facilities for Beacon Education Management. An artist, poet, musician, vocalist and church choir director, Patricia spends her spare time in her garden, happy when her grandchildren, Lisa, Tr'e and DeVonte come over to see her.

Sandra Rockman is a writer, playwright and theater director. Her recent work includes a cycle of personal essays chronicling her mother's dementia. Her essays have been published in the *San Francisco Chronicle* and the *Hartford Courant*. She lives with her husband, Tony Giacalone, in northern California and is currently working on a novel.

Ronna Rowlette is the mother of two daughters and a son. She is president of Rowlette Research Associates, Inc., in Tampa, Florida, specializing in community research with nonprofit organizations. Dr. Rowlette is also an adjunct professor, a freelance writer and photographer.

Nancy L. Rusk lives in Florida with her husband, her son, two dogs, one cat, one iguana, one rabbit, one turtle and fifteen ducks. She writes women's fiction and inspirational nonfiction.

Doris Sanford is a registered nurse with a master's degree in psychology. She has taught a college course in death and dying for the past thirty years and authored twenty-nine books for or about children. She provides seminars worldwide on meeting the needs of abused children. Please reach her at: *dorissanford@webtv.net.*

Lynn Schnurnberger has authored several books, and is a freelance writer living in Pelham, New York.

Mike Shapiro has been working as a cartoonist since 1987. His work has appeared in many publications, including *The Wall Street Journal, Harvard Business Review, Forbes, Reader's Digest* and *National Review*. In addition, his cartoons have been published in books, on the Internet and on T-shirts. Mike currently resides in Virginia.

Steve Smeltzer is a native of Fort Wayne, Indiana. In addition to cartooning, he makes his living by teaching and playing drums. He and his wife Cynthia enjoy traveling and eating in small-town diners. Steve's cartoons have appeared in *USA Weekend, Better Homes & Gardens, Saturday Evening Post* and *Woman's World.* His e-mail address is: *smeltzer@fwi.com.*

Dixie Jane Sokolik is a retired registered nurse. She and her husband, Jim, live in Winona, Minnesota. They have four grown children, five grandchildren and one very spoiled cat. She loves writing and is currently writing columns for a local newspaper. Her other interests include music, hiking, reading and traveling.

Linda Stafford is the author of over twenty novels. She lives on an island where she enjoys sailing and riding her horses on the beach. She has four grown children who are shocked that their mother is learning to fly an airplane (at her age!).

Lynn Stearns has had poetry, essays and stories in numerous publications including *The Baltimore Review, Mentor* and *Women Today.* She and her husband enjoy life in Maryland, and playing with their grandson, (the subject of her story, "The Secret Handshake") and his little brother whenever possible. Lynn can be reached at *lynnstearns@starpower.net.*

B.A. Sutkus was born and raised in Olyphant, Pennsylvania, and spent her youth listening to the stories told by the people in the area who worked in the coal mines. They kept their heritage and traditions alive by passing down from generation to generation the same tales that were told to them by their families. Today, she enjoys working with the American Legion Auxiliary, watching her grandchildren grow and devising ways to avoid her "attack cat," Miss Fluffer Nutter, who only attacks her. She often asks her cat, "Why can't you be more like Smokey?"

Janis Thornton lives in Tipton, Indiana. A staff writer for the *Frankfort* (Ind.) *Times,* she also operates a writing and graphic design service from her home. A part-time student at Indiana University, Janis is continuing her studies in creative writing. Her "mother's soul" is nourished daily by her eleven-year-old son, Matthew.

Elizabeth Thring is a native Washingtonian and currently resides in Silver Spring, Maryland, where she is a licensed real estate agent. She enjoys jogging, hiking, sailing and horseback riding. Bill is her only child.

Beth Copeland Vargo is a museum curator, freelance writer and poet. Her poetry collection, *Traveling Through Glass,* received the 1999 Bright Hill Press National Poetry Book Award. She received her M.F.A. degree in Creative Writing from Bowling Green State University and has taught writing to children and adults. Her personal essays have appeared in the *Chicago Tribune, Christian Science Monitor* and other publications.

Phyllis I. Volkens (1935–1996). Phyllis began her career on a used Smith-Corona and a dare, which she won! In the beginning, she wrote for the *Denver Post*. From there, *Reader's Digest* took her words to the world. Phyllis left us in 1996, but her writing remains. Her estate, via her daughter, Heather, can be reached at 310-444-9793 or at: *farraway7@yahoo.com*.

Patricia Walters-Fischer has been in the medical field for over seven years. She has worked in the adult critical care and emergency areas as well as pediatric emergency room and trauma in hospitals around Texas. Presently, she lives in St. Louis, Missouri, with her husband Steve and has entered into the field of preventive medicine through journalism.

Marion Bond West is the mother of two daughters and twin sons, grandmother of six. She lives with her husband Gene Acuff, in Georgia. She's contributing editor for *Guideposts* and has written for them since 1972 and contributed to a number of the *Chicken Soup* books, as well as authoring six Christian books. She's an inspirational speaker and may be contacted at 1330 DaAndra Dr., Watkinsville, GA 30677.

Tina Whittle is a wife, a mother and a freshman composition instructor at Georgia Southern University, where she encourages her students to use creative writing as personal exploration, not just in the classroom but throughout their lives. She has been published in *Alfred Hitchcock's Mystery Magazine* and *Writer's Digest*.

Sharon Wright, a freelance writer, lives in Houston, Texas, with her husband. Her articles and essays have appeared in *McCall's, Cowboy Sports & Entertainment Magazine, The Houston Writer* and *Science Fiction & Fantasy E-Zine*. She also writes contemporary novels. You may contact her at P.O. Box 724, Bellaire, TX 77402-0724.

Susan Alexander Yates is a bestselling writer and speaker. Her newest book, *And Then I Had Teenagers, Encouragement for Parents of Teens and Pre-Teens,* has just been published by Baker Publishers. She is the parent-child columnist for *Today's Christian Woman Magazine*. She and her husband, John, have five children and two grandchildren. They speak at Family Life Conferences throughout the country.

A Christmas Memory. Reprinted by permission of Lenore Gavigan. ©1999 Lenore Gavigan.

Grandma's Soup Night and *The Christmas I Was Rich.* Reprinted by permission of Joan Cinelli. ©1984 and 1993 Joan Cinelli.

Becoming a Grandma. Reprinted by permission of Robin Lim. ©2000 Robin Lim.

The Secret Handshake. Reprinted by permission of Lynn Stearns. ©1995 Lynn Stearns.

Second Chance. Reprinted by permission of L. D. Hindman. ©1998 L. D. Hindman.

The Surrogate Grandmother. Reprinted by permission of Pat Curtis. ©2000 Pat Curtis.

Lessons on Napkins. Reprinted by permission of Caurie Anne Miner. ©1999 Caurie Anne Miner.

A Worthy Investment. Reprinted by permission of Allison Yates Gaskins. Excerpted from *Thanks, Mom for Everything* by Susan Alexander Yates and Allison Yates Gaskins ©1997.

Unstoppable. Reprinted by permission of Dixie Jane Sokolik. ©1999 Dixie Jane Sokolik.

The Power of My Mother's Love. Reprinted by permission of Shana Helmholdt. ©1999 Shana Helmholdt.

A House for Momma. Specified excerpt from *All Over But the Shoutin'* by Rick Bragg. ©1997 by Rick Bragg. Reprinted by permission of Pantheon Books, a division of Random House, Inc., and International Creative Management on behalf of the author.

More Soup to Warm Your Heart

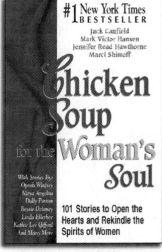

Celebrate Family

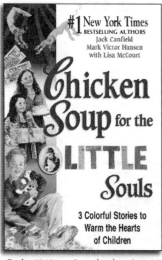

Code #8121 • Paperback • $12.95

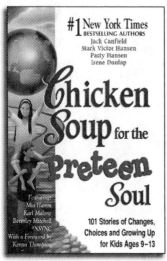

Code #8008 • Paperback • $12.95

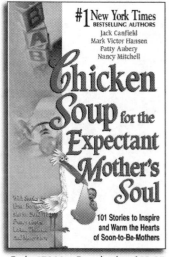

Code #7966 • Paperback • $12.95

Code #7478 • Paperback • $12.95

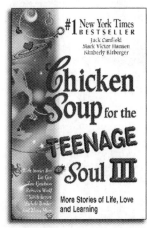

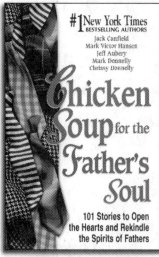
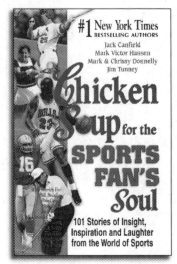